Pro HTML5 Accessibility

Building an Inclusive Web

Joshue O Connor

Apress®

Pro HTML5 Accessibility: Building an Inclusive Web

ISBN-13 (pbk): 978-1-4302-4194-2

ISBN-13 (electronic): 978-1-4302-4195-9

President and Publisher: Paul Manning
Lead Editor: Susan Ethridge
Technical Reviewer: William Seyler
Editorial Board: Steve Anglin, Ewan Buckingham, Gary Cornell, Louise Corrigan, Morgan Ertel, Jonathan Gennick, Jonathan Hassell, Robert Hutchinson, Michelle Lowman, James Markham, Matthew Moodie, Jeff Olson, Jeffrey Pepper, Douglas Pundick, Ben Renow-Clarke, Dominic Shakeshaft, Gwenan Spearing, Matt Wade, Tom Welsh
Coordinating Editor: Stephen Moles
Copy Editor: Roger LeBlanc
Compositor: Bytheway Publishing Services
Indexer: SPI Global
Artist: SPI Global
Cover Designer: Anna Ishchenko

Distributed to the book trade worldwide by Springer Science+Business Media New York, 233 Spring Street, 6th Floor, New York, NY 10013. Phone 1-800-SPRINGER, fax (201) 348-4505, e-mail orders-ny@springer-sbm.com, or visit www.springeronline.com.

For information on translations, please e-mail rights@apress.com, or visit www.apress.com.

Apress and friends of ED books may be purchased in bulk for academic, corporate, or promotional use. eBook versions and licenses are also available for most titles. For more information, reference our Special Bulk Sales–eBook Licensing web page at www.apress.com/bulk-sales.

Any source code or other supplementary materials referenced by the author in this text is available to readers at www.apress.com. For detailed information about how to locate your book's source code, go to www.apress.com/source-code.

For Ruairí Michael and Lorraine.

"Go raibh maith agaibh as a thabhairt áthas agus leighis le mo shaol"

Contents at a Glance

Contents

Everyone is a genius. But if you judge a fish on its ability to climb a tree it will live its whole life believing it is stupid.

A. Einstein

About the Author

Joshue O Connor is Senior Accessibility Consultant with NCBI Centre for Inclusive Technology (CFIT) based in Dublin, Ireland. He is a leading expert on web accessibility and digital inclusion and is skilled in the design and development of accessible websites/applications. Josh has many years of experience as both a graphic designer and web developer and has spent the last 10 years working directly with people with disabilities. First, as an assistive technology (AT) specialist and then as a usability analyst undertaking user testing of web interfaces and software applications directly involving people with a wide range of disabilities and AT requirements. He has an MSc in Computing (Assistive Technology and Universal Design) from DIT.

Josh is a member of several Worldwide Web Consortium (W3C) working groups—including PFWG, WCAG, and HTML5—and has written research papers on topics relating to accessibility, usability, and web development. His previous book, *Joomla Accessibility*, was about the open-source CMS Joomla.

When not playing some jazzy guitar or cooking Indian vegetarian food, he currently jams with "The Cookie Monsters," records abrasive electronic weirdness as "2Track," and records left-field electronica as "Head Noise," "My Favourite Weirdo," and "Fuzzy Systems." For more information, see techrecord.net.

About the Technical Reviewer

 **William Seyler** was born in Sisters Hospital, Buffalo, NY, USA, and things got more confusing after that. For professional education and job history, see his CV at www.WilliamSeyler.com. He is 6 ft. and 180 lbs., has brown hair, cut short, and green/hazel eyes.

Acknowledgments

Many thanks—for advice, help, and input or the use of materials they created—go to the following people:

Jared Smith (WebAIM), Michael Cooper (W3C/WAI), Janina Sajka (Linux Foundation, W3C/WAI), Steve Faulkner (TPG/WAT-C), Bryan Carver (Freedom Scientific), Jason Kiss (accessibleculture.org), Becky Gibson (IBM), Anne Van Kesteren (Opera, Standards suck/annevankesteren.nl), Roger Johansson (456bereastreet.com), Ian Devlin (iandevlin.com), Christopher Giffard (captionatorjs.com), John Foliot (W3C Invited expert/john.foliot.ca), Peter Krantz (peterkrantz.com), Damian Gordon (DIT).

Some special thanks are due to Gez Lemon (TPG/Juicystudio.com) for his friendship, scripting expertise, and generous advice throughout. Rich Schwerdtfeger (IBM) for his guidance and expertise, which greatly helped me articulate what goes on under the hood when AT interacts with a browser. Thanks to Mark Boas (Happy Worm/JPlayer happyworm.com) for scripting advice when developing an accessible HTML5 video player and to Dr. Silvia Pfeiffer (W3C Invited Expert/gingertech.net) for the same.

A very special thanks last of all (but certainly not least) to the Apress team for their professionalism, support, and generous assistance.

Take a bow: Ben Renow-Clarke, Stephen Moles, Susan Ethridge, Wil Seyler, Roger LeBlanc, Debra Kelly.

Introduction

This book aims to help web designers and developers come to grips with building exciting, accessible, and usable web sites/applications with HTML5. The book looks at using HTML5 to serve the needs of the widest possible audience, including people with disabilities using assistive technology (AT) and older people. It aims to be a useful go-to guide by giving you practical advice. The book explores the new semantics of HTML5 and how to combine them with authoring practices you may know from using earlier versions of HTML. It also aims to demonstrate how HTML5 content is currently supported (or not) by assistive technologies such as screen readers, and what this practically means for you as you endeavor to make your HTML5 projects accessible.

The HTML5 specification is huge, with new APIs and patterns that can be difficult to understand from an accessibility perspective. Accessibility itself can also seem complex and nuanced, in particular if you have no experience dealing with the needs of people with disabilities. This book aims to hold your hand through the process of gaining an understanding of the needs of people with disabilities, as well as the new specification.

Accessibility isn't a mysterious or esoteric subject, but it is nuanced. And HTML5 is a game-changer. Ultimately, creating accessible content is really a quality design issue. (Good design enables; bad design disables.) And getting design right is often a matter of choosing the correct approach. This book hopes to be your companion in understanding both, HTML5 and good accessibility design.

Who This Book Is For

Pro HTML5 Accessibility is for the intermediate to more advanced web designer and developer who is already building websites and applications but may need some help in understanding accessibility and transitioning to HTML5.

Prerequisites

The book can be read as a basic introduction to HTML5 and accessibility, but it may be more suited to the professional or experienced designer who already has knowledge of HTML4 as well as CSS, WAI-ARIA, and JavaScript experience. While no detailed knowledge of CSS, WAI-ARIA, or scripting is really required, it will help the reader to understand some of the design patterns and examples discussed in the book.

Downloading the Code

The code for the examples shown in this book is available on the Apress web site, `www.apress.com`. A link can be found on the book's information page under the Source Code/Downloads tab. This tab is located underneath the Related Titles section of the page.

Contacting the Author

The author has a general aversion to social media but will use Twitter occasionally. You can follow him on Twitter as @joshueoconnor.

CHAPTER 1

Introduction to HTML5 Accessibility

In this chapter, I will introduce accessibility, define what it is, and discuss why you should be paying attention to reducing the barriers to access that might exist for many people in the systems you build. We will also look at HTML5 and examine its main differences from HTML 4—and you'll see what this means for accessibility as well as how those differences will impact the way you build web sites and applications.

Introduction to HTML5: The New Wave

HTML5 is here. It is the new lingua franca for the Web. So what is it? HTML5 is the new version of HTML 4, XHTML1, and DOM Level 2 HTML. It has moved HTML from being a relatively simple document markup language to being a sophisticated platform for web applications with a host of new, rich application programming interfaces (APIs).

As with all major changes in life, the transition might not be smooth. Such a major shift that adds a host of new elements and attributes presents particular challenges for you as an author as well as, potentially, for the consumer.

HTML 4 was readily understood and offered features that could be used in imaginative ways. By leveraging these features in combination with other languages like Cascading Style Sheets (CSS) and JavaScript, developers could do things that were increasingly complex, pushing the models of user interaction.

With the advent of Web 2.0–type content such as AJAX, dynamic content updating, and more client-side processing, we saw a variety of terrific, sophisticated applications being developed out of what were often semantically limited markup languages.

This new wave of glossy widgets—and sometimes bizarre interaction models—often present many challenges to the user. If the user has a disability, the challenge is greater, because that user might not be able to access important widget functionality from the keyboard or content updates might be lost on the screen-reader user. Long before HTML5, many web designers started to really care about accessibility and look for ways to ensure their web sites and applications were usable by the widest audience. So grassroots movements like the Web Standards Project were born. An active and vibrant community arose that saw the challenges of improving the user experience and quality of design as a call to arms.

If you are reading this, chances are you are a web designer or developer and you would like to know more about HTML5 and how it relates to accessibility. So you're in the right place. This book assumes you have a decent level of knowledge of HTML 4, as well as some CSS experience and maybe some JavaScript experience. It also assumes you're keen to learn about developing robust web sites and applications by using HTML5.

If you're not an expert CSS or JavaScript person and don't even know much HTML, don't worry! This book is designed to provide sufficient references to online materials and resources that will soon get you up to speed. The HTML5 spec is notoriously large (about 800 pages), so what this book tries to do is distill the parts that relate most to developing accessible web sites. This book (in tandem with some other more generic HTML5 resources) should help you come to terms with the game-changer that is HTML5, as well as accessibility.

In this book, I will attempt to share with you what I know about both—as a web designer and developer and as someone who has worked with people with disabilities for nearly 10 years. I am also a member of the HTML5 working group, where my input has had particular emphasis on accessibility and on trying to ensure (with many others) that the HTML5 specification will best serve the needs of the broadest range of users, including people with disabilities.

HTML5 vs. HTML 4

So what's new in HTML5, and how does it differ from HTML 4? First, HTML5 is designed to do an awful lot more than just mark up text or be a hypertext markup language. (You are forgiven if you thought it was.) Second, many new APIs are now contained within the new specification that might not seem, at first glance, to belong in a document markup language at all.

These APIs are many and varied, and include Web Workers (an API for running scripts in the background independently of any user interface scripts), Web Storage (similar to HTTP session cookies, for storing structured data on the client side), and Web Sockets (for bidirectional communications with server-side processes). When you factor in native, "in the browser" support for video and audio via the `<video>` and `<audio>` elements—which signal a significant move away from browser plugin solutions like Flash, as well as the new 2D drawing API `<canvas>`—it's obvious that HTML5 is far more than a mere document markup language and really is a quantum leap beyond the other earlier versions of HTML.

▓ **Note** The added features are a mixed blessing. With these new language features, there will be more functionality but also more complexity both for you as an author and for your users. However, employing best practices in terms of user interface design and also in how you approach coding your projects will stand you in good stead. So while it might feel a little like you have to start all over again, I hope you will see that it doesn't entirely have to be like that. You will just have more choice and, of course, learn a few things. I hope also that the good things you might know about making stuff accessible using a combination of HTML 4 and CSS/JavaScript will often still apply. Don't be worried about keeping things simple—just using the right tool for the right job can get you very far.

HTML5 Syntax

In terms of syntax, HTML5 is a language that wears two hats. It can be written as both HTML and XML (also known as XHTML, which is an XML serialization of HTML—or put another way, an XML-like version of HTML that brings some of the rules of XML syntax to HTML).

Depending on your own requirements, you might need to serve more strictly well-formed XML-type documents to your users. Doing that will require the use of an XML parser, which is used to process XML documents. Alternatively, content comprised of HTML that is syntactically more lax HTML might suffice for your needs, in which case you can use an HTML parser. "More lax HTML" refers to code that might be a little sloppy but still works.

The HTML5 <!DOCTYPE>

In earlier versions of HTML and XHTML1, whether your documents were HTML or XHTML was defined primarily by the DOCTYPE (which was that kind of scary code in the header of your webpages that no one really knew what it did and that seemed arcane and pointless, although it was neither of these things). The DOCTYPE is really meant for machines to handle as a way of identifying the vocabulary that the document contents are meant to conform to.

In previous versions, you had the following DOCTYPES:

For HTML 4.01 Strict:

```
<!DOCTYPE HTML PUBLIC "-//W3C//DTD HTML 4.01//EN"
    "http://www.w3.org/TR/html4/strict.dtd">
```

For HTML 4.01 Transitional:

```
<!DOCTYPE HTML PUBLIC "-//W3C//DTD HTML 4.01 Transitional//EN"
    "http://www.w3.org/TR/html4/loose.dtd">
```

or for XHTML 1.0 Strict

```
<!DOCTYPE html PUBLIC "-//W3C//DTD XHTML 1.0 Strict//EN"
    "http://www.w3.org/TR/xhtml1/DTD/xhtml1-strict.dtd">
```

or XHTML 1.0 Transitional

```
<!DOCTYPE html PUBLIC "-//W3C//DTD XHTML 1.0 Transitional//EN"
    "http://www.w3.org/TR/xhtml1/DTD/xhtml1-transitional.dtd">
```

In HTML5, it is much simpler. Here is the new HTML5 DOCTYPE:

```
<!DOCTYPE html>
```

It's kind of neat, and certainly easy to remember. There are other advantages, as well. For example, you're no longer required to reference a DTD (Document Type Definition), as you were in previous versions of HTML, so it's pretty elegant and will trigger Standards Mode in all newer browsers.

Some DOCTYPE History

Triggering Quirks Mode is a technique used by developers to ensure backward compatibility with older browsers. The need to do this came about because of the practical peculiarities of different browsers when rendering code, and poor or incomplete implementations of technical specifications like the W3C DOM.

Since different browser manufacturers choose to implement the specifications differently, developers were forced to leverage the various rendering modes that were triggered by the DTD in a page in order to see how the document would be parsed, testing their content in Standards Mode, Almost Standards Mode, and Quirks Mode.

I hope now with HTML5 we are getting closer to the "author once then publish to many devices/platforms" model. If you don't remember all this, consider yourself lucky – it wasn't fun and made web development torturous. If you do remember all this, have a stiff drink. If you wish to read up on it, visit http://en.wikipedia.org/wiki/Quirks_mode.

■ **Note** In XHTML, no DOCTYPE is actually required, but you might need to use one when you have, for example, what's called a *polyglot document* (which is a hybrid document that can be served as both XHTML or HTML) or you need to declare entity references (symbols, mathematical symbols, language characters, so forth) for use within the document.

It makes sense when you think about it. If you and I are at a party and I say, "The veggie samosas are on the table, beside the woman with the great figure," you would know what I mean. For a browser, the use of the word *table* and *figure* mean totally different things; therefore, a way to explain to the browser what language is being used in a document that it must parse is vital in order for the software to know what to do with its contents.

If a load of browsers were at a party that line would mean something totally different (not that browsers eat veggie samosas) than it would in the context of our daily lives.

■ **Note** It's important to understand that with previous versions of HTML developers often struggled with whether to use "strict" or "transitional," and confusion as to how the browser would treat content, given a specific DOCTYPE, was common. For a very interesting overview of the whole history of DOCTYPES, parsing rules, and the MIME type (more on that later), I recommend reading Ian Hickson's article, "Sending XHMTL as text/html Considered Harmful," which explains some history, how these things came to be, and some best practices. You can find it at `http://hixie.ch/advocacy/xhtml`.

HTML5 and XHTML as text/html (It's a MIME Field)

Now, in HTML5, how your content is parsed is dependent more on the choice of the media type than the DOCTYPE.

This means that XML-type documents need to be given the XML media type, such as `application/xhtml+xml` or `application/xml`. By contrast, if you're using HTML syntax, you serve the document as `text/html`. This is often done in the HTTP - Content type Header, which takes the following form:

```
<meta http-equiv="Content-Type" content="text/html; charset=utf-8">
```

This tag appears inside the header of your document. (If you have server-side coding chops, you can use Content Negotiation. For more details, see `www.w3.org/2003/01/xhtml-mimetype/content-negotiation`.)

Listing 1-1 is an example document that conforms to the HTML syntax.

Listing 1-1. HTML Syntax

```
<!DOCTYPE html>
<html>
  <head>
    <meta http-equiv="Content-Type" content="text/html; charset=utf-8">
    <title>HTML Syntax Document</title>
  </head>
  <body>
    <p>This doc is HTML.</p>
  </body>
</html>
```

The other syntax that can be used for HTML5 is XML. Some things to note are the following:

- All documents with a text/html media type (such as older languages prior to HTML5 or documents having an XHTML1 DOCTYPE) will be parsed using the algorithm as defined by the current HTML spec.

- XHTML must no longer be served as text/html, and it must use application/xhtml+xml or application/xml.

- HTML documents must be served as text/html.

- For most of this book, we will be dealing with HTML and the content type text/html, which is included in the document header as shown earlier.

- <meta charset="UTF-8"> can now be used to specify the UTF-8 encoding. This replaces the need for the longer <meta http-equiv="Content-Type" content="text/html; charset=UTF-8">, although that syntax is still allowed.

What Syntax Should I Use?

You should be able to make the call yourself about what way you wish to author, as this should already be clear to you in terms of your previous authoring practice. You might, however, currently be asking, "What syntax do I use?" The chances are that if you're asking this question you can stick with serving your content as HTML using the text/html mime type because you don't have the requirements beforehand in your project to use more strict XML-type syntax.

XML follows simple rules such as requiring all content to be case sensitive, requiring you to close all tags, and to follow other such guidelines, whereas HTML content is more lax, it is not case sensitive, unclosed tags won't break your page, and so on.

■ **Note** If an incorrect or badly authored XML document is parsed by the more strict XML parser that doesn't match the rules of well-formedness, the document might not display—and that's a critical error which you probably don't want.

If the same rules were applied for all HTML documents on the Web (whether they are earlier versions of HTML or the latest), the Web would break, nothing would work! So, while HTML5 needs to have rules for dealing with both kinds of content (which it does), it must also treat badly formed HTML (or *tag soup* as it came to be known) in a way that can still be usable.

New Elements

Now we will look at some of the new elements that have been introduced in the HTML5 spec, as well as what they are for. There are quite a lot, and one of the tricky things is to determine where and when to use them. This is made somewhat easier by the fact that most of the new elements "do what they say on the tin." To use most elements, you won't have to think too deeply. It might be a little less clear what some others are for or when you would use them.

■ **Note** Don't be worried about adding HTML5 elements to your projects right now, even if you are not totally sure about support for an element or whether it will work 100 percent. When a new element is parsed by a browser or piece of assistive technology that it just doesn't understand, it is dealt with as plain text—and generally will not break anything.

Some HTML5 elements might not actually render or display in the browser (primarily because they might not be understood by it yet, although support is rapidly improving). It's also possible that while they might display visually, their semantics might be misunderstood or ignored by assistive technology. When this happens, you don't need to worry about them triggering any unusual behavior *most* of the time. However, if there is some strange behavior that gets triggered in the browser or some weird rendering quirk (anyone involved in web development for more than the past five years should be familiar with those quirks from the joy that was CSS coding), you've found a bug!

The best way to deal with bugs is to report them to the W3C and/or to the browser manufacturer. These nuggets of information really can help to make things better and improve future versions of software.

More than likely, you will find that someone, somewhere has found the bug and a group of developers have worked out a fix or *hack*. Hacks are a mixed blessing. Ideally, we wouldn't have to do them, but the world isn't a simple place, is it?

While we will go into much of the following in later chapters, here is an overview of some of the new elements that have been introduced in HTML5 for better structure:

- `<section>` represents a generic document or application section. It can be used together with the h1, h2, h3, h4, h5, and h6 elements to indicate the document structure.

- `<article>` represents an independent piece of content of a document, such as a blog entry or newspaper article.

- `<aside>` represents a piece of content that is only slightly related to the rest of the page.

- `<hgroup>` represents the header of a section.

- `<header>` represents a group of introductory or navigational aids.

- `<footer>` represents a footer for a section and can contain information about the author, copyright information, and other such details.

- `<nav>` represents a section of the document intended for navigation.

- `<figure>` represents a piece of self-contained flow content, typically referenced as a single unit from the main flow of the document, as shown here:

```
<figure>
 <video src="example.webm" controls></video>
 <figcaption>Example</figcaption>
</figure>
```

- `<figcaption>` can be used as caption for an image or other graphical content (it is optional), as shown in the preceding code example.

Then there are several other new elements:

- `<video>` and `<audio>` are for multimedia content. Both provide an API so that application authors can script their own user interface, but there is also a way to trigger a user interface provided by the user agent. source elements are used together with these elements if multiple streams of different types are available.

- `<track>` provides text tracks for the video element.

- `<embed>` is used for plugin content.

- `<mark>` represents a run of text in one document marked or highlighted for reference purposes, due to its relevance in another context.

- `<progress>` represents the completion of a task, such as downloading or performing a series of bandwidth expensive operations. This information can be very useful for people on limited broadband connections or for those using a dial-up service.

- `<meter>` represents a measurement, such as disk usage.

- `<time>` represents a date and/or time.

- `<ruby>`, `<rt>`, and `<rp>` allow for marking up ruby (an Open Source Object Orientated programming language) annotations.

- `<bdi>` represents a span of text that is to be isolated from its surroundings for the purposes of bidirectional text formatting.

- `<wbr>` represents a line-break opportunity. Word break can be used within a string.

- `<canvas>` is used for rendering dynamic bitmap graphics on the fly, such as graphs or games.

- `<command>` represents a command the user can invoke.

- `<details>` represents additional information or controls the user can obtain on demand. The summary element provides its summary, legend, or caption.

- `<keygen>` relates to more secure form creation and represents a control for generating a *key pair*, where a private key or code is stored on the client side (locally) and the public key is sent to a server (remotely).

- `<output>` represents some type of output, such as from a calculation done through scripting.

- The `<input>` element provides a field for the user to input data. In HTML5, it has new types and attributes. You might have some predefined input that you require from the user that you can define as option values (such as a Guitar type, as shown in the next example). We'll look at this in more detail in Chapter 8 on HTML5 forms.

```
<input list="guitars" />
<datalist id="guitars">
 <option value="Fender>
 <option value="Gibson">
 <option value="Martin">
 <option value="Gretsch">
</datalist>
```

- The `<input>` element has a type attribute, which now has the following new values:

  - tel

  - search

  - url

  - email

  - datetime

  - date

  - month

  - week

  - time

  - datetime-local

  - number

  - range

  - color

These new input types are provided to the user interface via the browser. They provide better, more sophisticated methods of form validation that can be done on the client side without calls to the server. There are also a host of new attributes that we'll look at as they arise throughout the book.

Also in HTML5, several attributes from HTML 4 now apply to all elements. These are called *global attributes* and include the following: accesskey, class, dir, id, lang, style, tabindex, and title. There are also several new global attributes:

- The contenteditable attribute indicates that the element is an editable area. The user can change the contents of the element and manipulate the markup.

- The contextmenu attribute can be used to point to a context menu provided by the author.

- The data-* collection of author-defined attributes allows authors to define any attribute they want as long as they prefix it with data- to avoid clashes with future versions of HTML. The only requirement on these attributes is that they are not used for user agent extensions.

- The draggable and dropzone attributes can be used together with the new drag-and-drop API.

- The hidden attribute indicates that an element is not yet, or is no longer, relevant.

- The role and aria-* collection attributes can be used to instruct assistive technology. There will be more about WAI-ARIA in Chapter 3, "JavaScript Isn't a Dirty Word, and ARIA Isn't Just Beautiful Music," where we will look at what it is, how to add it to your projects, and why it's important for accessibility.

- The spellcheck attribute allows for hinting whether content can be checked for spelling or not.[1]

HTML5: Accessibility and Feature Detection

So, that was an introduction to some of the new features of the HTML5 language. As I mentioned earlier, in later chapters we will be looking at how these new features relate to accessibility and what you can do with them to build accessible interfaces, as well as some of the challenges that await you.

The bad news is that many of the new HTML5 features are only starting to be supported by both browsers and assistive technology. From an accessibility perspective, this means you might have to be creative to make sure your content actually works, rather than taking an "in the spec it says do it this way, so that means it's supported" approach. The cookie doesn't crumble that way, unfortunately.

What's more, the specification doesn't entirely define the user experience. (And it could be reasonably argued that this is out of scope for the spec; however, I am inclined to side the other way.) So care must be taken to apply code in a practical way that can support the greatest range of users. And that's why you're reading this book, right?

The good news is that support for HTML5 is improving all the time, for both browsers and assistive technology (AT), so the future is bright. You might find that some of the elements or attributes you want to use are poorly supported in either the browser or by the assistive technology (and sometimes both), and I am very aware of this as I write the book. Where possible, I will try to illustrate how you can use

---

[1] Much of the section on new elements comes from www.w3.org/TR/html5-diff/, thanks to Anne Van Kesteren and Simon Pieters. Copyright © 2011 W3C® (MIT, ERCIM, Keio). All Rights Reserved.

HTML5 in a way that can be supported by older markup also, or by other accessibility languages like WAI-ARIA (which I'll say more about later).

▓ **Note** At time of this writing, many of the big players in the browser market have really good HTML5 support. It is often the AT that doesn't.

This book pays particular attention to backward compatibility in its general tone and tries to help you support what is known as *legacy user agents,* or older browsers and AT. Approaching the markup and design of your web content in a way that supports both the newer user agents that understand it, as well as those that don't (by giving them something to get their semantic teeth into), is the bedrock of *progressive enhancement,* which is the more enlightened approach to design.

▓ **Note** Throughout this book, I will often suggest that you borrow from other more accessibility-focused languages, like WAI-ARIA, because this is a really useful way of bridging the semantic accessibility gap in your projects. WAI-ARIA is now also officially a part of the HTML5 spec anyway, and it's a perfect tool to use to describe a widget's role, its state, or other properties to AT. It also has improving support in both the browser and AT.

There are also interesting techniques that can be used in HTML5, such as feature detection. This allows you, as an author, to query the user agent that your web content is being served to, in order to see if a given browser has support for specific features of HTML5 and then serve that browser that content—or don't serve it if the browser does not provide support. If that is all a little scary for you, there are tools such as Modernizr that can be used to do much of this for you.

▓ **Note** Modernizr is an open-source JavaScript library that uses media queries and scripted feature detection. It can be a useful tool in building your HTML5 pages. You can find out more at `http://www.modernizr.com`.

Now let's look at some background information about accessibility—what it is and why you need to make it part of your design.

Defining Accessibility

There are several definitions of accessibility. The International Standards Organization (ISO) defines accessibility this way:

"The usability of a product, service, environment or facility by people with the widest range of capabilities."

(ISO TC 16071, 2003)

Applying this definition to the Web ensures the interfaces that you design can be used by the widest possible audience, and therefore ensures there are no users who are left out. This sounds like a lofty ideal, and it might even seem daunting (and this is understandable), but don't worry. It really is amazing what you can do with HTML5, CSS, and JavaScript when you combine them the right way.

The W3C, in its "Introduction to Web Accessibility," defines accessibility as this:

"Web accessibility means that people with disabilities can use the Web. More specifically, Web accessibility means that people with disabilities can perceive, understand, navigate, and interact with the Web, and that they can contribute to the Web. Web accessibility also benefits others, including older people with changing abilities due to aging."

(WAI Introduction to Accessibility, 2010)

You will notice that the first definition does not mention blind users or other people with disabilities at all, yet it talks about general usability (which I'll discuss in more detail later). I prefer the second definition presented, because I think of accessibility as being "about people with disabilities." This helps me to theoretically understand the group I am trying to serve in a clear way, and it also removes some ambiguity in the definition. I find that if something is defined in too broad a way or is vague, it can be difficult to get a bead on what to do or where to start. By narrowing the definition, you have a more clearly defined point of reference.

Technically, accessibility can be defined as a subset of *usability* and thought of as a child of another discipline. Then again, *usability* can be understood as a child of Human Computer Interaction (HCI), which used to be called "Human Factors Engineering," more commonly known as *ergonomics*.

Accessibility: From Theory to Practice

Leaving the pros and cons of various definitions aside, in practice it is very important as a designer to try to understand the diverse needs of your audience. These needs vary greatly, and they cover a broad range of people of varying technical knowledge, manual-dexterity abilities, visual acuity, cognitive capacity, and speed.

So how can the average designer account for all this effectively? Are there ways to accomplish this goal that are accessible (to the designer, without taking on a degree in the area!) that will help you find your way through the maze of sometimes arcane or esoteric recommendations? This pursuit can be very daunting, but the answer is a resounding "Yes!"

This book aims to help you critically assess not only the design decisions you make, but also the sometimes contradictory advice you get from various guidelines and best practices so that you can be sure it is suitable for your needs. What's more, don't make the assumption that because "The spec says *x*" that *x* must automatically be true or that *x* even works at all. This warning is even more pertinent when it comes to accessibility.

Many HTML5 elements and attributes either are not, or will not, be supported by various browsers and/or assistive technologies, such as screen readers that are used by people with disabilities. Although the specification might clearly outline how a particular feature is to be implemented in the real world, it is often left to the vendor (or manufacturer) of a particular *user agent* (which is a catch all term for a browser, or even piece of AT) how to actually implement the spec. So this does affect the user experience in a big way. If you think back to the "browser wars," when there was no standard way for rendering different elements/attributes and when CSS had to be tweaked according to what devices it was being served to, you can see what I mean.

It will be the same with HTML5, and this book aims to practically show you how to future-proof your web content (regardless of what level of support is currently available for different HTML5 elements) in a way that is also backward compatible, which pretty much means that you need to ensure that it will work with older browsers and AT. Doing this successfully will sometimes mean playing loose with the rules. For example, when it comes to validation you might have to live with a few big red X's when the validator parses your content and you have added some specific accessibility markup, such as WAI-ARIA (which I'll say much more about later), to build an accessible JavaScript widget. However, the validator parsing rules often don't make proper provisions for these kind of documents, so you get errors. But we can't always have it every which way—such is life. If you are more concerned with building accessible stuff that really works, read on. But be warned: you might have to learn to think beyond the validator!

Later in the book, when we look at user-centered design, you'll see the benefits of really connecting with your users and how to use alternative user-evaluation methods and techniques, such as user testing, which can really show you what works and what doesn't work in your design.

User testing is a fantastic way to help you connect with your users and get a practical feel for the rights and wrongs of design. Implementing user testing is also a remarkable way of bridging the gap between you, the designer, and your end users. It also acts as a powerful way of moving from a theoretical understanding to a practical understanding of how design decisions impact the user.

User testing can be expensive, however, or just not practical. So we'll also look at ways you can do quick and dirty guerilla testing and some simulation techniques that might help you get a feel for the user experience that people with disabilities encounter. You might also benefit from the advice I give later on regarding testing yourself with a screen reader. This process can be a mixed blessing, and it needs to be approached with caution. This is because you need to be confident that any problems you experience when testing a web site with a screen reader are actually the result of an accessibility problem with the site, and not you having difficulties getting to grips with the AT!

This is a very common problem, but I aim to show you how to up your game when it comes to testing with common screen-reading software like JAWS or VoiceOver. I'll discuss how to approach the tests, explain what's going on when you are using the screen reader, and describe some common errors to avoid.

Understanding Accessibility

Good, accessible web sites are genuinely a natural by-product of good design. Good design comes from understanding some core things:

- What you are designing for and what the purpose of your site is

- Your audience's needs

- What visitors really wish to do when using your site

As stated previously, accessibility can at first seem abstract or esoteric. Many developers can find it difficult to grasp it fully as a practical discipline. Many people just don't get accessibility.

There are some aspects of accessibility that are initially easier to understand than others, but gradually, as their knowledge of best practices deepens, developers can quickly grasp that accessibility is rather practical.

Accessibility is an ever-evolving line, a continuum. However, for users of AT there are some core issues for each user group that don't really change—even if the technology does. For example, blind users need to be able to access equivalent content that describes to them what a particular image is all about, people with limited physical mobility really appreciate not having a lot of useless links to tab through, and so on.

Legislation

Depending on the country you live in, there will be different legislative requirements you might need to consider when building your web site. The degree to which legislation affects you depends on the purpose of your web site, whether you intend to do business with the federal government, or whether you are designing and developing for a public sector agency.

Understanding the law and how it relates to your project is very important. The following is a brief overview of legislation in different domains, covering the USA first and then the UK. Many thanks to Jared Smith of WebAIM from where much of the following is drawn from.

Rehabilitation Act

In the United States, the Rehabilitation Act of 1973 was the first major legislative effort to secure an equal playing field for individuals with disabilities. This legislation provides a wide range of services for persons with physical and cognitive disabilities. The Rehabilitation Act has been amended twice since its inception, once in 1993 and again in 1998. Two sections within the Rehabilitation Act, as amended, have an impact on accessible web design: sections 504 and 508.

Section 504

Section 504 of the Rehabilitation Act is a civil rights law. It was the first civil rights legislation in the United States designed to protect individuals with disabilities from discrimination based on their disability status. The nondiscrimination requirements of the law apply to employers and organizations that receive federal financial assistance.

Section 504, 29 U.S.C.§794, states the following:

> *"No otherwise qualified individual with a disability in the United States... shall, solely by reason of her or his disability, be excluded from participation in, be denied the benefits of, or be subjected to discrimination under any program or activity receiving Federal financial assistance."*

Therefore, any programs receiving federal funds cannot discriminate against those with disabilities based on their disability status. All government agencies, federally-funded projects, K-12 schools, and postsecondary entities (state colleges, universities, and vocational training schools) fall into this category.

Section 508

The Reauthorized Rehabilitation Act of 1998 included amendments to Section 508, which you can access at `http://webaim.org/articles/laws/usa/rehab`. This section bars the federal government from procuring electronic and information technology (E&IT) goods and services that are not fully accessible to those with disabilities. This includes the services of web design because the Internet is specifically mentioned.

Influence of Section 508

Why is Section 508 such a big deal? Although it's limited to federal agencies, Section 508 is an extremely influential piece of legislation. There are at least four reasons why this is so.

Section 508 provided the first-ever US federal accessibility standard for the Internet. The Web Content Accessibility Guidelines existed prior to this; however, these guidelines created by the Web Accessibility Initiative (WAI) were not intended to be written as standards. Plus, these guidelines came from a voluntary international body with no regulatory power.

This section provides compliance language that can be monitored at a distance. As stated earlier, guidelines did exist, but not in statutory language. Section 508 outlines binding, enforceable standards that must be adhered to in order for E&IT products to be accessible to persons with disabilities. A list of the Section 508 standards that apply to web accessibility is provided in the WebAIM Section 508 Checklist.

State governments might be held accountable for complying with Section 508. All states receive funding under the Assistive Technology Act of 1998. To gain access to this funding, each state must assure the federal government it will implement all conditions of Section 508 within their state entities (including institutes of higher education). Many states (for example, Arizona, Nebraska, and Wisconsin) have codified Section 508 to be state law, which requires state institutions to comply with these requirements.

Businesses must comply with Section 508 when supplying E&IT goods and services to the federal government. The influence of web accessibility on business and industry is more significant when the demands of a client, or potential client, like the US federal government must be met.

Section 508 Enforcement

The US Department of Justice Office of Civil Rights is charged with enforcing Section 508. When complaints arise, members of the public, students, and employees with disabilities can do the following:

- File an administrative complaint with agencies they believe to be in violation of Section 508.

- File a private lawsuit in federal district court.

- File a formal complaint through the US Department of Justice Office of Civil Rights.

The Office of the Attorney General is required to evaluate how well the government is conforming to Section 508. It is also required to provide updated reports to the President and Congress on both the accessibility of federal electronic and information technology to people with disabilities and the resolution of Section 508 complaints filed against federal agencies. The first such report was given in August 2001, and others have been given every two years thereafter.

Voluntary Product Accessibility Template

Voluntary Product Accessibility Template (VPAT) provides the details of how you comply with Section 508. It is a way of stating (up front) how accessible your product or service is. This can help with the procurement process because federal agencies can get an overview of how well your site or product performs compared to others.

■ **Note** For more information on VPATs and how to use them, see `www.evengrounds.com/articles/creating-an-effective-vpat`.

Other Relevant Legislation

While compliance with Section 508 is the main focus for most federal web projects, there are other acts to consider that have a bearing (while not explicitly referring to the Internet).

Americans with Disabilities Act

The Americans with Disabilities Act (ADA), passed in 1990 in the US, is civil rights legislation governed by the Department of Justice. The goal of this law is to make sure that people with disabilities can have an equal opportunity to participate in programs, services, and activities. Note that the ADA does not deal directly with the accessibility of the Internet. This might be because the Internet was just emerging as a widespread tool around the same time as the passage of the ADA. There are, however, two major sections in the ADA that might apply to web accessibility:

- Title II, which states that communications with persons with disabilities must be "as effective as communications with others" [28 C.F.R. ss 35.160 (a)]

- Title III, which deals with public accommodation of people with disabilities

Individuals with Disabilities Education Act

The Individuals with Disabilities Education Act (IDEA), as amended in 1997 in the US, provides for a "free appropriate public education," from preschool through high school, for all children with disabilities.

The IDEA relates to the Web in the following ways:

- The Internet is being used to a greater degree each year in the K-12 school systems. In fact, it is being used in two distinct ways:

  - Teachers use it to provide students with a general education curriculum in areas like history, science, English, or math. Students can explore materials and information, conduct research, engage in activities, and even take tests online.

  - An education goal found in most US states is that students will learn to use the Internet. Therefore, this becomes a curriculum in its own right.

15

- Another relevant piece of legislation is Section 255 of the Telecommunications Act of 1996, which "requires manufacturers of telecommunications equipment and customer premises equipment to ensure that the equipment is designed, developed, and fabricated to be accessible to and usable by individuals with disabilities."

Disability Discrimination Act 1995

In the UK, the Disability Discrimination Act (DDA) was introduced to end discrimination against disabled people and give them new rights in the areas of employment, access to goods and services, and buying or renting land or property.

There are some provisions in the Act (Part III) that arguably apply to web sites and have been in force since 1 October 1999.

However, the original Disability Discrimination Act 1995 was limited and missed some important areas, such as education. This meant that universities did not have to ensure that their educational services were accessible. This was dealt with by the passing of the Special Educational Needs and Disability Act 2001.

Special Educational Needs and Disability Act 2001

The Special Educational Needs and Disability Act 2001 (SENDA) was introduced as an amendment to the Disability Discrimination Act 1995 (DDA).

SENDA introduces provisions for people with disabilities in education in England, Wales, and Scotland. It aims for "comprehensive enforceable civil rights" for people with disabilities at school in England, Scotland, and Wales. It has major implications for further-education institutions, for the way the curriculum is delivered, and for the way students are supported.

PAS78, the DDA, and the Equality Act 2010

A very useful document for procurers of accessible web sites in the UK is PAS78. This publication provides guidance to organizations regarding how to commission an accessible web site from a design agency. It describes what is expected from web sites to comply with the UK Disability Discrimination Act 1995 (DDA), making web sites accessible to and usable by disabled people. In 2010, the DDA was superseded by the Equality Act. You can find more detail at the following sites:

- PAS78: www.equalityhumanrights.com/footer/accessibility-statement/general-web-accessibility-guidance

- The Equality Act 2010: www.legislation.gov.uk/ukpga/2010/15/contents

European Legislation

There are many individual pieces of legislation for each European Union (EU) member state, but there are also some overarching pieces of EU-wide legislation that relate to the Web and e-Inclusion.

■ **Note** The term *e-Inclusion* is the idea that no one should be left behind in enjoying the benefits of information and communication technologies (ICT). According to the European Commission e-Inclusion means "both inclusive ICT and the use of ICT to achieve wider inclusion objectives."[2] It focuses on participation of all individuals and communities in all aspects of the information society. e-Inclusion policy, therefore, aims at reducing gaps in ICT usage and promoting the use of ICT to overcome exclusion, and improve economic performance, employment opportunities, quality of life, social participation, and cohesion."

EU Charter of Fundamental Rights

The EU Charter of Fundamental Rights makes reference to people who are disabled:

- Article 21 prohibits discrimination based on grounds of disability, among other things.

- Article 26 provides explicit recognition of the rights of persons with disabilities and the need to ensure their independence, social and occupational integration, and participation in the life of the community.

i2010: A European Information Society

i2010 was the EU policy framework for the information society and media (2005-2009). It promoted the positive contribution that information and communication technologies (ICT) can make to the economy, society, and personal quality of life. The strategy is now coming to an end and is going to be followed by a new initiative—the Digital Agenda for Europe. For more information, see http://ec.europa.eu/information_society/digital-agenda/local/index_en.htm.

eEurope 2005

Before that, the eEurope 2005 Action Plan was launched at the Seville European Council in June 2002 and endorsed by the Council of Ministers in the eEurope Resolution of January 2003. It aims to develop modern public services and a dynamic environment for e-business through widespread availability of broadband access at competitive prices and a secure information infrastructure. This was preceded by eEurope 2002.

---

[2] http://ec.europa.eu/information_society/activities/einclusion/index_en.htm

---

▓ **Note** OK, scared? Well don't be. This is all included here just to paint a picture of how accessibility is taken seriously. Yes, the degree to which it is varies in different countries, but there is an imperative. So you should feel motivated to do the right thing.

The good news is that even if you don't totally get there with an "all-singing, all-dancing, full-on accessibility in-your-face" web site, making a sincere effort with your projects (in my experience) means an awful lot to the people with disabilities who use it.

It's when people feel they are being actively discriminated against and that an organization just doesn't care that there can be trouble. Actually, an "Accessibility" statement on a web site is really an "Inaccessibility" statement—and this makes sense if you define the scope of what you have done, or not done, and the work that is in progress. If you are up front about this kind of thing, it can certainly contribute to openness, transparency, and general good will—which is always a good thing.

Dealing with Change and Diversity

In many ways, the discipline of accessibility encompasses our ability, as designers, to deal with change and develop designs that can accommodate diversity in a positive way. There are natural changes that many of us will go through, such as failing sight and other physical and mental changes, as we get older. Therefore, our ability to perform certain tasks and the equipment we need may also change. Really understanding accessibility involves expanding our ability to deal with these changes.

The success of designers' efforts often depends on how well they can accommodate diverse user requirements. Using new tools, languages, and development methods is really just a test of our ability to do that, and the advent of HTML5 is no different. If as a developer you have some previous experience with building accessible interfaces, the hard-won knowledge you have gained will benefit you. You don't have to re-invent the wheel or start from some kind of "year zero" when you develop with HTML5. You might have to rethink your approaches to some kinds of content, because there have been some game-changers, but mainly, you will be able to nicely build on what you have learned previously.

The reality is that even though the languages and development methods that are used will often change rapidly, the needs of people with disabilities are pretty constant. This book focuses on some of the core aspects of designing for people with disabilities, which will hopefully simplify and enhance your understanding of the process.

What Are the Benefits of Accessibility?

There are some substantial benefits of accessible web design and development:

- **It makes good business sense:** Building accessible web sites can actually increase revenue for a business by ensuring that no one is excluded from its web site. There are some well-documented case studies that outline the business benefits of accessibility, such as the ones experienced by the following companies:

  - **Legal & General Group:** Doubled visitor numbers, cut maintenance costs by two-thirds, and increased natural search traffic by 50 percent.

  - **Tesco:** Spent 35 thousand GBP to build its web site, and had 13 million GBP per year in resultant revenue.

- **CNET:** Experienced a 30 percent increase in traffic from Google after it started providing transcripts. "We saw a significant increase in SEO referrals when we launched an HTML version of our site, the major component of which was our transcripts," said Justin Eckhouse of CNET. (W3C Business Case Examples, 2009)

These benefits can be generally categorized as follows:

- **Social Factors:** Increased web accessibility provides equal opportunities for people with disabilities by removing barriers to communication and interaction.

- **Technical Factors:** Increased Web accessibility improves interoperability, and quality, and reduces site development and maintenance time and server load. It also helps to ensure that content is enabled on different configurations, and that developers are prepared for advanced web technologies.

- **Financial Factors:** Greater accessibility improves search engine optimization (SEO)and enhances direct cost savings due to easier maintenance etc.

- **Legal and Policy Factors:** Increased Web accessibility addresses requirements for Web accessibility from governments and other organizations in the form of laws, policies, regulations, and standards.

- **Better design:** Graphic designers often design for themselves. This is not always the case, but it is often true. As a result the Web is littered with sites that use tiny text that can't be resized, illegible fonts, and bad color contrast. This often renders the site content unreadable to many. (WAI Business Case for Accessibility, 2010)

▓ **Note** A good design principle is that "form should follow function." This is a simple but effective rule of thumb that is unfortunately often ignored or just forgotten. As you progress with this book I hope that you will start to see that what you need to do to develop accessible interfaces really boils down to good design and coding practice. Accessibility is very practical and comes down to well-formed code, good User Interface design, solid Information Architecture, Human and Accessible Form Validation, and Error recovery. And the good news is all of this good stuff isn't just of benefit for people with disabilities, but for everyone.

Accessibility Should Enhance Your Design—Not Destroy It

In practice, accessibility brings some important fundamental design issues back into sharp focus for designers. This is a good thing. We often see shiny new things being built on the Web, and then people like me come along, look more closely, and see that it just doesn't work from an accessibility perspective. Then we have to be ones who say, "Hang on a minute." So the perception is that the accessibility community is anti-progress or anti-design.

This isn't the case, and no, we don't want to ruin the party. We just know a bit about what works and what doesn't. The Web is full of inaccessible stuff. In fact, the Web is inherently broken, and much of it shouldn't work, but does, which is pretty amazing in itself.

Let's look at how accessibility can limit a project in a positive way. Consider the following:

- To be *accessible* means that the designer must carefully consider how he or she presents content visually (in terms of clear design and color contrast) as well as how the underlying semantic structure of a web site is geared toward people with disabilities, or how a complex dynamic control can be used by someone with a disability. The effect of these "constraints" is that the designer must ideally use only whatever development techniques, elements, or attributes are suitable for the task at hand—the right tool for the right job. This approach is very important when developing HTML5 web content (as shall be demonstrated later when we look at new elements like <canvas>).

So accessibility is not anti-design, but merely a challenge. In reality, it helps to ground your designs in best practice across the board, and therefore brings extra benefits such as more future-proof, interoperable applications and web sites.

WCAG 2.0 and HTML5

The Web Content Accessibility Guidelines (WCAG 2.0) has been very carefully designed to be technologically agnostic, and I trust you will see the common sense in them when you are building your web sites and applications. Building accessible stuff that works is a very nuanced area. As I mentioned previously, you will have to balance real-world application of both the code and these guidelines in a way that is practical. Accessibility is not theoretical, mystical, or ethereal.

The needs of people with disabilities are very real and these guidelines are just that—guidelines and not a standard. They are meant to be informative and instructive, with the net result being that you have more accessible and usable interfaces.

■ **Note** Currently, there aren't a lot (or any) HTML5 test cases for WCAG 2.0. However, as I write, there are efforts to develop guidance and test suites for accessible and WCAG 2.0–conformant HTML5, and there will be more available as time goes on. So keep an eye on `www.w3.org/WAI/GL`.

WCAG is primarily intended for the following:

- Web content developers (page authors, site designers, and other such professionals)
- Web authoring tool developers
- Web accessibility evaluation tool developers
- Others who want or need a technical standard for Web accessibility

WCAG and related resources are also intended to meet the needs of many different audiences, including people who are new to Web accessibility, policy makers, managers, and others. WCAG 1.0 had various priority checkpoints; WCAG 2.0 has *success criteria*. While WCAG 1.0 was organized around a set of guidelines, WCAG 2.0 is organized around four simple principles, which form the acronym POUR.

- Principle 1: Content must be Perceivable (P). This principle refers to all content, including multimedia, video, and audio:
  - Provide a text alternative for all non-text content.
  - Provide synchronized alternatives for multimedia (such as captioned video, audio descriptions, and so forth)
  - Information and structure must be separate from presentation.
  - Make it easy to distinguish foreground information from the background (for example, have good color contrast).
- Principle 2: Interface elements must be Operable (O):
  - All functionality must be operable via the keyboard.
  - Users must be able to control limits on their reading or interaction.
  - Users must be able to avoid content that can cause seizures due to photosensitivity.
  - Provide mechanisms for users to find content, orientate themselves, and navigate through it.
  - Help users avoid mistakes, and make it easier to correct mistakes when they do occur.
- Principle 3: Content and controls must be Understandable (U):
  - Make text content readable and understandable.
  - Make the placement and functionality of content predictable.

- Principle 4: Content should be robust enough to work with current and future technologies (R):

  - Support compatibility with current and future user agents.

  - Ensure that content is accessible, or provide accessible alternatives (from WAI Introduction to WCAG, 2010).

I hope you can see that much of the advice is quite practical. In reality, it is often a case of "It doesn't matter how you get there as long as certain criteria are met," such as those just outlined.

The Challenge of HTML5 Accessibility

As you can see, there are a lot of changes afoot! As with any new major change, it may not all be smooth sailing. Dealing with this change can be difficult because the goalposts are actually moving. This is partially because HTML5 is itself still in draft. However, it has reached its first LC (or Last Call) for comments. As such, it is approaching a steady state.

This presents some challenges when writing about HTML5 because its support in browsers and AT is only starting to come on-stream. However, as the browsers implement them, so then the AT technologies often follow. This happens because vendors can then see that certain features are gaining use, and they will therefore make choices about what they support and how this will impact the user experience. Ultimately, the good news is that the toolkit has been dramatically expanded with HTML5, though you may often be faced with the problem of too much choice when it comes to approaching how to mark up your web projects.

As I touched on earlier, the semantic feast that follows from HTML 4 is pretty amazing.

Conclusion

In this chapter, I introduced you to the wonderful world of accessible web design and gave you a flavor of some of the challenges that lie ahead. There will be ups and downs, but it really can be fun. You won't always get things right, but trying to goes a long way. In the next chapter, we will look at disability in more detail as well as some of the more commonly used assistive technologies.

CHAPTER 2

Understanding Disability and Assistive Technology

In this chapter, we will look at a range of different types of disability and examples of some of the assistive technology (AT) that is used by people with disabilities. This chapter will help you to gain a greater understanding of what it means to have a disability and how having a disability changes the way web content is consumed by a user of AT.

Understanding Your Users

One of the hardest things for developers who are trying to build accessible web sites is to successfully understand the needs of their users. You should consider the potential needs from a couple of different angles. First, you must think about the functional requirements of the users, such as the tasks they wish to achieve while using the site. That has an obvious impact on the functionality that the site requires, as well as the approach you should take toward information architecture.

Then there are the devices that your audience will use. Leaving aside AT for a moment, with the growth of smartphone usage, many of us now are using the Web on the go, so the mobile space is really important.

■ **Note** There is a very tight mapping between accessibility and the mobile Web. So many of the development practices you bring to creating content for mobile devices are also really good for accessibility!

It's All Me, Me, Me with Some People!

Many designers build things for themselves, or for their friends, whether consciously or unconsciously. However, there has been a greater awareness in the design community about accessibility over the past few years and a buzz about the challenge of building accessible interfaces that has captured the imagination of developers.

The following text will help you come to grips with what it means to have a disability and how this can affect how you perceive the world and interact with it. This understanding can be used to better understand how to accommodate the diverse range of interaction needs that people with disabilities have. It isn't exhaustive, nor is it meant to be, but it should serve as a good introduction.

▓ **Note** Keep in mind that you cannot reasonably be expected to know every detail about every kind of disability, every piece of AT, and the corresponding techniques for designing custom Web interfaces that will work with them! So don't worry. Let common sense be your guide, and learn to embrace feedback, even if it initially appears to be negative. It's really valuable! When one person has a problem trying to perform a task on your web site, it means that there are many more who are also having problems but just haven't said anything. So be grateful that someone was grumpy enough to complain! By reacting positively, you will be able to improve the quality of your design projects as well as improve as a developer. So it's a win-win situation. It might hurt your pride a little, but you'll get over it.

We'll look at some User Centered Design techniques in a Chapter 9, "HTML 5, Usability, and User-Centered Design," but right now let's look at some different disability types.

Overview of Blindness

There are many degrees of blindness. The common perception is that a blind person cannot see anything at all, but this is often not the case. A blind person might be able to make out some light, shapes, and other forms.

One friend of mine actually has good sight, but he is registered as legally blind because he has a severe form of dyslexia that renders him functionally blind because his condition creates cognitive confusion. So there are many interesting edge cases.

There are also reasons that a person has to be defined as officially having a disability. These reasons include such things as eligibility for state aid, welfare, and other services.

For example, in the US under the Social Security laws, a person is considered blind if the following applies:

> *"He has central visual acuity of 20/200 or less in the better eye with the use of a correcting lens."* [1]

In the UK, the Snellen Test is a common way of measuring visual acuity by using a chart with different sized letters in order to evaluate the sharpness of a person's vision. If a person is being assessed for a vision impairment, the test looks specifically for

- Those below 3/60 Snellen (most people below 3/60 are severely sight impaired)

- Those better than 3/60 but below 6/60 Snellen (people who have a very contracted field of vision only)

- Those 6/60 Snellen or above (people in this group who have a contracted field of vision especially if the contraction is in the lower part of the field) [2]

---

[1] www.who.int/blindness/causes/en/.

■ **Note** The definitions of disability vary from country to country, and there are international efforts to synchronize these definitions under initiatives such as the International Classification of Function (ICF). These are classifications of health and health-related domains from body, individual, and societal perspectives. Classifications are determined by looking at a list of body functions and structure, as well as their level of activity and participation. Because an individual's functioning and disability occurs in a context, the ICF also includes a list of environmental factors. Therefore, the twin domains of activity and participation are a list of tasks, actions, and life situations that are used to record positive or neutral performance, as well as any activity limitations and participation restrictions that a person may encounter. These are grouped in various ways to give an overview of an individual's level of ability in areas such as learning and applying knowledge, communication, mobility, self care, community, and social and civic life, for example.

Some of the most common causes of blindness worldwide are the following

- Cataracts (47.9%)

- Glaucoma (12.3%)

- Age-related macular degeneration (8.7%)

- Corneal opacity (5.1%)

- Diabetic retinopathy (4.8%)

- Childhood blindness (3.9%)

- Trachoma (3.6%)

- Onchocerciasis (0.8%) [3]

■ **Note** In terms of computers and the Web, blind users in particular are a group that have benefitted from technological developments in a very real way. The development of text-to-speech software has allowed blind users of AT to work at a broad range of jobs (and not all IT) and to participate strongly with various online communities. This all helps with the sense of inclusion a person feels.

---

[2] The definition also considers the angle of vision or visual field. You can find out more at www.ssa.gov/OP_Home/ssact/title16b/1614.htm.

[3] www.who.int/blindness/causes/en/

Blindness and Accessibility

Most of the time when people think of Web accessibility, they think of blind people! You could be forgiven for thinking this was the case—because blind users are often the most vocal group online.

However, Web accessibility is not solely about blind computer users. When you read a lot of discussion online about both subjects, don't fall into the trap of associating Web accessibility with only blind people and screen readers. The idea that "If it works with a screen reader, it is accessible" is only partially true. But that is a little like saying, "Function x is defined in the HTML5 spec like this, therefore you should do it that way and it will just work." In an ideal world, yes, it would work for sure, but in the real world you have to consider the browser, its support for any given functionality, and the user modality (or method of interaction—are they sighted or blind users of AT, and so on?).

There are other aspects to consider for users of more serial devices, such as single-button switches for people with limited mobility. A screen-reader user might have no problems navigating or interacting with a widget or with page content that could be very difficult for someone with limited mobility. Computers users with limited mobility will often tire very easily or even get exhausted tabbing through the 20 links that you thought were a good idea to include at the time!

So try not to just consider blind users (although they are, of course, very important) and screen readers when you are thinking about accessibility. However, because the screen-reading technology in use is very sophisticated, as you shall see later, there is a degree of complexity in both correctly serving content to these devices as well as using them.

Vision Impairment

There is a very broad range of vision impairments. Some of the most common are outlined here, with some photographic examples included that attempt to simulate what vision might be like for a person with the condition. It isn't really the case that a person with vision impairment just can't see very well. As these examples hope to illustrate, there can be greater problems for the person with the condition, depending on the impairment itself.

Figure 2-1 is a picture of my desktop before I created any of the simulations that follow.

Figure 2-1. My desktop, as seen by someone with relatively good vision

Glaucoma

There are many causes for glaucoma, from simple aging to smoking. People with glaucoma might experience a total loss of their peripheral vision, as depicted in Figure 2-2. In the early stages, glaucoma can cause some subtle loss of color contrast, which can lead to difficulties seeing things around the environment or using a computer.

Figure 2-2. My desktop, as seen by someone with glaucoma (residual vision sample)

A person with peripheral sight loss might have difficulty seeing dynamic content updates if they are not near a particular element or widget. This can also be an issue for screen magnification users (more on this later).

Macular Degeneration

Macular degeneration is common among older people and causes a loss of vision in the center of the eye, as shown in Figure 2-3. This makes reading, writing, doing any kind of work on a computer, or performing up-close work very difficult. Recognizing certain colors can also be a problem.

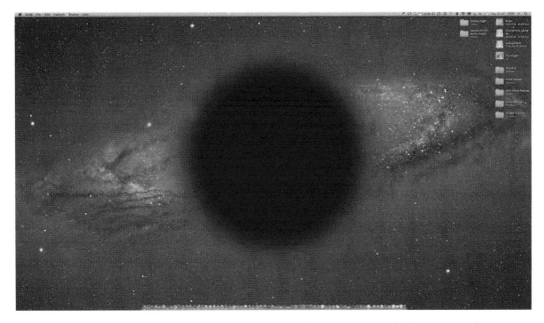

Figure 2-3. *My desktop, as seen by someone with macular degeneration (residual vision sample)*

Retinopathy

This condition causes a partial blurring of vision or patchy loss of vision, as shown in Figure 2-4. It can be brought on by advanced diabetes. The person's near vision may be reduced, and they may have difficulty with up-close reading.

Figure 2-4. My desktop, as seen by someone with retinopathy (residual vision sample)

Detached Retina

A detached retina can result in a loss of vision where the retina has been damaged. A detached retina might cause the appearance of dark shadows over part of a person's vision, or the person might experience bright flashes of light or showers of dark spots. See Figure 2-5.

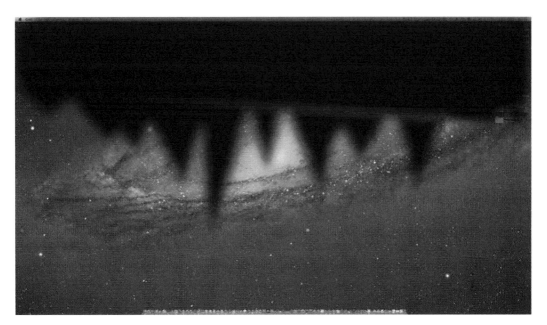

Figure 2-5. My desktop, as seen by someone with a detached retina

▓ **Note** There are some useful online tools that can act as *vision simulators*, such as the one developed by Lighthouse International. The simulator is designed to help inform, educate, and sensitize the public about impaired vision. Using filters that simulate macular degeneration, diabetic retinopathy, glaucoma, hemianopia, and retinitis pigmentosa, over YouTube videos of your choice, the simulator suggests some of the visual problems that a person with eye conditions experiences every day.[4]

For a more immersive simulation experience, the University of Cambridge has developed a very useful set of glasses that are designed to simulate a general loss of the ability to see fine detail, but are not intended to represent any particular eye condition. This type of loss normally occurs with aging and the majority of eye conditions, as well as not wearing the most appropriate glasses. The Cambridge Simulation Glasses can help to

- Understand how visual acuity loss affects real-world tasks

- Empathize with those who have poor vision

---

[4] www.lighthouse.org/about-low-vision-blindness/vision-simulator/

- Assess the visual demand of a task, based on the level of impairment [5]

Physical Disability

There are many kinds of physical disabilities that can manifest in different ways and range from the moderate to the more severe. Physical disabilities can be conditions present from birth, or they can be acquired later on in life due to accident.

Some common mobility problems include either a lack of physical control of movement or unwanted spasms, such as tremors. Often people with physical disabilities become easily exhausted and find many forms of movement very tiring.

When it comes to the use of a computer, people with physical disabilities often cannot use a mouse. The devices that are used (switches, joy sticks, and other AT, which we will look at shortly) can be a great help when trying to interact with a computer.

Some people with physical disabilities might not use any kind of AT but will find it hard or even impossible to use web sites and applications that are not keyboard accessible. In fact, ensuring your web sites are keyboard accessible is probably one of the single greatest things you can do to help users with physical disabilities. Doing this as a rule of thumb is a great idea and will also help to support users of switches and other serial input devices.

Cognitive and Sensory Disabilities

Computer users with cognitive and sensory disabilities are probably the hardest to accommodate. This is pretty much because it is such a new area of research and there is little conclusive evidence about what works and what doesn't.

Accessibility-related web-development techniques are also underspecified. However, as time goes on, there is a greater understanding of cognitive and sensory disabilities and there will be a greater suite of accessible development methods that can be used to accommodate this user group's needs.

Some of the challenges that the designer faces when building interfaces that can be used by people with cognitive and sensory disabilities are outlined in the sections that follow.

Perception

This is a visual and auditory difficulty where certain shapes, forms, and sounds can be hard to recognize. Understanding how to serve the needs of users with perception difficulties can be hard, because it is difficult to know just how they might perceive certain items, such as unusual user interfaces.

Care must be taken when combinations of visual and auditory cues are used in rich media interfaces, because this can cause problems such as *sequencing* (which is explained in an upcoming section).

Consistent and clear design will certainly help, and the use of distinctly designed components that clearly illustrate their inherent functionality and are easy understand will help as well.

Memory and Attention

Problems with short-term memory and attention can have a profound impact on a person's ability to perform the most basic tasks, and it can make using more complex technologies very challenging. People experiencing issues with memory loss can find that it severely impacts their ability to understand and react to user-interface feedback (such as form validation) and that it makes responding appropriately or in the required way in any given situation very difficult.

Chunking content into small, related blocks can be a great help to people with memory problems. This is where you divide related content and interface elements into groups of five to seven *chunks*, which is a useful method to aid comprehension as well as to help users with short attention spans.

Sequencing

Sequencing relates to the ability to associate auditory and visual cues over time, or knowing what steps are required to perform a given task. Difficulties with sequencing can be reduced by providing *cues* in the interface that, for example, will help your users understand when input is required.

Also, sequencing-related problems can be minimized if you avoid using unnecessary flashing content, animation, or movement that can be distracting to the user and divert their attention away from core functionality, or that can just be distracting when the user is trying to read. Many other users would also thank you for doing this, including me!

Dyslexia

The term *dyslexia* comprises a range of conditions that relate to difficulty interpreting words and numbers or math.

The use of clear, concise language for Web content can be a great help to people with dyslexia, as can the font you use. People with dyslexia have problems with characters that include *ticks* or *tails*, which are found in most Serif fonts. The size of ascenders and descenders on some letters (such as the downstroke on *p* and the upstroke on *b*) can get mixed up, so the visual shape of the characters must be clear. Dyslexic people rely on this as a visual clue to help them distinguish one letter from another.

Some general advice on fonts to use can be found at `Dyslexic.com`, specifically `www.dyslexic.com/fonts`.

▓ **Note** Comic Sans seems like a great font, but most designers would rather gnaw off their own leg than use it. A groovier and more designer friendly font is the rather nice "Dyslexie: A Typeface for Dyslexics." This font was developed at the University of Twente in the Netherlands to help dyslexic people read more easily.

It's based on the notion that many of the 26 letters in the standard Latin-based alphabet, as used in English, look similar—such as v/w, i/j and m/n. Thus, people with dyslexia often confuse these letters. By creating a new typeface where the differences in these letters are emphasized, it was found that dyslexic people made fewer errors.

There is also a really nice video on dyslexia at the following web site: `www.studiostudio.nl/project-dyslexie`.

What Is Assistive Technology?

The range of assistive technology (AT) devices and controls is really varied. There are also many definitions. I like this one:

"A term used to describe all of the tools, products, and devices, from the simplest to the most complex, that can make a particular function easier or possible to perform."

US National Multiple Sclerosis Society

You might have noticed that disability isn't explicitly mentioned at all, and this is important. You don't think of your glasses or your TV remote controls as assistive technology, but that is exactly what they are.

▓ **Tip** For a great introduction to AT, watch the AT boogie video by Jeff Moyer with animation by Haik Hoisington. It's fun and educational, and it can be found at `http://inclusive.com/assistive-technology-boogie`.

Why can't technology be used by many different people regardless of their ability? Can good design make this a reality? Good design should enable the user to perform a desired task regardless of the user's ability.

As a designer or web developer, you don't need in-depth knowledge of how assistive technology works. In fact, this range and depth of knowledge is likely difficult to achieve because it will take a lot of time and energy.

Many assistive-technology devices are serial input devices. They accept one binary input, on/off. Others are much more complex (like screen readers) and can be used in conjunction with the browser to do very sophisticated things and develop new interaction models. In the next section, we will look at screen readers—what they are, how they work, and how you can use them in your testing (with warnings) of the accessibility of your web sites.

You don't really need an exhaustive understanding of every type of AT, but a good understanding of screen-reader technology is a valuable foundation for successful accessible design, regardless of the AT used.

What Is a Screen Reader?

Screen readers are mainly used by blind and visually impaired people, but they can also be beneficial to other user groups, such as people with dyslexia or people with literacy issues.

A screen reader will identify what is on the screen and output this data as speech. It is text-to-speech software that literally reads out the contents of the screen to a user as he or she gives focus to items on the screen and navigates by using the keyboard. Screen readers are used to interact with and control a PC, Mac, web browser, and other software.

Screen readers can work very well with the operating system of the host computer itself, and they can give a deep level of interaction with the computer, letting the user perform many complex system administration tasks. In fact, the screen reader usually performs much better when interacting with the host operating system because they are tightly integrated. It's when the screen reader user goes online that problems often start. The online world isn't a controlled or well-regulated place, so there are reasons why the safe and well-engineered environment of the operating system is generally much more accessible.

Screen readers can be used to simulate right-mouse clicks, open items, and interrogate objects. Interrogating an object really means to query—rather like focusing on an object and asking it "What are you, or what properties do you have?" Screen readers also have a range of *cursor types* and can be used to navigate the Web and control the on-screen cursor, as well as simulate mouse-over events in Web environments that use JavaScript. In short, pretty much all sighted user functionality can be done using a screen reader.

▦ **Note** The term *screen reader* is quite misleading. A screen reader does much more than just read the screen. A more accurate term would be *screen navigation and reading device* because the software is used to navigate not only the user's computer but the Web.

Many different screen readers are available, such as JAWS, Window-Eyes, the free open-source Linux screen reader (ORCA), and the free NVDA, as well as the constantly improving VoiceOver that comes already bundled with Mac OS X. There are others, such as Dolphin Supernova by Dolphin, System Access from Serotek, and ZoomText Magnifier/Reader from Ai Squared. Coming up next is an overview of some of the more commonly used screen readers. It's not exhaustive coverage of the available products, and the different packages basically do the same thing. What people use is largely determined by budget and preference.

JAWS

JAWS for Windows is one of the most commonly used screen readers and is developed by Freedom Scientific in the US. JAWS stands for *Job Access With Speech*, and it's an expensive piece of software that costs about $1,000 for the professional version.

There are also many *JAWS scripts* available, which expands its functionality to enable access to some custom interfaces and platforms. JAWS was originally a DOS-based program. It gained popularity due to its ability to use macros and quickly access content and functionality.

Around 2002, this ability was brought into the more graphical Windows environment with the addition of being able to navigate around a webpage using quick keys and giving focus to HTML elements like headings. This kind of functionality and user interaction with screen-reading technology has become a cornerstone of accessible web development.

JAWS functionality expanded as the years went by, with the ability to query the fonts used in a page, specify what web elements had focus, and more advanced features like *tandem*, which allows you to remotely use another person's screen reader to access a computer. Tandem is very useful for troubleshooting and remote accessibility testing.

JAWS 12 saw the introduction of a virtual ribbon, for use with Microsoft Office and other applications, as well as the introduction of support for WAI-ARIA.

So How Does a Blind Person Access the Web and Use a Screen Reader?

The following will help you come to grips with how the screen reader is used, as well as help you if you decide to manually test your HTML5 interfaces with a screen reader.

First off, JAWS uses what's called a *virtual cursor* when interacting with Web content. So you are not actually interacting directly with the webpage itself but with a virtual version or snapshot of the page that is loaded on a page refresh. The virtual cursor is also used for reading and navigating Microsoft Word files and PDF files, so some of the tricks you will learn here can be applied when navigating accessible offline documents.

■ **Note** With JAWS, interacting with Web content involves using an *off-screen model (OSM)*, where HTML content from the page is temporarily buffered or stored and the screen reader interacts with that rather than the page directly. There are times, however, when the DOM is used, and other screen readers don't use an off-screen model anymore because it is seen as slightly outdated and problematic. So interacting with the DOM directly is preferable. Don't worry too much about this now because I'll cover it in more detail in a Chapter 4, "Understanding Accessibility APIs, Screen Readers, and the DOM." The details of how screen readers use an OSM and interact with the DOM become important later when we talk about dynamic content and using JavaScript.

Starting with JAWS

The type of JAWS voice that you use—as well as its pitch, its speed, and the amount of punctuation that JAWS outputs—can be controlled via the Options menu > Voices > Voice Adjustment.

■ **Tip** You might also wish to make some adjustments like turning off the *echo* for when you are typing. In my experience, many blind users do this right away; otherwise, when you type a sentence, each character you input will be announced and that can get very annoying, very fast.

Many of the speech functions in JAWS are accessed via the numeric keypad. The INSERT key is very important also (commonly called the JAWS key), because it is used to access some more advanced functions when online.

The number pad is used to query text and controls how and what is read. So using the arrow keys will move you up and down and read on-screen content, while going LEFT and RIGHT with the arrow keys will bring you forward and back, respectively, through text.

■ **Note** To stop JAWS from talking at any time, press the CTRL key!

The most common keys for interacting with text are

- NUM PAD 5—Say character
- INSERT+NUM PAD 5—Say word
- INSERT+NUM PAD 5 twice—Spell word
- INSERT+LEFT ARROW—Say prior word
- INSERT+RIGHT ARROW—Say next word
- INSERT+UP ARROW—Say line

- INSERT+HOME (the 7 key) —Say to cursor

- INSERT+PAGE UP (the 9 key) —Say from cursor

- INSERT+PAGE DOWN (the 3 key) —Say bottom line of window

- INSERT+END (the 1 key) —Say top line of window

As mentioned earlier, the LEFT ARROW and RIGHT ARROW keys are used to move to and read the next or previous character, respectively. The UP ARROW and DOWN ARROW keys will allow you to move to and read the previous or next line, respectively. If you hold down the ALT key and press the UP ARROW or DOWN ARROW key, you go through a document by sentence. Or you can use CTRL to navigate a document by paragraph.

Using Dialog Boxes with JAWS

To shift between different programs you have open on your PC, you use the CTRL+TAB and CTRL+SHIFT+TAB keys to toggle forward and back, respectively. To navigate options in a dialog box, you use the TAB key to go forward and SHIFT+TAB to go back.

JAWS and the WEB

JAWS provides a killer way to browse the Web easily. When you open your Web browser—for example, Internet Explorer (IE)—you can jump to any HTML element on the page of your choice by pressing a single key. To find the headings on a page, press H; for all tables, press T; for form controls, press F; and so on. Pressing any of these keys more than once will result in the next desired element within the document source order being announced and given focus. This is a fantastic way to browse the Web, use headings to navigate, and jump over sections of content and quickly give focus to whatever element you wish!

■ **Note** Being able to browse the Web as I just described is entirely dependent on the page having a suitable semantic structure for the assistive technology to use in the first place. If a webpage has no headings, for example, this method of browsing just won't work. Given this, the important role that well-formed markup plays in accessibility, as discussed in the previous chapter, should be crystal clear.

Displaying HTML Items as Lists

Expanding on the preceding method of user interaction, JAWS can also be used to create lists of all the headings, links, and other HTML elements in a page and present them to the user in a dialog box the user can easily navigate through using the cursor keys.

If you press the JAWS (INSERT) key and a corresponding function key, you get a list of HTML elements displayed nicely in a dialog box. For example, you can press INSERT+F7 to display a list of all links on the current page, as shown in the dialog box in Figure 2-6.

Figure 2-6. The Links List dialog box

Another example is that you can press INSERT+F6 to display a list of all headings on the current page, as shown in Figure 2-7.

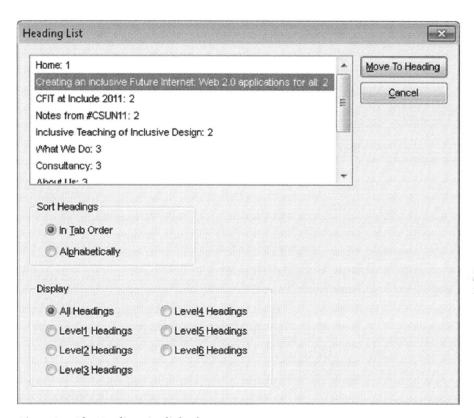

Figure 2-7. *The Heading List dialog box*

Or you can press INSERT+F5 to display a list of all form fields on the current page, as shown in Figure 2-8.

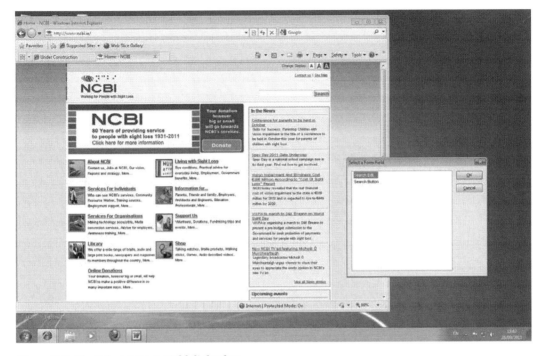

Figure 2-8. *The Select A Form Field dialog box*

You can then use the arrow keys to select an item, and press ENTER to activate or give it focus.

■ **Note** Once the dialog is open, you can also browse the list alphabetically—a really handy feature. So if you have a long list of links, rather than using the arrow keys to go through them one by one, if you know the name of the link you want you can press the key of its first letter and bounce to that link directly. So (once the link dialog box is open) if you want the Contact link, press C; if you want About Us, press A; or if you want Sales, press S; and so on.

JAWS and Forms

As mentioned earlier, JAWS uses a virtual cursor for interacting with webpages. The screen reader can be thought of as not interacting with the page directly, apart from when the user needs to input some data, such as with a form. This is when the virtual cursor is switched off, and JAWS disables the quick navigation keys and functions and enters Forms Mode.

▒ **Tip** The quick navigation features that were described earlier are turned off when you are in Forms Mode because you need the keys to type! When using the JAWS virtual cursor (which is the default when browsing the Web), the keyboard input is captured by the screen reader and used to navigate the Web.

In earlier versions of JAWS, when you moved into a form control and wanted to type or select a radio button or other element, you had to manually select Forms Mode. The newer versions of JAWS have an Auto Forms Mode and are on by default. More advanced users can turn this feature off if they choose and go back to manually selecting Forms Mode in their screen reader. This can give the user more control, as they can choose to enter the Input Mode or not – rather than it being the default in their AT. It is largely a matter of preference; other screen readers like VoiceOver will allow you to enter text in an input field when it has focus and doesn't have a user controlled Forms Mode.

▒ **Note** To manually control a form using JAWS, press F to move to the next form control on the page. Press ENTER to enter Forms Mode. Press the TAB key to move between form controls while in Forms Mode. Type in edit fields, select check boxes, and select items from lists and combo boxes. Press NUM PAD PLUS to exit Forms Mode.

There can be problems with the JAWS screen reader not being able to pick up on some content in forms because the virtual cursor is off. When you build forms, you should be sure that your forms are well labeled, and by keeping them clear and simple in layout and design you should avoid these issues. However, user testing your projects with people with disabilities is a great way of highlighting problems that you couldn't anticipate. We'll look at this in Chapter 9, "HTML5, Usability, and User-Centered Design." Also at this stage, getting into the details of Forms Mode and the various cursors that are used is a little more of a post-graduate topic, but I will try to highlight some of these issues in the later Chapter 4, "Understanding Accessibility APIs, Screen Readers, the DOM," as well as Chapter 8, "HTML5 and Accessible Forms."

VoiceOver and the Mac

There have been huge improvements with the quality of the native, out-of-the-box VoiceOver screen reader that comes bundled with every Mac. It is safe to say the quality of the voice, its integration with the operating system, and its usefulness on the Web have resulted in many blind users making the switch to the Mac. The cost of the JAWS screen reader alone is equivalent to buying a lower spec Mac. Also, I have heard some blind friends say that they prefer it because it just "feels nicer."

VoiceOver is also suitable for you, as a developer, to use in your testing of the accessibility of web sites—and in some ways, it is preferable to using JAWS because you can start testing it right out of the box and the learning curve isn't as steep.

Before we look at VoiceOver in more detail, I need to mention something important that you really should do to configure your Safari browser. To be able to give focus to items on the page such as links (which is very important for accessibility testing), you need to enable this feature in the browser under Universal Access, as shown in Figure 2-9. This feature will work whether VoiceOver is on or off—it's a pain that it's not enabled by default.

Figure 2-9. You must select the Press Tab To Highlight Each Item check box

▨ **Note** If you are vision impaired, VoiceOver can be used to configure your Mac straight out of the box. This is a really useful feature.

So where to start with VoiceOver? If you are running the Mac already, you can start VoiceOver by pressing CMD+F5. You'll see a change to your screen on the bottom left, as shown in Figure 2-10.

Figure 2-10. *VoiceOver screen reader dialog*

This dialog box can be very helpful for testing, because it represents the text output of VoiceOver. So if you are a sighted person testing a page, you can get a visual heads up about what the screen reader will be outputting. Any items you focus on using the keyboard (or the trackpad or mouse) will also have their name (and sometimes certain properties) announced by VoiceOver, and you will be able to see this info in this box.

The Control (Ctrl) and Option (alt) keys are very important when using VoiceOver and are known as the VoiceOver or VO keys. You will pretty much need to press these in conjunction with other keys to get VoiceOver to do stuff, like bounce to a heading, go to links, and other such actions.

You can also assign VO commands to things like trackpad gestures and number pads to perform commonly used tasks with fewer keystrokes. You might want to emulate the swipe gesture to navigate between HTML items, such as when using the iPhone and VoiceOver (which is a really cool way to be able to browse the Web). I'll say more on that a little later. The VoiceOver Utility is used to tweak the screen reader to your needs.

You access the VoiceOver Utility by selecting Universal Access in the Systems Preferences dialog box, as shown in Figure 2-11.

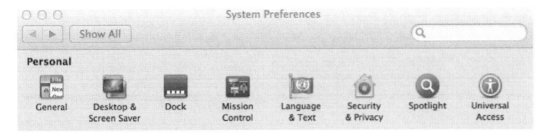

Figure 2-11. *Accessing the Universal Access options*

Then you will see the accessibility options relating to the Mac, as shown in Figure 2-12.

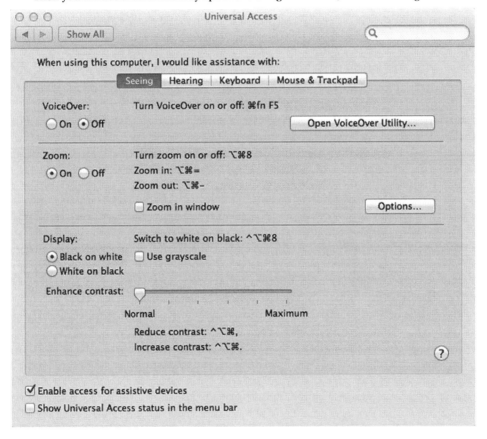

Figure 2-12. *Universal Access options*

■ **Note** There are several other accessibility features already on your Mac, such as a pretty good screen magnifier for people with impaired vision. (This is also available with every Windows PC and Linux Box.) It's worth spending some time getting familiar with them.

Opening the VoiceOver Utility will bring you into the area where you can customize your screen reader settings, as shown in Figure 2-13.

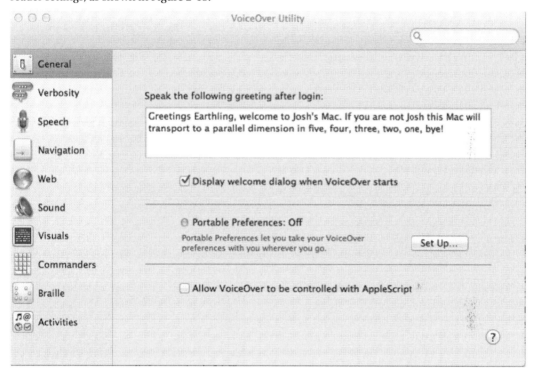

Figure 2-13. VoiceOver Utility

The VoiceOver Utility allows you to select the voice, pitch, speed, and other settings that you want to use. You might want to adjust the voice to speak to you fast or slow, depending on what you are doing. I really like the Vicki voice, set at the values shown in Figure 2-14.

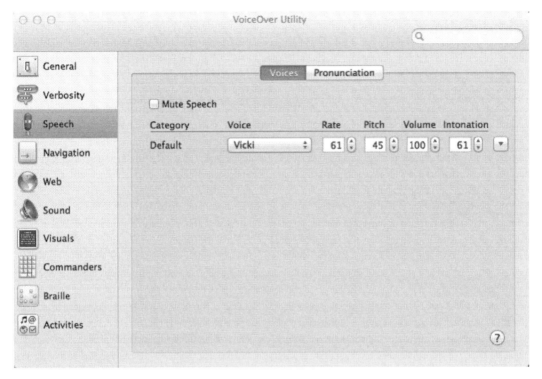

Figure 2-14. VoiceOver Utility—speech configuration options

▨ **Note** There are a couple of other features that you might want to tweak. For example, I like to switch off the Announce When A Modifier Key Is Pressed option and the Announce When The Caps Lock Key Is Pressed option. Although both are important when a visually impaired person is using the screen reader, when testing webpages for accessibility I find the first option really annoying because every time the shift key is pressed (if I am typing) "Shift" gets announced. These options are shown in Figure 2-15, which displays the Verbosity options.

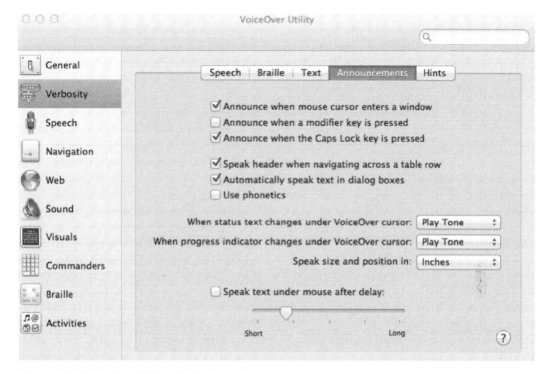

Figure 2-15. VoiceOver Utility—Verbosity options

The Web options, shown in Figure 2-16, are also important. I recommend that you have a look and tweak them a little, because this might help with your testing and with browsing the Web.

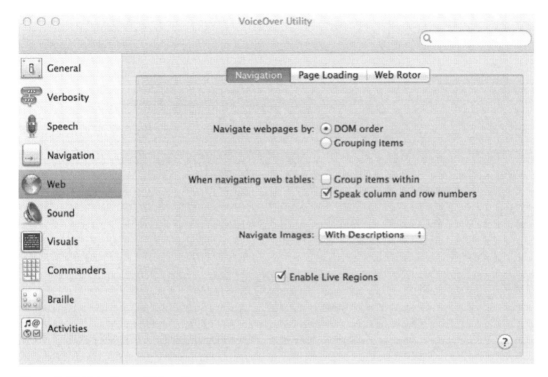

Figure 2-16. VoiceOver—Web options

You can see three tabs in Figure 2-16: Navigation, Page Loading, and Web Rotor.

▨ **Tip** VoiceOver offers a couple of ways to navigate webpages. The first is the default DOM Order, which allows you to navigate in the way I outlined previously, such as going from heading to heading or link to link. The navigation order is determined by the source order in which the items appear in the code. The second option is Grouping Items, which lets you use gestures like swiping left and right, or up and down, to get a spatial feel for a page and where items are positioned. Although this might be useful for some blind users, it's not really useful for a developer to test the accessibility of a page. So I would leave the DOM Order option selected.

I recommend leaving the Page Loading options, shown in Figure 2-17, as they are.

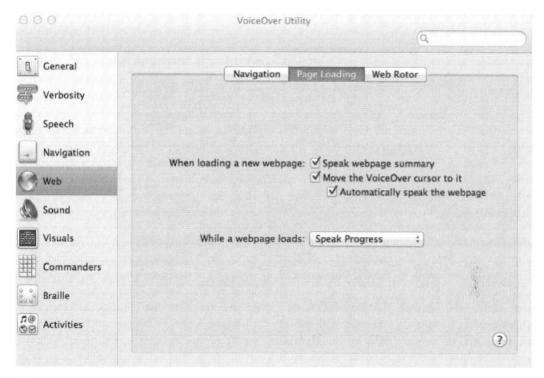

Figure 2-17. More VoiceOver Web options

The last option we shall tweak slightly. This is the preferences pane for the Web Rotor, which is an important feature in VoiceOver for you to understand because it is at the core of the new wave of gesture-based interaction.

Using the Web Rotor

The Web Rotor acts as a way to use simple gestures to access certain kinds of HTML and other elements. As shown in Figures 2-18, 2-19, 2-20, and 2-21, it is a virtual dial that you access by pressing your thumb and your forefinger at say 6 o'clock and 12 o'clock, respectively, and then turning your fingers clockwise or counterclockwise. You will then see a dial appear that shows the various options for you to choose, as you continue to turn. When you have chosen a particular kind of content (such as a link or headings), you can use, via the trackpad, a simple swipe gesture (to the right or left) to navigate. Each gesture will highlight the desired items as they appear in the source code, outputting them as speech as you swipe. Pretty neat.

Figure 2-18. *VoiceOver—Choosing links with the Web Rotor*

Figure 2-19. Choosing tables with the Web Rotor

Figure 2-20. *Choosing buttons with the Web Rotor*

Figure 2-21. Choosing form controls with the Web Rotor

As you can see from those four screen shots, this is an elegant and clever solution that takes full advantage of using the trackpad and some simple gestures. As you play with it, you'll see that it's pretty easy to switch between content types and get a feel for how accessible the page is.

■ **Note** You must have Trackpad Commander enabled for this to work, and doing so will disable the click functionality of the trackpad. Also, this functionality works best with Safari.

You can customize the rotor so that you can tweak the order in which the rotor items appear, as well as what does or doesn't appear.

Another adjustment I would make is to select the Enable Live Regions check box, as shown in Figure 2-22, to add live regions to the rotor choices. Live regions and landmarks are a part of the WAI-ARIA specification. Live regions dynamically update areas of a page for things like up-to-the-minute weather information, stock prices, and shares data—or anything that is constantly updating. Landmarks are a way of distinguishing between sections of content like the header, a banner item, and so forth.

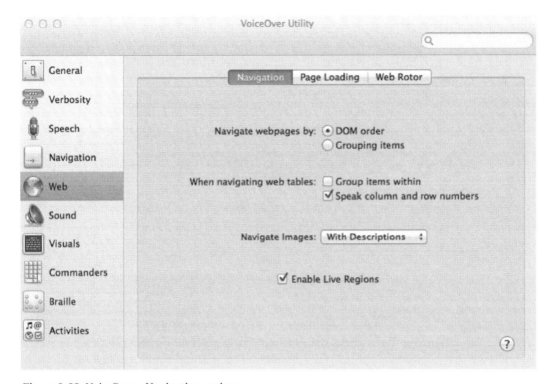

Figure 2-22. *VoiceOver—Navigation options*

Although Enable Live Regions is selected by default, it's not enabled by default within the Rotor. So if you wish to see this feature in your Web Rotor preferences (and yes, it's going to be useful), I recommend that you select Web Rotor in your VoiceOver Utility preferences and activate live regions and landmarks, as shown in Figure 2-23. In the figure, I have rearranged things slightly to suit my needs for accessibility testing.

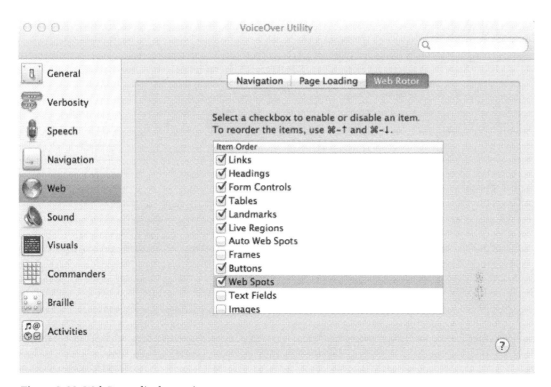

Figure 2-23. Web Rotor display options

VoiceOver has tons of other great features, such as user-defined Web Spots. By pressing the VO keys, CMD and Shift, and the right brace (}), you can create a list of custom spots (or functions that might get used a lot on a webpage, for example) and then navigate to them using the rotor. This is very useful for repeated use of a page that you visit very often.

▪ **Note** These examples are all relevant to MAC OS Lion (10.7.1) and using Safari 5.1. The Rotor can also be accessed using the VO keys and pressing U, and navigating via the arrow keys. You can also start to type an HTML element's name to get a list of items that can be accessed, rather like a clever search engine feature.

All of the features included with the JAWS screen reader (when using the Web, anyway) pretty much have their functional equivalent in VoiceOver, although there are subtle differences in the realization of the interface. They can't really be considered exactly the same, because they operate in different ways and JAWS is the older kid on the block and therefore has some more advanced functions.

▓ **Tip** The new version of VoiceOver that comes with Lion (10.7) has a handy new feature called QuickNav. It's a way of interacting with the Rotor in a more direct fashion. Press the left and right cursor keys together, and then enter QuickNav mode. By pressing the left arrow and up arrow together you can move the Rotor backward and then navigate the webpage by the chosen item with the up/down arrow keys. By using the right arrow and the up arrow, you can move the Rotor forward. For more information, as well as a video on how to use this feature see: `www.apple.com/accessibility/voiceover`.

Window-Eyes

GWMicro is the developer of Window-Eyes (for Windows operating systems), which is a screen reader that is similar to JAWS and worth a mention because it was one of the first to support WAI-ARIA. It operates slightly differently than JAWS in that it doesn't use an off-screen model (OSM) and interacts with the DOM directly, but its core functionality is very similar to JAWS. I have heard blind friends and colleagues express a preference for it because it was a little faster and more responsive, but functionally it is very similar. It is, however, much cheaper than JAWS, which is a good thing.

NVDA

The NVDA screen reader is also worth a mention because it has many positive things going for it (such as being completely free and open source). It's also a strong supporter of WAI-ARIA.

It can also provide feedback via synthetic speech and Braille. NVDA allows blind and vision-impaired people to access and interact with the Windows operating system and many third-party applications.

Major highlights of NVDA include the following:

- Support for popular applications, including web browsers, email clients, Internet chat programs, and office suites

- Built-in speech synthesizer supporting over 20 languages

- Announcement of textual formatting where available, such as the font name and size, the text style, and spelling errors

- Automatic announcement of text under the mouse, and optional audible indication of the mouse position

- Support for many refreshable Braille displays

- Ability to run entirely from a USB stick or other portable media without the need for installation

- Easy-to-use talking installer

- Translated into many languages

- Support for modern Windows operating systems, including both 32-bit and 64-bit variants

- Ability to run on Windows logon and other secure screens

- Support for common accessibility interfaces such as Microsoft Active Accessibility, Java Access Bridge, IAccessible2, and UI Automation

- Support for Windows Command Prompt and console applications

NVDA has its own speech synthesizer that comes bundled with it (called *eSpeak*), but it can be plugged into common existing speech synthesis engines such as SAPI 4/5.

Screen Readers and Alternatives

If you don't want to use a screen reader (and you may have good reasons, because it's difficult to learn how to use them properly), you could try using a screen-reader emulator such as Fangs.[5] Fangs can be used as a plugin for Firefox and to demonstrate what the output of a webpage would be to a user of JAWS. This approach, however, isn't a silver bullet either, because it won't give you a feel for the user experience of a blind person, which is what really learning the ropes of using a screen reader will do. Having said that, it's a useful tool you can turn to if using a screen reader doesn't go well.

■ **Tip** A trick you can use with VoiceOver, if you don't want to listen to the entire speech output—VoiceOver will display the text that it is outputting as speech in a little window at the bottom of the screen. For developers, this is useful for understanding what the screen reader will output when any HTML element has focus.

In Chapter 4, "Understanding Accessibility APIs, Screen Readers, and the DOM," we will take a more advanced look at how the screen reader works under the hood; this will help you understand just what is going on when you use a screen reader. Finally, in Chapter 10, "Tools, Tips, and Tricks: Assessing Your HTML5 Project," we will further explore some common strategies used by blind people when they're navigating the Web and outline how you might be able to simulate these browsing strategies in your accessibility testing with a screen reader. We'll also look at some other tools you can use in your browser to understand what the screen reader "sees" under the hood.

Technologies for Mobile Device Accessibility

This short section on mobile device accessibility is designed to give you a brief introduction to the range of mobile devices that can be used by people with disabilities—in particular, vision impairments. It doesn't go into developing for these devices, as many of them require platform-specific apps, though they can of course consume your HTML5 content also.

---

[5] www.standards-schmandards.com/projects/fangs/

VoiceOver and the iPhone

The functionality of VoiceOver on the iPhone is pretty much the same. There are a couple of very neat things that it does, however. For example, it has a new way of selecting items on the iPhone, so a person using VoiceOver will move her finger over the screen and any objects that are hit will be announced. When an onscreen item is active (has been announced) and the user has her finger on the item, tapping anywhere else on the screen will select it.

That's really clever, and while it can take a little getting used to, it makes a lot of sense. Typing out text messages and emails can be a lot slower than with a dedicated keyboard, but external keyboards can be added. I have also seen a blind friend use a dedicated Braille input device.

The standard swipe gestures also work the same as with the MacBook Pro, as well as the Web Rotor. You might even find yourself using VoiceOver outside on a sunny day when listening to iTunes—it can be very useful even for a sighted person when it's hard to see the screen.

▓ **Note** It is truly amazing to see the quantum leap that is the iPhone. In accessibility terms, it was a total game-changer that introduced a whole new interaction model using touch and gestures. If anyone had told me even four or five years ago that a touch screen device with one button would be used successfully by blind and vision-impaired people as an input device, I would have said they were crazy.

Talks and Symbian

For many years, the main mobile screen reader was Talks. It could be used on Symbian phones (such as Nokia) as a way of accessing the phone, the phone's functionality, and so forth. It is still reasonably popular but has lost a lot of ground due to the popularity of other, newer mobile operating systems.

RIM and BlackBerry Accessibility

The BlackBerry was never really considered a very accessible device, but that is about to change. I have heard positive things about RIM's initiative to improve the accessibility of the BlackBerry platform.

Here are some of the accessibility features that are available for the new wave of BlackBerry smartphones:

- Clarity theme for BlackBerry smartphones—These include a simplified Home screen interface, large text-only icons, and a high-contrast screen display.

- Visual, audible, and vibration notifications of incoming phone calls, text messages, emails, and so forth.

- Customizable fonts—You can increase the size, style, and weight of fonts.

- Audible click—A confirming audio tone useful for navigating using the trackpad or trackball.

- Reverse contrast—You can change the device display color from dark on light to light on dark.

- Grayscale—You can convert all colors to their respective shades of gray.

- Browser zoom—A screen-magnification function.

A range of other enhancements on the platform are designed to serve the needs of users with mobility, cognitive, and speech impairments. So it looks really promising. Another big plus is that Aaron Leventhal, who was the chief accessibility architect at Mozilla and was driving Firefox accessibility, is now the senior accessibility product manager at RIM and will bring a lot of skill and experience to the platform.

Android

The Android platform is gaining ground in usage, and as of version 1.6 there has been in-built platform features for people with vision impairments. However, it still requires that you download the appropriate software and configure the phone. This can be a little complicated, but in principle a visually-impaired user can access just about any function, including making phone calls, text messaging, emailing, web browsing, and downloading apps via the Android Market.

▓ **Caution** Talkback is a free screen reader developed by Google. It is important to be aware that to get the most out of using these screen readers, you must use a phone that has a physical navigational controller, for navigation through applications, menus, and options. This can be a trackball, trackpad, and so on. It's also a good idea to select a phone that has a physical keyboard, because there is very limited accessibility support for touch-screen devices.

I am a fan of the Android platform. I love its customizable nature and its flexibility, and you can twiddle away with it for hours on end. However, from an accessibility perspective, the whole experience leaves a lot to be desired—especially on a touch-screen device. There is a night-and-day difference between the complexity involved in configuring and enabling accessibility for an Android device and the out-of-the-box accessibility experience of the iPhone. The iPhone is far superior, which is a pity because the Android platform has much to recommend it. You can use various screen readers with Android, for example, and there are other useful accessibility features. However, in terms of the user experience, it is currently just very fiddly and is not for the faint hearted.

Speech Synthesis: What Is It and How Does It Work?

Now that you've had an introduction to how to use a screen reader, how about a little background on what's actually going on under the hood?

Text that is to be outputted as speech is transformed into very small atomic components called *phonemes*. These are the building blocks of our language (and yes, they are smaller than syllables). For example, the English language alphabet has 26 characters and about 40 phonemes.

The main kind of synthesis used to actually create the voice output are these:

- Formant synthesis

- Concatenative synthesis

- Articulatory synthesis

Of the three, formant is the earliest used and most common. It is also the easiest method for quickly creating recognizable sounds because formants are real-time generated sounds that represent the main frequency components of the human voice. Formants occupy a rather narrow band of the frequency spectrum (just like the human voice) and are created by combining these commonly used frequencies at various levels of amplitude.

Formant synthesis has a distinct advantage over the other types of synthesis because it can be used to output text at quite high speeds and still be intelligible and understandable, which is more difficult with either concatenative or articulatory synthesis. However, formant-based speech output can sound rather robotic.

Concatenative synthesis is when a database of pre-recorded sounds is used to represent the text output as speech. It can result in a more human voice, but it has some disadvantages—such as loss of clarity at high-speed output (which is important for many screen-reader users who have a preference for high-speed speech output).

Articulatory synthesis uses a model that copies the human vocal tract and how sounds are actually created. It is more complex, but it leads us nicely into some of the other models, such as HMM, which try to predict what will be coming next on the basis of the previous or current output. These models do this by using hidden Markov chains (which is bringing us into the territory of probabilistic modeling, so let's leave it there!).

■ **Note** If you'd like more information, there is an interesting working group looking at HMM-based speech synthesis systems, which you can find at `http://hts.sp.nitech.ac.jp`. You can also find some real-time HMM generators there.

Screen Magnification

Screen-magnification software is used by people who are vision impaired. These products are used to literally magnify the screen, in whole or in part. This magnified view is then the principle view for the user and can be moved around the screen by the mouse or other device.

You might be aware that this kind of feature is already a part of the Windows operating system and Mac OS X and be wondering why someone would spend their hard-earned money on a dedicated software package. The difference between a dedicated package and the feature in your operating system is one of quality and clarity, and it is very noticeable when you compare a screen-magnification product like SuperNova or ZoomText with the in-built operating system products. The fact is that when you use (and really push) the magnification features of your operating system, you can get artifacts and, more importantly, blurred text that can become illegible at high magnification levels.

A screen-magnification package like SuperNova or ZoomText will redraw the screen at a higher resolution. What's more, such packages also have other in-built features that provide high-quality anti-aliasing, so any re-drawn text that is viewed at high magnification levels is much sharper and clearer. While the inbuilt screen magnification features of your chosen operating system can certainly be used by someone with a mild to moderate vision impairment, very often more severely vision-impaired people will need to use an off-the-shelf package.

▦ **Note** Some things to be aware of when you are building web sites and applications is making parts of the page change in a way that can be seen by someone using screen-magnification software. A rule of thumb is to avoid things like having a control on the far left of your page that updates something on the far right when activated, which the user can easily miss when he or she is looking at a rather narrow part of the screen. It might be more accurate to say "When the user might not expect it." If the command updates a shopping cart or similar item, it's probably fine because the user is primed to expect this to happen. This design pattern can be a problem when it is unexpected, because the screen magnifier's view is often rather small. So just bear that in mind.

Switch Access

Enhanced informational design is also good for users with very limited physical mobility or movement. Users with physical disabilities often use a device called a *switch*, shown in Figure 2-24, to interact with their computer and access the Web.

Figure 2-24. A variety of single-button switches

Switches vary in form. They really should be considered binary input devices, or simple 'on' 'off' input, rather like a light switch. What is amazing is just how much can be done using these very simple input devices in conjunction with a suitable software interface.

As shown in Figure 2-24, a switch is often really just a single large button designed so that the user can press it with minimal effort. (Also, some switches need to have their sensitivity reduced because the user might hit them quite hard.) There are also switches that are controlled by other methods of interaction, such as the user blowing into them or wobbling them. There are a variety of other forms of interaction that meet the ability of the user.

Some users often use a combination of two or more of these switches. A switch can be configured to perform a default action, like opening a commonly used application, or a macro can be added to it. This kind of powerful customizable functionality can really help to increase the user's ability to interact with the computer, the web browser, or other applications as desired.

How Do Switches Work?

Switches are generally used in conjunction with other software. They are commonly called *scanning software*, and there are several in use, such as Grid, Clicker, and EZ-Keys.

In general, these scanning packages work by dividing the screen into a grid-type layout and initially highlighting each row of content of the grid (for a defined period of time according to user preference— say, two seconds). When the specified time period has lapsed, the next row is automatically highlighted, and then the following one, and so on.

When the user sees that the row containing the item he wants to choose is being highlighted, he presses or activates the switch. The individual items in the row then start being highlighted one at a time, column by column, until the desired item is highlighted. The user can then activate the switch button to select it. This temporary highlighting happens in a linear fashion (first by row, and then when a row is selected, row by row). This process is referred to as *scanning*.

The output can be displayed as text (as in Figure 2-25, where text output appears in the box at the top while the user is typing) within the scanning software, but usually this output is routed to another application.

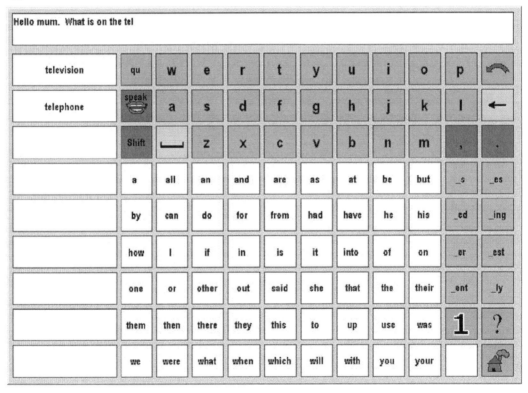

Figure 2-25. The original Grid software

Sometimes a customized skin is used for email as shown in Figure 2-26.

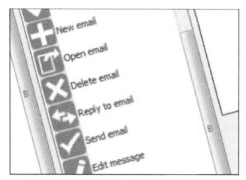

Figure 2-26. *A custom skin for using email*

Skins can also be designed for navigating the Web, including browsing specific sites. Figure 2-27 shows a skin for browsing YouTube.

Figure 2-27. *A custom skin for browsing YouTube*

Finally, Figure 2-28 shows a Grid 2 interface that can be used to make typing messages easier.

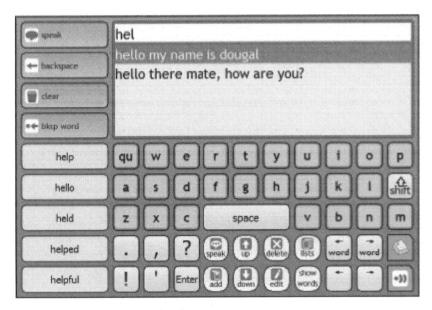

Figure 2-28. The Grid 2 interface for typing

This combination of single-switch, multiple-switch, and grid-type software is very empowering technology for many people with disabilities. These technologies enable them to fully use their computers, communicate with family and friends, and surf the Web.

Mouse Emulation

Another (more advanced) scanning type of application that operates slightly differently is EZ-Keys XP. Shown in Figure 2-29, EZ-Keys XP is software that provides complete mouse emulation using alternative inputs, such as a keyboard or even a slight movement of the eye using switch activation. It allows the user to control the mouse using an innovative radar-type mode, and it has other features such as a standard keyboard, an expanded keyboard, a joystick, and single-switch and multiple-switch scanning.

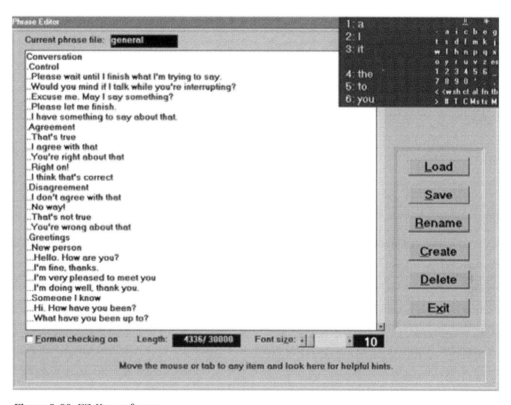

Figure 2-29. *EZ-Keys software*

Switch Access, Mouse Emulation, and the Web

A switch access system really needs to be seen in action to be understood. So here is a link to a YouTube video that demonstrates how a switch can be used to access the Web, using software like EZ-Keys: www.youtube.com/watch?v=6xLkPuGvSQc.

For videos that show switch access using the Grid, go to the following site: www.youtube.com/watch?v=OpGleNU2Jtw.

▓ **Note** I also recommend the Enable Ireland AT YouTube channel, which has lots of great videos relating to AT. Here, you can see a wide variety of AT in use. These videos also have closed captioning (CC).

www.youtube.com/user/enableirelandat

The Accessibility Overlap

To help you parse the information we covered in this chapter, keep in mind that many of the WCAG 2.0 guidelines and practices overlap. This means that they affect various user groups in positive ways. For example, keyboard accessibility and being able to access all vital functionality from the keyboard is a core requirement for creating accessible web sites, which will help reduce barriers for all users with a disability regardless of the AT they use. That's a useful piece of information!

Keyboard access is the closest thing there is to a silver bullet, in accessibility terms, because it impacts a broad range of disability types, interaction models/modalities, and AT. By providing reliable keyboard access, you will help to make your web sites more accessible to blind users of screen readers, people with limited mobility who use a switch, people who cannot use a mouse due to tremors, spasms, and/or involuntary movements and thus rely on the keyboard alone, as well as to nerds like me who just like being able to access stuff quickly via power-user shortcuts. So that's a win/win from what is, I hope, a simple enough interaction model for you to understand and implement.

As mentioned earlier, accessibility is not just about blind people. However, (and I will backpedal a little here) the accessibility best practices you apply to your projects to make your content accessible to blind screen-reader users will also really help many other user groups.

Sometimes a little empathy will also go a long way. For example, if a little voice in the back of your mind tells you that your new Web 3.0, dynamic-interaction widget might be a bit overengineered and complicated—guess what! It's probably overengineered and complicated!

Simplicity is your friend. Many graphic designers, when they first start out and are learning about PhotoShop and how to do adjustment layers and use filters, will go nuts. (I did.) They'll end up designing images with loads of layers and filters that are interacting with each other, and the result can be a mess. (I made plenty of those.) However, if you strip things back, look at the core of what image you want to produce, and give elements a little space to breathe, a certain harmony will emerge that is inherent within the objects themselves.

Applying this more practical aesthetic to your design and code using the mantra "Form follows function" will help you. Also, looking at what your users want and trying to project a mental model your users can understand.

Conclusion

In this chapter, I introduced some different types of disability, or shall I say we looked at diverse ranges of ability. We also looked at the various kinds of technology available to help people engage with computers and the Web. In the next couple of chapters, we are going to look at JavaScript and then a new accessibility markup language called *WAI-ARIA*, which can be used in conjunction with HTML5 (and earlier versions of HTML) to make accessible, rich Internet applications. We'll also look at how screen readers work in more detail by examining the off-screen model, and you'll meet the DOM and Accessibility APIs.

CHAPTER 3

JavaScript Isn't a Dirty Word, and ARIA Isn't Just Beautiful Music

For a long time, JavaScript was a very dirty word in accessibility circles. It was pretty much a pariah, found in the bargain basement of web development among the Bread albums and unloved Pokémons. This wasn't helped by the first version of Web Content Accessibility Guidelines (WCAG) pretty much banning it from use, and there was a division among developers regarding their attitude to using JavaScript. There was also snobbery that questioned whether it was even a proper coding language at all. The low barrier to entry, as well as its ability to work even when poorly written, didn't help its image either. This has now all changed.

In this chapter, we'll look at how JavaScript and other technologies can be used to build dynamic accessible web sites and Rich Internet Applications (RIAs). These are commonly developed using a combination of HTML, Cascading Style Sheets (CSS), JavaScript, and the new kid on the block, WAI-ARIA. WAI is the Web Accessibility Initiative, which is based in the W3C, and ARIA stands for *Accessible Rich Internet Applications*. Sometimes it is referred to as just *ARIA*.

This chapter covers some common approaches to accessible design using these languages and developing dynamic content that works for everyone—by paying attention to some basic good-scripting practices. We'll also look at the current more *accessibility friendly* JavaScript libraries. This chapter also gives you a good basis to help you transition to accessible HTML 5 development, because much of what is covered here can be applied equally to HTML 4 and HTML5. I'll also outline some backward-compatibility techniques you might still need to use when developing to support older assistive technologies (AT).

▓ **Note** The part of this chapter about scripting is not intended to be an exhaustive JavaScript how-to guide; instead, it presents an overview of some simple principles. I've taken some good advice from friends when writing this. (Take a bow, Gez Lemon. I owe you one.) I also borrowed some examples from existing resources. When it comes to scripting in general, there really are lots of ways to do similar things, so I'll leave a lot of the nitty-gritty details of how to apply the scripty bits to your own preference, and concentrate instead on some simple principles you should stick to that will make your projects more accessible.

If you need a good introduction to JavaScript, I recommend books by Christian Heilmann, who has written extensively on the subject and is an expert in accessibility, as well as DOM Scripting: Web Design with JavaScript and the Document Object Model (friendsofED, 2010) by Jeremy Keith and Jeffrey Sambells, which is also excellent. This chapter assumes you have some scripting experience, but don't worry if it isn't that advanced—you'll get the general idea.

A useful tool to help you to write better JavaScript is JSLint, which was originally developed by Douglas Crockford. This will show you common errors, such as missing semicolons at the end of a line; curly braces without an `if`, `for`, or `while` statement; or those pesky `return`, `throw`, `continue`, or `break` statements that stop your code from running. There is an online version available at `www.jslint.com`.

JavaScript: Useful When Used Well

Previous versions of HTML were primarily document markup languages. They were designed at a time when webpages were pretty much just that—pages. They were the online equivalent of a textual Word document. As time went on, they became more sophisticated, and images (then video content) could be embedded within them. Ultimately, the web evolved into the application space that it is today, where web sites behave more like desktop applications and the user can do far more sophisticated stuff within the browser.

All of this Web 2.0 stuff (for want of a better term for *more advanced functionality*) was made possible by a relatively simple document markup language combined with CSS and, yes, some JavaScript. The fact is, there are times when you just cannot use HTML on its own and some tasteful use of JavaScript can really add to the accessibility of your web sites by providing extra instructions for your users, helping with form validation, and providing more meaningful alerts.

▨ **Note** The Section 508 guidelines in the US that state when a timed response is required from the user (when booking concert tickets, for example), you must inform the user. This would be practically impossible using HTML alone—JavaScript needs to be used.

Note that JavaScript is totally independent of HTML or any of the host of other languages that it can be applied to. It consists largely of a host of behaviors and can be thought of as occupying that layer in the web development stack. It is used largely for determining how your content will behave when activated or moved around, and how it will respond to particular events that *fire*.

JavaScript is a client-side language, which means that it operates entirely within the browser. There are other languages, such as PHP, that operate on the *server side* and can be used together with JavaScript for more sophisticated server/client interaction.

WAI-ARIA: What Is It?

Later in this chapter I'll talk a lot about WAI-ARIA (or ARIA, as it is sometimes called). As previously mentioned, WAI-ARIA is a technology specification that was developed by the Web Accessibility Initiative (hence the WAI) in the W3C to bridge the semantic gap between markup languages like HTML 4 and HTML5.

■ **Note** Over the past few years, the web moved from the static webpage to the AJAX/Web 2.0 space and became more application-like. The idea with ARIA was to develop a language that could be plugged in to a host language like HTML/XHTML (it can also be used with SVG), and that could make these applications more accessible to people with disabilities using AT.

HTML5, of course, has a whole new range of controls (which we will look at later) that improve the accessibility of web sites and applications. However, while developers were waiting for HTML5 (and let's face it, it was a long wait), there was a need for something that could describe the purpose, sometimes the state, and other properties of hand-rolled dynamic interactive widgets and components that developers were making for assistive technologies. So some very clever people got their heads together and WAI-ARIA was born.

What's Wrong with HTML 4, 3, 2…?

I'm amazed at how much has been achieved in terms of sophisticated online applications, using what was practically a limited document markup language. (This is a posh way of saying, "How the hell did the web develop the way it did?")

Only two types of elements within HTML 4 could natively receive focus via the keyboard alone: `<ahref>` anchor tags and `<form>` controls. As stated earlier, keyboard accessibility is the bedrock of accessible web development. In HTML5, a great many controls are already keyboard accessible to several of the main browsers like Opera 11, Safari 5, IE 9, Firefox 6, and Chrome 13—either fully or partially. These include the `<audio>` element; the `<datalist>` element; the `<color>` input element; the `<date>` input element; the `<month>`, `<number>`, `<range>`, and `<search>` input elements; as well as `<time>`, `<week>`, and `<summary>` elements.

Even though the palette of focusable elements and controls isn't nearly as limited anymore, it's worth noting some of the techniques that were developed to make elements focusable within the browser, because they will still be very useful—in particular, for issues like backward compatibility with older AT and browsers that don't yet (or won't) support HTML5.

You should also realize that while many of the new controls in HTML5 can be accessed via the keyboard, this doesn't mean they're fully accessible. For this to happen, their role and other information need to be exposed via an accessibility API to the assistive technology. This isn't yet the case with several of the new HTML5 controls I just listed.

So technically while the user might be able to get to the control using the keyboard alone, it doesn't actually mean they can find out what the control actually is or what it does!

■ **Tip** To handle situations like the one just described, you might need to add accessibility information using WAI-ARIA. I'll go into more detail later on how accessible the new HTML5 controls are and how well they expose their role and other information to AT via the native accessibility APIs.

Accessible JavaScript

In terms of accessibility and barriers that poor scripting practices could create for the end user, many developers didn't really care. This attitude wasn't consciously directed at people with disabilities. Developers just liked that they could do more stuff with scripting that made pages more interesting to author and use, as well as more dynamic, and they got caught up in the new language. However, the barriers created were often very real to people using AT.

Some of these barriers were due to the fact that back then some users had JavaScript turned off or the user was behind a firewall or somehow just in a limited browsing environment. (Corporate environments can be very locked down.) So not having access to JavaScript meant that many of these scripted interfaces just wouldn't work properly.

However, over the past few years this has all changed (apart from the locked-down corporate environment). JavaScript is enabled by default in many browsers, and users of AT such as a screen reader can happily use many JavaScript-heavy web sites and applications without too much trouble, as long as the principles and practices that I outline here are followed.

▒ **Note** WebAIM, one of the world's leading online web-accessibility web sites, researched screen reader usage and found that 98 percent of screen-reader users had JavaScript enabled.

For more information, see `http://webaim.org/projects/screenreadersurvey3/#javascript`.

Progressive Enhancement

One of the first principles of developing accessible scripted content is the idea of *progressive enhancement*. To build sites according to this principle, you think of your scripts like you think of your CSS—you separate them into their own files, or layers. Your HTML is the *content layer*, the CSS is the *presentation layer*, and the JavaScript is the *behavior layer*. This way of thinking of scripts has been well documented and makes a lot of sense, because it helps with code management and makes project hand-offs easier and less confusing. As an extra benefit, it's good for people with disabilities using AT, because the basic content is always available and not totally dependent on scripting to work. That means progressively enhanced content can also be parsed more easily by your favorite search engine.

▒ **Note** You can think of the Google search engine as a blind user. It will parse the code that people don't see on the surface—rather in the same way that a screen reader will—and then work its algorithm magic and return results. So be nice to people with disabilities in your designs and you will also serve Big G.

When you do separate your stuff, you start with an accessible webpage (well-structured HTML content, correctly labeled form controls, suitable alternate text, and so on), add a separate CSS file for all your presentational stuff, and then add JavaScript functionality to aspects of the site to enhance its functionality to user agents that can handle them correctly.

The core idea of progressive enhancement is that user agents (browsers) that can take full advantage of newer technical specifications and authoring methods can and will, and your code won't break those that can't, don't, or won't. A progressively enhanced web site, therefore, will be keyboard accessible and keyboard-only users will be able to perform the tasks they need to when they visit your web site.

That being said, JavaScript must still be applied in a way that is *device independent*, meaning that it doesn't require a mouse to be used for the JavaScript to work (as can often be the case).

Unobtrusive JavaScript

It is also vital that the use of JavaScript is *unobtrusive*. This approach aims to give a diverse range of your users a more seamless user experience. They might not recognize the technology (all good technology should be, to some degree, invisible), but they'll recognize unwanted behaviors when they come across them, and they'll certainly recognize things that just don't work. Unnecessary movement on a webpage, complex and generally unintuitive widget functionality, and weird or unfamiliar controls are all over the web. Don't contribute to the canon.

▨ **Note** What's the difference between *progressive enhancement* and *unobtrusive JavaScript*? Well, it's a little like ying and yang, because they are intertwined. They both support the idea of layered development, but progressive enhancement outlines the model of serving behaviors in a staggered way to user agents that support them, and not breaking content for those that don't. Something that is unobtrusive doesn't get in the way or disturb the user experience if unsupported. A good example is the NOSCRIPT issue. (See the upcoming section.) They are different sides of the same coin.

Tidy Coding

In CSS, you write declarations that are defined globally, use them to control appearance via `<div>` elements or `id` or `class` attributes (also known as *hooks*), and then tell the browser to present it, or render it, in different ways. Rather than adding lots of fussy CSS code to your HTML, you can add more discreet hooks that you then write presentational rules for in your CSS file. You can think of JavaScript in the same way. One good practice is to define global behaviors in your JavaScript file that attach themselves to the ID and class hooks in your HTML, so that the behaviors will cascade (if you will) down through your HTML file.

Note that you can give your ids and class names *behavior-like*' names, such as *popup* or *expand_menu*, that are easy to understand while you are coding. Or you can piggyback on existing ID and class names. For example, consider this snippet: `<a href="http://www.somewebsite.com" class="expand_menu">Expand me</a>`

▨ **Note** The proper method for adding many JavaScript events to your hooks is to define the element, then the event, and finally the action. There are several methods for doing this, such as `getElementbyId`, `getElementsByTagName` (when you want to target several elements with a similar behavior), and `getAttribute`. Each method can be used to traverse the DOM of the HTML document; look for specific IDs, element types, or attributes; and then do something to them when the document loads. Adding the `window.onload=prepareLinks();` function will also ensure that your JavaScript doesn't fire before the page has loaded. This is important if your scripts are in an external file that might load before the rest of your HTML!

Common JavaScript Accessibility Problems

▨ **Note** The term *event handler* will be used a lot in the coming section. An event handler is really a method containing program statements executed in response to an event, so *event handler* and *method* can be used interchangeably. Event handlers are added to your HTML code and activated, or triggered, by some kind of user interaction. They can also be triggered by the browser itself, when a page loads for example, or when some section of the webpage has been updated asynchronously using the XHR object (which is common with AJAX development).

Most of the accessibility problems that arise from the use of JavaScript come about because it has been used incorrectly, or because there is a general lack of awareness about the impact your code can have on the user experience for people with disabilities in particular. It is largely understandable how this happens, because the developers might just be unaware that how they are actually applying scripting is even a problem.

There are also lots of ways to do similar things with JavaScript that appear to produce the same result but might be more "black hat" than "white hat." It's only when you look at a heavily scripted interface from the perspective of someone with a disability that you can appreciate that adopting methods like progressive enhancement really makes sense. This chapter is a call for more "white hat" JavaScript, so be good to your users!

There are more low-hanging fruit accessibility issues—or more accurately, usability issues—for which you can just use common sense as a guide to fix. If you think your scripted web site or interface is complex and difficult to use, then guess what—it's probably complex and difficult to use for lots of other people! It seems kind of daft when it's spelled out like that, but it's true.

However, there are other less obvious accessibility issues:

- **Lack of keyboard accessibility:** JavaScript has some event handlers that can be activated only by using the mouse, such as onClick, onMouseOver, onMouseOut, and onDblClick. Other methods are less device specific—such as onFocus, onBlur, onSelect, and onChange. They're activated when an item or object receives focus, and this can be via the mouse, the keyboard, or any input devices, such as a switch (as described in the previous chapter). The latter method is a *device independent* way of adding a behavior to an object in your webpage, and it's a simple but powerful example of a more accessible way to add JavaScript to your content.

- **Lack of Control:** Taking the previous example a step further, if a webpage has been developed with only onClick methods, these functions often are not accessible to a keyboard user. The user might not be able to use the widgets/controls at all and therefore is blocked out of the web site. This can also be an issue when content is hidden or removed on certain events and the user either cannot undo an action or just can't get to some content.

  Approaches for handling a variety of such situations are outlined in detail in the WCAG 2.0 Success Criteria. We'll look at some of their advice for accessible scripting in the upcoming section "JavaScript and WCAG 2.0."

- **Too much going on:** Overengineered, overcooked interfaces have become more common these days. They are tolerated less and less as the user experience has become much more important in an age of seemingly infinite choice. When users have a bad experience with a web site, they are fortunate enough to not have to go back, and there are plenty of competing web sites that will be glad to acquire their business. When an organization is a public sector or federal agency, that's a different situation, and there is a mandate to ensure that their web interfaces meet a certain standard.

However, we've all seen pages where functions, animations, and dynamic behaviors have been added for their own sake. Many webpages clearly reflect the era of their design, as they feature behaviors that were fashionable at a particular time. Someday, AJAX interfaces, rounded corners, and the like will seem like old effects, but nothing is as bad as a confusing and disorientating interface where the designer has gone nuts adding extras to an unintuitive interface that only he or she can use or understand. These interfaces can be confusing, especially for older people and people with cognitive impairments, and they can be totally counterproductive, actually blocking many people from using the site's functionality.

Keyboard Accessibility, Mouse-Only Events, and Keymapping

There are many other event handlers that can be layered on top of a simple onFocus method, which is the bedrock of accessible scripting. If you pay attention to these foundations of your scripts, you will find that you can develop sophisticated sites and applications that are also highly accessible. I also mentioned earlier that the user might not be able to use the controls because onClick will actually work very well for a keyboard-only user (or indeed any other switch device that simulates an Enter keypress).

I'll group all of these devices under the umbrella of *keyboard accessible*. This is because you can call a scripting function (like onClick) and attach it to a control within the browser that has native keyboard-accessibility (such as a link or button), or you can make a <div> focusable by the keyboard by using tabindex="0". Under the hood, the onClick event is actually mapped to the default action of a link or button. The name is misleading because the event will activate upon the pressing of the Enter key. There are situations where you have to be a little careful, however—in particular, when you add onclick events to <div> elements. This is because the onclick events will fire fine on elements within the natural source order of a document and often <div> elements don't follow this. I noticed this in particular when building the HTML5 video player (which is coming up in Chapter 6) because the onclick events wouldn't fire from the keyboard in Firefox, Safari, and Chrome. (IE 9 doesn't support the <video> element.)

It might also be a good idea in your projects to consider mapping some of the more commonly used mouse-only events with some keyboard-friendly and accessibility-friendly event handlers, such as those outlined in Table 3-1.

Table 3-1. Accessible Event-Handler Mappings

Mouse only event handlers...	...mapped to the more accessibility friendly
onmousedown	onkeydown
onmouseup	onkeyup
onclick	onkeypress
onmouseover	onfocus
onmouseout	onblur

You can provide the two event handlers if you need to, when building JavaScript controls, to ensure that they can be used both by the mouse and via the keyboard. You will see an example of this in Chapter 6, when we build an accessible HTML 5 <video> player.

To trigger a behavior via the keyboard, sometimes you might need to script the actual key that you want to fire the event. Some of the most commonly used are the Space and Enter keys. You have to be careful with event handlers like onkeypress because it will fire regardless of the key the user presses. So if you mean a specific key, it's best to define that.

For this to work you have to call a key code that you can map to the particular function. For the Space bar, the key code is *32*, and for the Enter key, the key code is *13*. Attaching these event types to various input keys takes the following form in order to activate the event. The following code sample is your playVideo function reworked to respond to the keypress event. It also checks to see whether it's the correct key:

```
function someFunction(objEvent) {
    if (objEvent.type == 'keydown')
    {
        var iKeyCode = objEvent.keyCode;
        if (iKeyCode != 13 && iKeyCode !=32) {
            return true;
        }
    }
    someFunction();
}
```

A nice live tool that gives you keycodes to help you figure out what code represents what key can be found at http://asquare.net/javascript/tests/KeyCode.html.

▓ **Caution** As mentioned previously, be careful not to confuse `onKeyPress` with `onClick`. `onKeyPress` (unless mapped to a specific key) will fire an event or call a function as soon as any key is pressed—so use it with caution. It can be a rather blunt instrument.

Some Event Handler Accessibility Best Practices

While we're on the subject of event handlers, here are some general good practices:

- Avoid using the `onDblclick` method because there is no accessible keyboard equivalent.

- Avoid mapping mouse co-ordinates to event handlers. This won't work because the user can't move the system caret or focus on these within the browser via the keyboard or other devices.

- Avoid using the `onChange` event handler in your drop-down boxes. A nonsighted person using a screen reader will use the arrow keys to navigate up and down between the options contained in the drop-down box and find out what the options are by having the screen reader output them as speech. If the `onChange` event handler is applied to the menu, rather than allowing the screen reader user to navigate through it, the event will be triggered when the user hits the arrow keys as she navigates the controls. The user will then be taken to whatever the default URL is, or the URL of the default item in the list. Generally, allowing the user to navigate the menu items and then let her press the Tab key to select a Go button or similar UI element is better.

- Coding items that can be activated only by a specific event handler is also not good practice. There should be a real URL or link that an event handler is added to, so when JavaScript is disabled the real URL can still be given focus.

- Don't use the `createEvent()`, `initEvent()`, and `dispatchEvent()` handlers to give an element focus. Use `element.focus()` instead.

- Don't use named anchors (# attributes within an `<ahref>` element) or inline code, such as `javascript:window.open()`, to control dynamic menus or popup windows. Neither of these will work if JavaScript is off, because the `href` element has no way of then passing an instruction to the browser (as it usually does when opening a URL) without scripting enabled. This is an example of how a native behavior has been hijacked by the script, making the interaction entirely dependent on the new technology (the JavaScript) and removing the ability of the `href` element to behave in its default manner, because it has no URL to give focus to.

Creating Accessible Pop-up Menus and Inline Event Handlers

When using pop-up menus, you should inform the user that a popup will be launched before they actually launch it by including this information—ideally, within the link text itself (whether you use script or not). However, pop-up menus should be used with caution, and only as needed. More often than not, you won't really need to. In the following examples, even if JavaScript is off, the user isn't left high and dry and can still get to a useful page:

```
<p> Here is a my <a href="http://www.myusefulpopup.html" target="_blank">really interesting
and useful pop box [Opens in new Window] </a></p>
```

To be sure that your popUp function degrades gracefully, use real URLs (as shown in the preceding example).

The following examples invoke a function called popUp, which takes the general form shown here:

```
<script type="text/javascript">
    function popUp(X)
    {
        window.open(X);
    }
</script>
```

The following are inline examples (which aren't best practice but are used here for illustration purposes):

```
<a href="http://www.myusefulpopup.html" onclick="popUp('http://www.myusefulpopup.html');
return false;"> Here is my really interesting and useful pop box [Opens in new Window] </a>
```

This seems like a duplication of functions, and it is. You can simplify it by using JavaScript to just point to the element it's attached to:

```
<a href="http://www.myusefulpopup.html" onclick="popUp(this.getAttribute('href')); return
false;"> Here is my really interesting and useful pop box [Opens in new Window] </a>
```

Or you can use the snazzier version:

```
<a href="http://www.myusefulpopup.html" onclick="popUp(this.href); return false;"> Here is my
really interesting and useful pop box [Opens in new Window] </a>
```

The point to remember is that the href value is a real URL, so when scripting is off it will still work. These are examples of *inline* scripting, or scripting that is contained in the code. It's better to have the script in a separate file, like you do with CSS, and then point to that file in your header, referencing IDs, referencing class names, or searching for element IDs and types as JavaScript allows you to do.

■ **Note** The "return false" bit of the script stops the event from firing. This is useful when you have lots of event handlers and you want to embed them and control how they behave in a more granular fashion. Don't want event propagation? Then use "return false" on your event handlers. That sends a big "Don't activate this" flag to the browser. Remember that the window object has an open( ) method that it uses to determine specific features. It takes the following general form:

```
Window.open(url, name, features)
```

Use of TabIndex and More Advanced Focus Techniques

The most common way of allowing any element to receive keyboard focus is by setting a `tabindex` value for the element. The `tabindex` attribute can take several values, and a common way to make sure it will receive focus is to add `0` or `-1` to the attribute (`tabindex="0"` or `tabindex="-1"`). A common way to then give focus is to use the `element.focus()` method. This allows the keyboard user to navigate via the arrow keys.

Using `tabindex="0"` on a `<div>` element as shown in the following code sample means the `<div>` can receive focus in the normal course of tabbing through the items on a page:

```
<div tabindex="0">
//Some content here
</div>
```

By using a negative value (`tabindex="-1"`), the element can receive focus but will be taken out of the tab order. Why would you want to do that? Well, you might have widgets that reveal functionality as the user progresses through them, so they are more customizable or responsive to the user needs.

```
<div id="some_control" tabindex="-1">
//Some content here
</div>
```

A simple bit of JavaScript will find the name element (in this case, I used the ID 'some_control') and call the focus method to do just that:

```
var objDiv = document.getElementById('some_control');
// Hit me
objDiv.focus();
```

Table 3-2 is an important chart that demonstrates how elements that have the `tabindex` attribute applied to them will behave. The `tabindex` attribute can take various arguments, and the argument used will affect how the attribute behaves. It is important to understand when to use them and how they will behave. For example, you might want to dynamically change the behavior of your control—sometimes giving it focus and sometimes not—or vary the order in which the items become focusable.

Table 3-2. *Use of the Tabindex Attribute*

Tabindex Attribute	Focusable with Mouse or JavaScript via element.focus()	Tab Navigation
not present	Follows default behavior of element (only form controls and anchors can receive focus)	Follows default behavior of element.
zero - tabindex="0"	yes	In tab order relative to element's position in document.
Positive - tabindex="X" (where X is a positive	yes	Tabindex value directly specifies where this

integer between 1 and 32768)		element is positioned in the tab order.
Negative - tabindex="-1"	yes	No, author must focus it with `element.focus()` as a result of arrow or other key press.

More information on these core behaviors can be found at `www.w3.org/TR/wai-aria-practices/#kbd_focus`.

▪ **Tip** Using the negative `tabindex="-1"` value will remove the element from the document source order, so the user cannot then tab to the element. Using `tabindex="0"` will give the element focus but still keep it in the document tab order.

▪ **Note** When I talk about "Tab order" or "source order," I'm talking about the sequence in which elements appear within the document source code. This is important because it defines exactly what links, buttons, and form controls get focused on, and in what order. So simply rearranging the order of elements can improve the accessibility and usability of your web site.

JavaScript and WCAG 2.0

In the first version of WCAG 1.0 (which you can find at `www.w3.org/TR/WCAG10/`), JavaScript was referred to under "Guideline 6. Ensure that pages featuring new technologies transform gracefully."

The full guideline covered issues that didn't relate entirely to JavaScript, such as using CSS and ensuring that documents could still be read if their style sheets were missing—still good advice. Here is an excerpt from the Web Content Accessibility Guidelines 1.0[1]:

> *"Ensure that pages are accessible even when newer technologies are not supported or are turned off."*

The idea was to encourage content developers to use new technologies that solve problems raised by existing technologies, while continuing to ensure that their pages work with older browsers and for people who choose to turn off features.

This is still sound advice and worth applying in your project. The checkpoints that related to JavaScript were as follows:

- 6.2 Ensure that equivalents for dynamic content are updated when the dynamic content changes. [Priority 1]

---

[1] `www.w3.org/TR/WCAG10/#gl-new-technologies`

- 6.3 Ensure that pages are usable when scripts, applets, or other programmatic objects are turned off or not supported. If this is not possible, provide equivalent information on an alternative accessible page. [Priority 1]

- 6.4 For scripts and applets, ensure that event handlers are input device-independent. [Priority 2]

- 6.5 Ensure that dynamic content is accessible or provide an alternative presentation or page. [Priority 2] For example, ensure that links that trigger scripts work when scripts are turned off or not supported (e.g., do not use "javascript:" as the link target). If it is not possible to make the page usable without scripts, provide a text equivalent with the NOSCRIPT element, or use a server-side script instead of a client-side script, or provide an alternative accessible page.

Why No NOSCRIPT?

I've covered most of the preceding issues already, and for the most part, this is good advice. However, I don't agree with the recommendation regarding NOSCRIPT. The use of unobtrusive scripting methods is a better idea than relying on the use of fallback content. This is to say, build your projects and add JavaScript in a way that won't break the experience for users who might not be able to access it for whatever reason. This approach will result in a more streamlined experience than fallback content can provide. There might be times when you have no alternative to the use of fallback content, but with the judicious use of unobtrusive JavaScript you can avoid doing so for the most part.

I'll talk about Checkpoint 6.2, "Ensure that equivalents for dynamic content are updated when the dynamic content changes. [Priority 1]," a little later and in the context of the new WCAG 2.0 guidelines, because the implications of this checkpoint have changed and become more technical since the advent of AJAX and asynchronous (clients-side) content updates.

NOSCRIPT is a little like the "You don't have the latest, grooviest browser, so we are blocking you out of our flashy, cool web site while you go back to your totally uncool life!" kind of messages that you used to get back in the day. It's amazing anyone ever thought serving these kind of condescending messages were a good idea, but there you go.

▒ **Tip** My friend Gez Lemon writes about how there are better alternatives to NOSCRIPT on his excellent JuicyStudio web site. And yes, <NOSCRIPT> is still technically allowed in HTML5. Evidently, someone still thinks <NOSCRIPT> is a good idea. Gez outlines why it isn't such a good idea in this article: http://juicystudio.com/article/say-no-to-noscript.php.

For an interesting article on how to replace NOSCRIPT with accessible and unobtrusive JavaScript, see Frank M. Palinkas' article on Dev.Opera at http://dev.opera.com/articles/view/replacing-noscript-with-accessible-un.

Client-Side Scripting Techniques for WCAG 2.0

One of the big differences between WCAG 1.0 and 2.0 is that the second iteration of the guidelines has been designed to be much more rigorously testable. There are also a lot of useful real-world examples for you to get your teeth into. There are techniques, guidelines, and outlines of the success criteria, as well as a list of common failures.

I am including the list of all the client-side scripting techniques here, and I've cherry-picked a few of them for you so that you can look at them in more detail. I want you to get a feel for them in total, and they are published here pretty much as is. I encourage you to study these and the others not shown here, which you can do online at www.w3.org/TR/WCAG20-TECHS/client-side-script.html. Of course, you can tweak them to suit your projects.

⧆ **Note** These scripting techniques relate to specific WCAG success criteria, and you can look at these online. Some of them might seem a little old. I'm including the techniques here so that you can get a feel for how scripting advice is related to WCAG 2.0, rather than this book being a WCAG "how to" guide. It should be pretty clear, however, that many of these techniques are still practical and useful.

You'll notice that the !DOCTYPE in these examples is for HTML 4, but the principles outlined here will apply equally well to HTML 5 (because it's just the host language for the script). There aren't currently any HTML5 test cases for WCAG 2.0, but they are being developed.

What follows is a list of the client-side scripting techniques[2] that you can find online at www.w3.org/TR/WCAG20-TECHS/client-side-script.html. A selection of them is available in full in Appendix A at the end of the book and has been included to reinforce some of what I covered earlier, as well as to introduce some new techniques you will find useful. All the following techniques are published in accordance with the W3C copyright policy. Thanks to Michael Cooper (W3C/WAI) for his advice and help.

Here is the full list of client-side scripting techniques:

- SCR1: Allowing the user to extend the default time limit

- SCR2: Using redundant keyboard and mouse event handlers

- SCR14: Using scripts to make nonessential alerts optional

- SCR16: Providing a script that warns the user a time limit is about to expire

- SCR18: Providing client-side validation and alert

---

[2] Copyright © 2007 W3C® (MIT, ERCIM, Keio). All Rights Reserved. W3C liability, trademark and document use rules apply.

- SCR19: Using an onchange event on a select element without causing a change of context

- SCR20: Using both keyboard and other device-specific functions.

- SCR21: Using functions of the Document Object Model (DOM) to add content to a page

- SCR22: Using scripts to control blinking and stop it in five seconds or less

- SCR24: Using progressive enhancement to open new windows on user request

- SCR26: Inserting dynamic content into the Document Object Model immediately following its trigger element

- SCR27: Reordering page sections using the Document Object Model

- SCR28: Using an expandable and collapsible menu to bypass block of content

- SCR29: Adding keyboard-accessible actions to static HTML elements

- SCR30: Using scripts to change the link text

- SCR31: Using script to change the background color or border of the element with focus

- SCR32: Providing client-side validation and adding error text via the DOM

- SCR33: Using script to scroll content, and providing a mechanism to pause it

- SCR34: Calculating size and position in a way that scales with text size

- SCR35: Making actions keyboard accessible by using the onclick event of anchors and buttons

- SCR36: Providing a mechanism to allow users to display moving, scrolling, or auto-updating text in a static window or area

- SCR37: Creating Custom Dialogs in a Device Independent Way

Common Scripting Failures in WCAG 2.0

The following are some of the common WCAG 2.0 failures that relate to dynamic content and scripting:

░ **Note** The list of all common WCAG 2.0 failures can be found here: www.w3.org/TR/WCAG20-TECHS/failures.html. Advice on how to fix them is also provided.

- F37: Failure of Success Criterion 3.2.2 due to launching a new window without prior warning when the status of a radio button, check box, or select list is changed

- F42: Failure of Success Criterion 1.3.1 and 2.1.1 due to using scripting events to emulate links in a way that is not programmatically determinable

- F44: Failure of Success Criterion 2.4.3 due to using tabindex to create a tab order that does not preserve meaning and operability

- F50: Failure of Success Criterion 2.2.2 due to a script that causes a blink effect without a mechanism to stop the blinking at 5 seconds or less

- F52: Failure of Success Criterion 3.2.1 and 3.2.5 due to opening a new window as soon as a new page is loaded

- F54: Failure of Success Criterion 2.1.1 due to using only pointing-device-specific event handlers (including gesture) for a function

- F55: Failure of Success Criteria 2.1.1, 2.4.7, and 3.2.1 due to using script to remove focus when focus is received

- F59: Failure of Success Criterion 4.1.2 due to using script to make div or span a user interface control in HTML

- F60: Failure of Success Criterion 3.2.5 due to launching a new window when a user enters text into an input field

- F61: Failure of Success Criterion 3.2.5 due to complete change of main content through an automatic update that the user cannot disable from within the content

- F62: Failure of Success Criterion 1.3.1 and 4.1.1 due to insufficient information in DOM to determine specific relationships in XML

- F85: Failure of Success Criterion 2.4.3 due to using dialogs or menus that are not adjacent to their trigger control in the sequential navigation order

■ **Note** I won't list them all here in any detail (but you should check them out online). Even a cursory look should help you to understand that they are related to several of the issues discussed previously, such as using device-independent event handlers, using accessible form validation, informing the user of content updates, and so on.

Accessible JavaScript Toolkits

As the use of JavaScript has become more common and important as a part of the web developer's toolbox, there has also been the rise of the library. JavaScript libraries are bunches of ready-made scripts, widgets, and components you can copy and paste, or generally just plug in—as is—to your web projects. You will then refer, within the header part of the document, to where these scripts reside on the client or server.

Using scripting libraries and toolkits is a mixed blessing. On one hand, it can save you the egregious task of having to learn a lot of JavaScript; on the other, it can be a pain because you have to trust that the components you use are quality components and accessible and usable by the widest audience. This isn't always the case. In fact, it's the exception rather than the rule.

▓ **Note** As with all things you don't build yourself, when you are not familiar with the architecture under the hood, it can be harder to modify the code without breaking internal dependencies that you are not aware of. Having said that, the better ones can provide good documentation and internal commenting that can make tweaking them to suit your needs easier.

However, there are a few JavaScript libraries that aren't bad when it comes to accessibility and that are worth exploring further. There are a couple that I suggest you avoid, but rather than explicitly mentioning them here, I'll stick with the ones that are worthy of attention because they considered accessibility in their architecture.

▓ **Note** The main reason that the following toolkits can be considered to be more accessible than others is because of their support for and implementation of the WAI-ARIA specification. WAI-ARIA provides a semantic toolkit that describes the function of widgets and other scripted controls via the Accessibility API to assistive technologies, such as screen readers. We will be looking at WAI-ARIA in some detail later on in this chapter.

DOJO (DIJIT)

DIJIT 1.6 is the DOJO core and has support for keyboard-accessible widgets and a high-contrast mode for vision-impaired users, as well as increasing support for WAI-ARIA. The range of widgets includes interactive menus, dialog boxes, progress bars, lightboxes, and so on.

- **DOJO Explorer:** Check out the Dojo Feature Explorer page, where you'll find useful demos of all of Dojo's features. All demos include their source code, either in HTML markup, JavaScript, or both. You can access the page at http://dojocampus.org/explorer.

- **DIJIT Accessibility (A11y):** You can find out more about how DOJO widgets are designed to be accessible and support device-independent interactions, as well as to provide role and state information for AT at the following web site: http://livedocs.dojotoolkit.org/dijit/a11y.

- **DOJO Accessibility Statement:** For the full DOJO accessibility statement and how the toolkit relates to WCAG 2.0 and Section 508 compliance, go to http://dojotoolkit.org/reference-guide/dijit/a11y/statement.html.

jQuery UI

The jQuery UI framework sits on top of the core jQuery toolkit. Several widgets have accessibility built in, and there are many accessible plugins you can add to your projects. jQuery UI has a very active accessibility team, support for CSS3, and a wide range of widgets that include accessible drag and drop, tabbed menus, sortable tables, accessible lightboxes, and form validation.

- **Download jQuery UI:** To download jQuery UI, go to `http://jqueryui.com`.

- **Accessible jQuery Plugins:** For the full range of accessible plugins, go to `http://plugins.jquery.com/plugin-tags/accessibility?page=1`.

FLUID Project: Infusion

Fluid Infusion sits on top of the jQuery toolkit and combines JavaScript, CSS, HTML, and user-centered design principles to provide a powerful inclusive toolkit.

Here are some interesting facts about Fluid Infusion:

- Flexible markup ensures you're free to change component designs as you see fit, without worrying about breaking JavaScript code.

- Infusion uses a powerful events system to notify your code when something has happened, so that you can take interactions even further.

- No black boxes. Everything in Infusion is designed to be modified, reworked, and adapted to suit your needs.

- Ideal for portals, mashups, and content management systems. Infusion is fully namespaced and plays nice with other code.

- Infusion comes with a lightweight and convenient CSS library to help you quickly flesh out your layouts.

Fluid "How-to" Guides

Fluid comes with some good tutorials for you to get started. For more information, see `http://wiki.fluidproject.org/display/docs/How-to+Guides`.

- **Fluid Components:** Fluid components are reusable user interfaces that take the hard work out of supporting rich interaction in a Web application. Components are often larger than familiar widgets in a UI toolkit, taking into account user workflows and sequences. For more information, see `http://wiki.fluidproject.org/display/fluid/Components`.

- **Fluid Demos:** The Fluid Demo page provides you with a nicely designed 'shop window' for the components. I like the way it is laid out and you can select a component and easily see the CSS, HTML and JavaScript that was used to create it. Everything from accessible drag and drop, the Grid reordering systems are available. For more information, see http://build.fluidproject.org/infusion/demos.

▨ **Note** Other toolkits that support WAI-ARIA to a greater or lesser degree are the YUI Library and GWT (Google Web Toolkit). There are others, and support is growing all the time. If you are not sure and you have a toolkit that you like, it's always a good idea to let the company know directly that accessibility is important to you. So drop them a line, and if you have a mind to, get involved!

▨ **Tip** If you use Wordpress, there are a slew of ARIA enabled plugins that were developed as a part of the AEGIS project. For a full list of the plugins, go to http://wordpress.org/extend/plugins/profile/theofanis1999.

WAI-ARIA: How to Do It!

WAI-ARIA provides a way for the developer to describe some new navigation structures, such as tree-type controls, create accessible drag-and-drop functionality, add accessible progress meters so that a blind user can be informed of how far a download is progressing (in real time), include accessible sliders to change the values of various kinds of user input, or modify a selection for a search query (such as minimum or maximum values if you are searching for a house to rent or buy).

For example, WAI-ARIA also allows you to mark *regions* of a webpage that are commonly used and lets you use them with AT. These can be menus, primary content, secondary content, banner information, and so on.

▨ **Tip** Using WAI-ARIA, you can identify *landmarks* and *live* regions of a webpages and a screen reader user will be able to "see" these in the same way that they can navigate by headings or links and bounce around the page.

For example, WAI-ARIA live regions are used on pages that update frequently, such as stock tickers and chat logs. The JAWS preferences ensure that the ARIA property value is not set to off. If it is on, the screen reader will automatically detect if there has been an update and will announce the update or the changed content. This is really useful because the screen-reader user does have to lose focus on whatever part of the page he happens to be browsing at any given time.

This issue of not losing focus and having a live update being announced is a powerful and useful new feature that enables a more complete user experience. Also, it's worth noting that not disrupting focus for the user is an important part of accessible web development, and care should be taken to support this—in particular, when you are developing heavily scripted applications.

■ **Tip** A common way to break current focus is to force unnecessary page refreshes. So keep these to a minimum and do as much form validation on the client side as possible. Or if you're using scripting to change the DOM and to add new content, wrap this functionality in a live region!

Live Region Properties

As with any live aspect of communication (among humans), you don't want to be the chatterbox or rudely interrupt a person when she's trying to tell you something or do something. Live regions have the ability to set the level of interruption in a way that won't disturb the user unnecessarily. These regions can be set to be off, polite, or assertive. Most of the time, you'll probably use the polite value, but there are times when you want to say to the screen-reader user, "This is really important—you must know about this right now," so you will vary the value to assertive. There used to be a rude property for live regions!

Setting the value to polite will not interrupt the screen-reader user. When there is a break or pause in the user interaction, the user will then be informed of the update. Setting the value to assertive will notify the screen-reader user immediately, and that setting is really useful when some user input is required or something critical has happened that needs attention.

There are many reasons why you would create a live region—among others, you can use them as containers for live streams of data, such as stock market info, weather, or updating new items.

■ **Note** Live regions can also be used for form validation or to inform the user that some action has been completed. Basically, any input/data source—whether it's PHP, ASP, JSON, or XML—can be used.

A basic live region takes the following form:

```
<div role="region">
<div id="SingleLiveRegion" aria-live="polite" aria-atomic="false"></div>
</div>
```

In the preceding example, the ARIA role region is added to the parent `<div>` element. This makes it "live." The ID of `"SingleLiveRegion"` provides the hook for your datasource. The use of `aria-live="polite"` causes the updated contents of the widget to be announced only when the user has finished interacting with the webpage—so the user won't be interrupted in the usual course of browsing the webpage with the screen reader.

The use of the `aria-atomic="false"` property determines whether the screen reader will update only some of the info contained within the live region (which is the entire `<div>` that has the role of Region applied), or all of it.

The default behavior is that the AT will not look at the contents of the entire region because it assumes the atomic-value is set to `false`. It's useful to use when there are several nodes within the same Live Region that will be updating, because it gives more granular control over what the AT will announce.

Consider the example in Figure 3-1, which displays a stock market widget with five separate live streams. The code used to create it is shown in Listing 3-1.

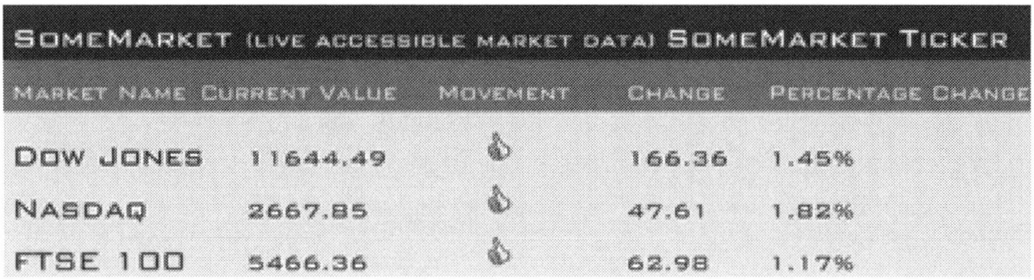

Figure 3-1. Fantasy accessible live region

▨ **Note** Sometimes in code examples I use ellipses such as "[…]" to indicate that some of the code in a sample isn't relevant or has been intentionally left out. Also, I haven't included the CSS because you can experiment with that yourself. This example and others that follow are presented primarily to illustrate the semantics needed to make these patterns accessible. You can style them to your own taste.

Listing 3-1. Semantic Code for Building the Fantasy Accessible Live Region Widget

```
<!DOCTYPE HTML>
<html>
  <head>
    <meta charset="UTF-8">
    <title>Multiple Embedded Live Region Table</title>
  </head>
  <body>
    <div id="marketwatch" aria-live="polite" aria-atomic="false">
      <h4><a href="http://www.somemarketurl.com">SomeMarket</a></h4>
      <span>(live accessible market data)</span>
      <span id="marketwatchTicker">
        <a href="http://www.somemarketurl.com/ticker.html">SomeMarket Ticker</a>
      </span>
    </div>
    <table id="somemarket_items" summary="A LiveRegion sample of current market values for
major international indexes. Data will update in a polite manner (unlike stock market traders)
which won't interfere with screen reader browsing"  class="marketdata">
      <thead>
        <tr>
          <th>Market Name</th>
          <th>Current Value</th>
          <th>Movement</th>
          <th>Change</th>
          <th>Percentage Change</th>
        </tr>
      </thead>
```

```
    <tbody>
      <div id="DowJones_LiveRegion1">
        <tr class="up">
          <td class="marketname" >
            <ahref="http://www.somemarketurl.com/dow_jones_live/">Dow Jones</a>
          </td>
          <td class="current">11644.49</td>
          <td class="movement"><span><img src="arrow.up"></span></td>
          <td class="change">166.36</td>
          <td class="percentageChange">1.45&#37;</td>
        </tr>
      </div>
      <div id="Nasdaq_LiveRegion2">
        <tr class="up">
          <td class="marketname">
            <ahref="http://www.somemarketurl.com/Nasdaq_live/">Nasdaq</a>
          </td>
          <td class="current">2667.85</td>
          <td class="movement"><span><img src="arrow.up"></span></td>
          <td class="change">47.61</td>
          <td class="percentageChange">1.82&#37;</td>
        </tr>
      </div>
      <div id="FTSE_LiveRegion3">
        <tr class="up">
          <td class="marketname">
            <a href="http://www.somemarketurl.com/FTSE_live/">FTSE 100</a>
          </td>
          <td class="current">5466.36</td>
          <td class="movement"><span><img src="arrow.up"></span></td>
          <td class="change">62.98</td>
          <td class="percentageChange">1.17&#37;</td>
        </tr>
      </div>

      [...]

    </tbody>
  </table>
 </body>
</html>
```

▪ **Note** The code in Listing 3-1 is a fantasy accessible live region widget not because it's inaccessible but because the stock is going up.

Rolling Your Own? Using ARIA to Label and Describe

Web developers and designers often want to design their own custom, hand-rolled components. This means you might wish to design your own graphics for use in your interfaces, such as for buttons and other customized controls.

For a sighted user, being able to look at the browser is often enough to be able to understand what the control is and even what it does. A good design has particular affordances that will intuitively lead the user to an understanding of what to do. If you have to explain it to the user, it might already be too complicated!

A nonsighted person cannot make these kinds of connections visually, and the identity of a hand-rolled graphic or entire widget is unknown unless the object is described somehow. When a user of AT activates it, what can that user expect? Describing both what an element is and what its function is, therefore, is at the core of accessible web development and the correct application of semantics to these controls.

If you use the native HTML controls, you should know that they have inherent semantics that are used to describe an element and what it will do when used with AT. If not, ARIA is an excellent way of providing these semantics. The following are examples of how you can do this using some of the new ARIA properties.

You're probably familiar with the accessibility poster child/rock star that is the alt attribute of the <img> element. This is the first thing most developers learn when they start to learn about accessible web development. This is where you describe an image by using alternate text. You can also describe the function of an image to assistive technology (when it is to behave like a link) by adding alternate text to your graphics. It takes the following form for descriptive images:

```
<img src="dir/somegraphic.jpg"alt="Picture of Ruairí bouncing in his bouncer!"> or for
functional images of <a><img src="dir/button_graph.png" alt="Submit your personal info"></a>
```

▓ **Tip** Sometimes you'll want to use alternate descriptions to describe what a hand-rolled element does and not what it looks like. I'll say more about this and the use of alternate text in HTML5 later.

So we've looked at using the alt attribute of the image element to provide some semantics for AT to understand the identity and sometimes the purpose of an object. ARIA expands on this idea and brings some powerful new properties to the table. You can use these to describe both the identity and purpose of custom controls to AT, as well as other relationships, states, and so on.

Here is a list of some of these:

- Aria-labelledby: This is a way of accessibly pointing to an existing element that labels the current hand-rolled element. You should use aria-labelledby when you're pointing to text from an element that is actually onscreen and you want to give an element a name (such as "button") that can be recognized by assistive technology. It can be used when you create bespoke controls and aren't using generic real HTML controls that have inherent semantics.

- Aria-label: This can be used like aria-labelledby when text is not positioned onscreen.

- Aria-describedby: This property is very similar to aria-labelledby but is designed to describe additional information about an object. If you create a web page component (such as a button) and you wish to describe the purpose of the button or what will happen when it is activated to assistive technology, you can do so by using aria-describedby.

Aria-describedby can be thought of as providing a cue for assistive technology. When a sighted person looks at a list of items on a webpage, say in an online shop, she can make the association between the picture of an item, the description of the item, and any controls such as buttons. Blind users cannot do this in the same way, so they rely on these cues to be provided programmatically.

Consider the following code example, in which the description of an item is clear visually and also programmatically:

```
<div>
  <label for="imei">IMEI Code</label>
  <input type="text" name="imei" id="imei" aria-describedby="imeidesc">
  <span class="cue" id="imeidesc">
   International Mobile Equipment Identity: 15-digit code to identify
 a mobile phone, found by dialing *#06#
  </span>
</div>
```

To see some of these new ARIA properties in action, have a look at the web site WebA11y: Adventures in Web Accessibility,[3] where there are some good examples of how to augment button text with ARIA. Many thanks to Becky Gibson (IBM) for allowing me to reproduce her samples here.

On the page www.weba11y.com/Examples/connectionsInvite.html, you'll find various examples of using ARIA to augment the text of a button. You'll find a set of sample invites to connect to various colleagues. There are a series of Accept and Reject buttons that are repeated for each invitation using a mixture of the ARIA property.

Different ARIA methods are used and documented in each of the following examples, and the screenshots show the various samples Becky created, followed by the code used:

- **Example 1:** The Amy Jones example uses a separate, offscreen span (pushed offscreen using a CSS declaration that's shown in Figure 3-2) to label the button. In the companion Listing 3-2, the span element contains the text for the label of the button, to be spoken by the screen reader when the button is given focus.

---

[3] www.weba11y.com

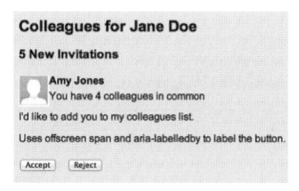

Figure 3-2. *Screenshot from weba11y.com*

Listing 3-2. A Spoken Button Label

```
.offscreen {
        position: absolute;
        margin-top: -9999px;
}

<button aria-labelledby="invite_1_accept"…>
<span class="offscreen" id="invite_1_accept">accept invitation from Amy Jones</span>
<span>Accept</span>
</button>
```

- **Example 2:** The Bill Green example shown in Figure 3-3 and Listing 3-3 uses an offscreen span inserted within the button element after the visible text. Thus, the visible text for the button, "accept" or "reject" is spoken before the offscreen text.

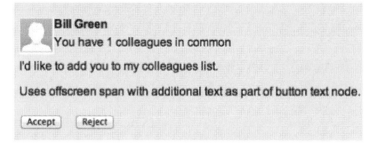

Figure 3-3. *Screenshot from weba11y.com*

Listing 3-3. CSS That Will Push the Description Off Screen, but Screen Readers Will See It

```
.offscreen {
        position: absolute;
        margin-top: -9999px;
}
```

```
<button…>Accept<span class="offscreen"> invitation from Bill Green</span></button>
```

- • **Example 3:** The Ima Clone example uses `aria-label`, as shown in Figure 3-4 and the snippet that follows it.

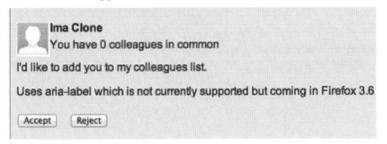

Figure 3-4. Screenshot from weba11y.com

```
<button aria-label="accept invitation from Ima Clone"…>Accept </button>
```

▪ **Tip** An elegant way to inform the user would be to create a live region in the webpage that updates when either button is activated.

ARIA Required

Adding info about required fields is an important part of accessible web development. There are a couple of things to note about the following example:

1. It's really easy to do.

2. It's pretty water tight (as you shall see).

3. It's really useful.

4. See point number 1.

The example in Figure 3-5 and Listing 3-4 contains the word "Required" inside the text label for each input box. This means that as soon as the input box is given focus by the screen-reader user, the contents of the label—both the name of the control and the keyword "Required"—are announced. This will also work with older screen readers, so it's already backward compatible. Sighted users (even those with poor vision) will see that the field is required also. This is a much better technique than using asterisks (*) to denote required fields. They are really, really easy to miss for users with vision impairments, and the screen-reader output of "star" might be missed in the course of general user interaction.

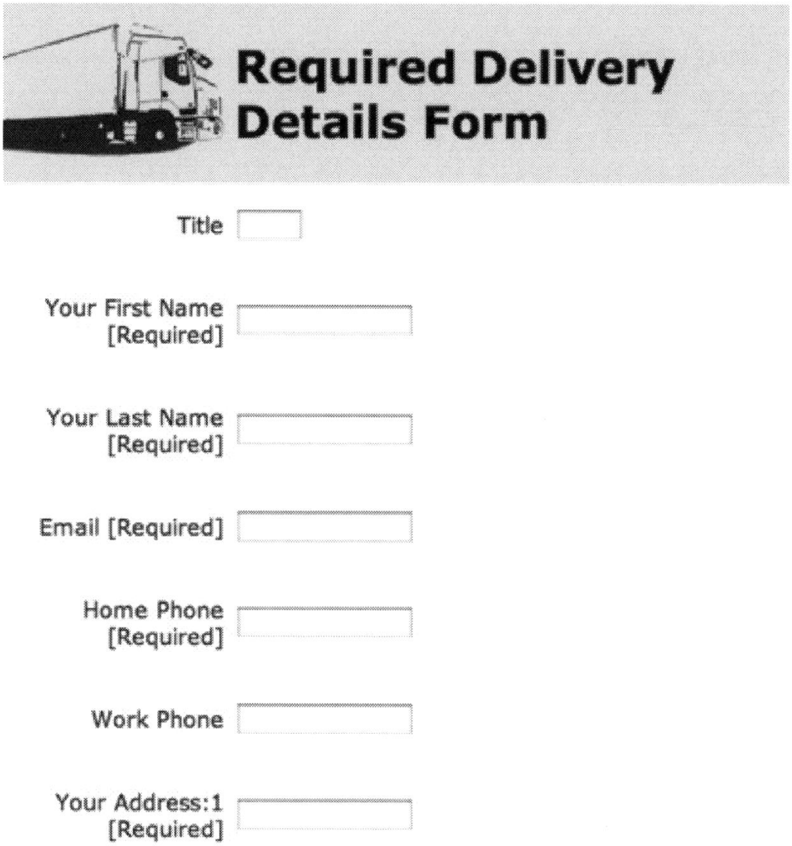

Figure 3-5. Basic form with inline [Required] text for backward-compatibility

Listing 3-4 shows the code that generates Figure 3-5.

■ **Tip** You can wrap the input controls in `<divs>` and style them as you please using CSS. I left that out here so that you can concentrate on the structural markup that is vital for the forms to be made accessible.

Listing 3-4. *Basic Form with Inline [Required] Text*

```
<!DOCTYPE html>
<html lang="en">
  <head>
    <meta charset="UTF-8">
    <title>Required Delivery Details Form</title>
  </head>
  <body>
    <h1>Required Delivery Details Form</h1>
    <form id="a11y_delivery">
      <div id="col-blk">
        <div class="colms">
          <label for="title">Title</label>
        </div>
        <div class="colms">
          <input id="title" type="text" name="title" />
        </div>
      </div>
      <div class="clrflt"></div>
      <div id="col-blk">
        <div class="colms">
          <label for="first_name">Your First Name [Required]</label>
        </div>
        <div class="colms">
          <input id="firstname" type="text" name="firstname" aria-required="true" />
        </div>
      </div>
      <div class="clrflt"></div>
      <div id="col-blk">
        <div class="colms">
          <label for="last_name">Your Last Name [Required]</label>
        </div>
        <div class="colms">
          <input id="lastname" type="text" name="lastname" aria-required="true" />
        </div>
      </div>
      <div class="clrflt"></div>
      <div id="col-blk">
        <div class="colms">
          <label for="email">Email [Required]</label>
        </div>
```

```
      <div class="colms">
        <input id="email" type="text" name="email" aria-required="true" />
      </div>
    </div>
    <div class="clrflt"></div>
    <div id="col-blk">
      <div class="colms">
        <label for="homephone">Home Phone [Required]</label>
      </div>
      <div class="colms">
        <input id="homephone" type="text" name="homephone" aria-required="true" />
      </div>
    </div>
    <div class="clrflt"></div>
    <div id="col-blk">
      <div class="colms">
        <label for="workphone">Work Phone</label>
      </div>
      <div class="colms">
        <input id="workphone" type="text" name="workphone" />
      </div>
    </div>
    <div class="clrflt"></div>
    <div id="col-blk">
      <div class="colms">
        <label for="address1">Your Address:1 [Required] </label>
      </div>
      <div class="colms">
        <input id="address1" type="textarea" name="address1" aria-required="true" />
      </div>
    </div>
    <div class="clrflt"></div>
    <div id="col-blk">
      <div class="colms">
        <label for="address2">Your Address:2 [Required]</label>
      </div>
      <div class="colms">
        <input id="address2" type="textarea" name="address2" aria-required="true">
      </div>
    </div>
    <div class="clrflt"></div>
  </form>
</body>
</html>
```

▪ **Note** You might be wondering why I have both an `id` value and a `name` value on the input controls. This is for backward compatibility with older browsers and AT that don't understand the `id` value. While you may say, "Wow, some people must be using ancient technology." Yes, that's right. They are.

You could go a little further and add some old-school HTML accessibility magic and wrap some of the controls in a `<fieldset>` and `<legend>`, to add some more useful data. (See Figure 3-6 and Listing 3-5.) Doing this will help a screen-reader user (as well as a sighted person) understand how the form controls are grouped. This relationship is announced by the screen reader when the various input fields that are wrapped in `<legend>` and `<fieldset>` elements are given focus by the keyboard. These two elements are well supported by older AT also, and they make your forms a bit more backward compatible and robust.

Required Delivery Details Form

A little about you

Title

Your First Name [Required]:

Your Last Name [Required]:

Email [Required]:

Home Phone [Required]:

Work Phone:

A little about where we are going

Your Address Line 1 [Required]:

Your Address Line 2 [Required]:

Submit to Deliver

Figure 3-6. *ARIA "Required" example with <fieldset> and <legend>*

Listing 3-5 shows how to produce Figure 3-6.

Listing 3-5. *Using <legend> and <fieldset>*

```
<h1>Required Delivery Details Form</h1>
<form id="a11y_delivery">
  <fieldset>
    <legend>A little about you</legend>
    <label for="title">Title</label>
    <input id="title" type="text" name="title" />
    <label for="first_name">Your First Name [Required]:</label>
```

```
    <input id="firstname" type="text" name="firstname" aria-required="true" />
    <label for="last_name">Your Last Name [Required]:</label>
    <input id="lastname" type="text" name="lastname" aria-required="true" />
    <label for="email">Email [Required]:</label>
    <input id="email" type="text" name="email" aria-required="true" />
    <label for="homephone">Home Phone [Required]:</label>
    <input id="homephone" type="text" name="homephone" aria-required="true" />
    <label for="workphone">Work Phone:</label>
    <input id="workphone" type="text" name="workphone" size="20">
  </fieldset>
  <fieldset>
    <legend> A little about where we are going</legend>
    <label for="address1">Your Address Line 1 [Required]: </label>
    <input id="address1" type="textarea" name="address1" aria-required="true" />
    <label for="address2">Your Address Line 2 [Required]:</label>
    <input id="address2" type="textarea" name="address2" aria-required="true" />
  </fieldset>
  <input type="button" value="Submit to Deliver" />
</form>
```

HTML5 also has a required attribute that we'll look at later. And, yes, applying it is very similar to how you do it with ARIA.

▦ **Note** Adding the inline word [Required] as a part of the label for the input box means that this will get announced by the screen reader (including some older ones) on focus. Also, when the user agent supports the aria-required="true" property, this will also get announced. So *Required* gets announced twice, using newer agents. The addition of <fieldset> will mean that the contents of the field set will be announced on focus for each item that you tab through. Although it's useful for the first one or two, it might not be needed, or it might get annoying for longer forms. Ultimately, you have to try to judge what will benefit your users most—there is a fine line between too much accessibility and a good user experience for people with disabilities.

Want a Desktop Type Menu? Use ARIA Menubar

Listing 3-6 is the basic outline of an ARIA-enabled menu bar, designed to look like and behave similar to the menu you would find in a desktop application.

Listing 3-6. *An ARIA Menu*

```
<h1> Menubar test </h1>
<ul role="menubar" id="menu_css">
<li role="menuitem" aria-haspopup="true" aria labelledby="OpenFileLabel">
<span id="OpenFileLabel">File</span>
<ul role="menu">
<li role="menuitem">New</li>
<li role="menuitem">Open...</li>
<li role="menuitem">Save</li>
<li roles="menuitem">Save As...</li>
<li roles="menuitem">Print</li>
</ul>
</li>
<li role="menuitem" aria-haspopup="true" aria-labelledby="ViewFileLabel">
<span id="ViewFileLabel">View</span>
<ul role="menu">
<li role="menuitem">Undo</li>
<li role="menuitem">Redo...</li>
<li role="menuitem">Cut</li>
<li roles="menuitem">Copy</li>
<li roles="menuitem">Paste</li>
</ul>
</li>
<li role="menuitem" aria-haspopup="true" aria-labelledby="EditFileLabel">
<span id="EditFileLabel">Edit</span>
<ul role="menu">
<li role="menuitem">Bullet List</li>
<li role="menuitem">Numbered List</li>
<li role="menuitem">Date</li>
<li roles="menuitem">Order ID</li>
<li roles="menuitem">Supplier</li>
</ul>
</li>
</body>
</html>
```

You can style it with CSS as you please, and you'll also need to provide some script (using your library of choice) to provide focus to the elements (such as Show and Hide within the menu) and to initiate whatever behaviors you wish them to have. This is a skeleton outline of an ARIA-enabled menu. As you can see, it's quite simple in that it is a basic series of HTML list items that are given the ARIA role of menubar:

```
<ul role="menubar">
```

The `<li>` elements are given the two extra properties of `aria-haspopup`, and `aria-labelledby`. The `aria-labelledby` property we have come across before, and it means that the contents of the `<span>` that have the label will be announced by the screen reader on focus—for example, File, Edit, View, and so on.

```
 <li role="menuitem" aria-haspopup="true" aria-labelledby="OpenFileLabel"><span
id="OpenFileLabel">File</span>
```

The following roles of menu and menuitem are natural subclasses, and they perform as their name implies:

```
<ul role="menu">
  <li role="menuitem">New</li>
  <li role="menuitem">Open...</li>
  <li role="menuitem">Save</li>
  <li roles="menuitem">Save As...</li>
  <li roles="menuitem">Print</li>
</ul>
```

▒ **Note** You can ascribe various JavaScript behaviors to the list items by giving them unique identifiers and then attaching a scripting function to them, or by using numbered arrays to ascribe different functions or behaviors to these nodes numerically, whatever you prefer. The following example gives an ID to each of the items. However, if you want them to behave in a common way, menu items should just receive a class identifier that can act as a hook for scripted behaviors.

```
<ul role="menu">
  <li role="menuitem" id="NewItem">New</li>
  <li role="menuitem" id="OpenItem">Open...</li>
  <li role="menuitem" id="SaveItem">Save</li>
  <li roles="menuitem" id="SaveAsItem">Save As...</li>
  <li roles="menuitem"id="PrintItem">Print</li>
</ul>
```

Document Landmarks and ARIA

Most web sites follow a well-established convention of form (well not most of them, but a lot do). This is similar to the following: a banner at the top, the navigation area to the left, and the content on the right, straddling the middle. Most developers (the good ones, using CSS to lay out pages—I hope that's you) will wrap each of these sections in a <div> and position them using CSS.

A sighted person can look at a page and quickly understand the purpose of each of these sections, how they relate to each other, and so on. This is not the same for nonsighted people. For them to understand the purpose of each of these sections, they need semantics that describe what the purpose of each of these sections or chunks of the page are. Earlier versions of HTML didn't have semantics for such common layout structures, and ARIA provides them.

▒ **Note** HTML5 also has a very similar set of semantics that will allow you to pretty much do the same thing as I describe here.

Figure 3-7 is a sample webpage design and layout along the lines of what I just mentioned. Note that any similarity to other Groovy organizations is entirely coincidental.

Figure 3-7. Groovy Times Inc web site

Here you have a banner at the top, a navigation menu on the left, and the main content to the right of the page that straddles the middle. There's also a footer.

As a wireframe, the basic outline looks something like Figure 3-8.

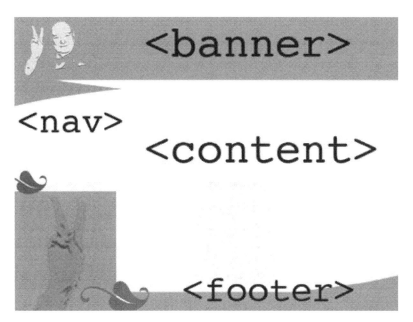

Figure 3-8. *Groovy Times Inc wireframe*

WAI-ARIA now provides a way to describe the purpose of these sections of web content to users of AT, like screen readers. This is shown in Listing 3-7.

Listing 3-7. *Describing Section Content*

```
<div role="banner">
[...]
</div>
<div role="navigation">
[...]
</div>
<div role="main">
[...]
</div>
<div role="contentinfo">
</div>
```

You can see that by simply adding the text role="banner" or role="navigation" or role="main" you can easily describe the purpose of each of these sections.

■ **Note** Remember that the `<div>` and `<span>` elements are *semantically neutral* elements. They have no meaning, poor things, and are merely empty hooks—ciphers for you to do with what you will. They cheer up to no end when you give them meaning. Existential crisis averted!

There are more landmark roles that you can use, and they are as follows:

- **application:** Represents a region of the page that executes a set of tasks for its users, or that is expected to behave like a desktop application. It can be an entire page or a section of a page. The `role="application"` attribute should not be used on an entire page, however. There are also some issues with how AT deals with sections that have the role of application, because the screen-reader virtual cursor is disabled and the screen-reader user cannot browse by headings, extract links, and so on. I'll say more about that in the next chapter.

- **banner:** As you saw earlier, this is the section that can contain the logo or the site title.

- **complementary:** Any section that is meaningful on its own but supports the main content of the site.

- **contentinfo:** This can be copyright info, accessibility statements, a footer, and so on. This can be thought of as child content.

- **main:** The main content in a document.

- **navigation:** A list of links used for navigating the web site.

- **search:** The sites search tool.

■ **Note** There are also landmark roles for Form and Search. You'll notice that they pretty much do what you expect and are easy to add to your pages. The great thing is that when older browsers come across these pieces of ARIA code and don't understand them, they just ignore them, so they won't break anything. Breathe a sigh of relief.

A more extensive list of ARIA roles and controls are contained in Appendix B at the end of this book. Look ahead now if you wish to familiarize yourself with them. Now we'll look at WAI-ARIA and see how it relates to HTML5.

WAI-ARIA and HTML 5

As you can see, lots of these roles are similar to some of the elements and controls you'll find in HTML5. The reason you might want to use them is that some of the HTML5 elements might not be supported by assistive technology, whereas many of the roles outlined here are.

Many of these ARIA roles can be used in conjunction with HTML5 elements as a way of making them backward compatible with legacy versions of AT. Also, when the browser comes across a combination of HTML5 controls and WAI-ARIA, in general the ARIA control will trump the HTML5 control and be rendered by the browser rather than the native functionality of the HTML5 element.

░ **Caution** When ARIA is added to any host language, it trumps the semantics of the host language. In general, adding ARIA functionality will override the default semantics of the element is attached to. The preceding examples of landmarks had no native semantics. By adding some, you give them meaning. Happy days.

WAI-ARIA also has other states and properties that can be used in conjunction with the more descriptive roles that you saw earlier to more fully describe to AT what the current state of a control is. This could be describing whether a check box is selected or deselected, to use a simple example. You'll recognize some of the states and properties from what we have covered in this chapter, but I'm including them in total so that you can get a feel for how flexible ARIA is. The following examples from the W3C are used with permission.

The following states and properties can be used to create sophisticated Web applications when used in conjunction with event handlers and listeners.

- `aria-activedescendant`: Identifies the currently active descendant of a composite widget.

- `aria-atomic`: Indicates whether assistive technologies will present all, or only parts of, the changed region based on the change notifications defined by the `aria-relevant` attribute. See the related `aria-relevant` attribute in this list.

- `aria-autocomplete`: Indicates whether user-input completion suggestions are provided.

- `aria-busy (state)`: Indicates whether an element and its subtree are currently being updated.

- `aria-checked (state)`: Indicates the current checked state of check boxes, radio buttons, and other widgets. See the related `aria-pressed` and `aria-selected` attributes in this list.

- `aria-controls`: Identifies the element (or elements) whose contents or presence are controlled by the current element. See the related `aria-owns` attribute in this list.

- `aria-describedby`: Identifies the element (or elements) that describes the object.

- `aria-disabled (state)`: Indicates that the element is perceivable but disabled, so it is not editable or otherwise operable. See the related `aria-hidden` and `aria-readonly` attributes in this list.

- `aria-dropeffect`: Indicates what functions can be performed when the dragged object is released on the drop target. This allows assistive technologies to convey the possible drag options available to users, including whether a pop-up menu of choices is provided by the application. Typically, drop-effect functions can be provided only after an object has been grabbed for a drag operation because the drop-effect functions available are dependent on the object being dragged.

- `aria-expanded (state)`: Indicates whether the element, or another grouping element it controls, is currently expanded or collapsed.

- `aria-flowto`: Identifies the next element (or elements) in an alternate reading order of content which, at the user's discretion, allows assistive technology to override the general default of reading in document source order.

- `aria-grabbed (state)`: Indicates an element's grabbed state in a drag-and-drop operation.

- `aria-haspopup`: Indicates that the element has a pop-up context menu or sublevel menu.

- `aria-hidden (state)`: Indicates that the element and all of its descendants are not visible or perceivable to any user as implemented by the author. See the related `aria-disabled` attribute in this list.

- `aria-invalid (state)`: Indicates the entered value does not conform to the format expected by the application.

- `aria-label`: Defines a string value that labels the current element. See the related `aria-labelledby` attribute in this list.

- `aria-labelledby`: Identifies the element (or elements) that labels the current element. See the related `aria-label` and `aria-describedby` attribute in this list.

- `aria-level`: Defines the hierarchical level of an element within a structure.

- `aria-live`: Indicates that an element will be updated, and describes the types of updates the user agents, assistive technologies, and user can expect from the live region.

- `aria-multiline`: Indicates whether a text box accepts multiple lines of input or only a single line.

- `aria-multiselectable`: Indicates that the user can select more than one item from the current selectable descendants.

- `aria-orientation`: Indicates whether the element and orientation are horizontal or vertical.

- `aria-owns`: Identifies an element (or elements) in order to define a visual, functional, or contextual parent/child relationship between DOM elements where the DOM hierarchy cannot be used to represent the relationship. See the related `aria-controls` attribute in this list.

- `aria-posinset`: Defines an element's number or position in the current set of listitems or treeitems. It's not required if all elements in the set are present in the DOM. See the related `aria-setsize` attribute in this list.

- `aria-pressed` (state): Indicates the current pressed state of toggle buttons. See the related `aria-checked` and `aria-selected` attributes in this list.

- `aria-readonly`: Indicates that the element is not editable but is otherwise operable. See the related `aria-disabled` attribute in this list.

- `aria-relevant`: Indicates what user agent change notifications (additions, removals, and so on) assistive technologies will receive within a live region. See the related `aria-atomic` attribute in this list.

- `aria-required`: Indicates that user input is required on the element before a form can be submitted.

- `aria-selected` (state): Indicates the current selected state of various widgets. See the related `aria-checked` and `aria-pressed` attributes in this list.

- `aria-setsize`: Defines the number of items in the current set of listitems or treeitems. It's not required if all elements in the set are present in the DOM. See the related `aria-posinset` attribute in this list.

- `aria-sort`: Indicates if items in a table or grid are sorted in ascending or descending order.

- `aria-valuemax`: Defines the maximum allowed value for a range widget.

- `aria-valuemin`: Defines the minimum allowed value for a range widget.

- `aria-valuenow`: Defines the current value for a range widget. See the related `aria-valuetext` attribute in this list.

- `aria-valuetext`: Defines the human-readable text alternative of `aria-valuenow` for a range widget.

WAI-ARIA and JAWS

Table 3-3 outlines how a major screen reader like JAWS currently supports many of the roles and states mentioned. Note this is very much subject to change. Table 3-3 is illustrative, and since the time of publication might have gotten better. Screen-reader support for WAI-ARIA is improving all the time. Several screen readers—like JAWS, NVDA, and VoiceOver—already have advanced support for ARIA.

Table 3-3. Roles That JAWS Recognizes

Role	Comments
alert	This role does not appear in either the virtual buffer or forms mode, but its contents are spoken by JAWS when an alert is made visible.

Role	Comments
button	
checkbox	
columnheader	
combobox	
dialog	This role will be announced only when a child of the dialog gets focus and will not appear in the virtual buffer.
document	This role might not be explicitly announced by JAWS, but it indicates that the area it occupies is meant to be read as a webpage. This is the default role of the topmost object in a webpage (that is, the "body" tag).
grid	
gridcell	
group	Like document, this role might not be explicitly announced by JAWS. However, when this role surrounds a group of form controls, JAWS should announce its name and description when entering the group.
heading	
img	
link	
list	
listbox	
listitem	
log	Presently, this role is known to work with JAWS in Firefox only, and it functions as a type of live region.

Role	Comments
menu	
menubar	
menuitem	
menuitemradio	
option	
presentation	This role indicates that a feature of a webpage exists for visual formatting only. Therefore, JAWS ignores objects with this role. (This role is known to work in Firefox.)
radio	
radiogroup	
row	
rowheader	
separator	
slider	
spinbutton	JAWS announces this role as a "spin box."
tab	
tablist	
tabpanel	
textbox	
toolbar	This role is indicated in the virtual buffer by start and end messages like those that exist for HTML lists.

Role	Comments
tooltip	This role is not shown by JAWS in the virtual buffer or in forms mode, but its contents are spoken when it becomes visible.
tree	When this role is in the virtual buffer, JAWS might show only one item of a tree control. This allows the user to navigate past the tree quickly.
treegrid	
treeitem	

ARIA States

The same principle of reasonable common usage applies to ARIA states as applied in Table 3-3 to the roles.

■ **Note** Some states, such as those related to drag and drop, have been omitted from the list in Table 3-4.

Table 3-4 provides a list of states that JAWS recognizes.

Table 3-4. JAWS-Recognizable States

State	Comments
aria-activedescendant	JAWS uses this state to locate the focused items in tree views, list boxes, and other such controls that manage multiple, focusable child objects.
aria-busy	Although JAWS does not presently use this state, its use is encouraged so that future versions of JAWS can take advantage of it.
aria-checked	
aria-describedby	JAWS announces this state for form controls.
aria-disabled	JAWS announces this state for form controls.

State	Comments
aria-expanded	JAWS announces this state when in forms mode in tree controls.
aria-haspopup	JAWS announces this state for menus and buttons that pop up a menu.
aria-hidden	
aria-invalid	JAWS announces this state for form controls.
aria-label	
aria-labelledby	JAWS announces this state for form controls.
aria-level	JAWS announces the level of tree items when in forms mode.
aria-multiline	JAWS uses this state to identify multiline edit controls.
aria-orientation	JAWS uses this state to determine if a slider is oriented horizontally or vertically.
aria-posinset	JAWS announces this information when in forms mode for trees and lists.
aria-pressed	JAWS announces the pressed state of a toggle button.
aria-readonly	JAWS uses this state to identify edit fields that are navigable with a caret, but whose content cannot be changed.
aria-required	JAWS announces this state for form controls.
aria-selected	
aria-setsize	JAWS announces this information when in forms mode for trees and lists.
aria-valuetext	

Copyright Freedom Scientific, used with permission.

Using JAWS and Landmarks

JAWS will announce the type of ARIA landmarks that you've defined. It also provides the screen-reader users the ability to navigate the page using the landmarks in the same way they would bounce around the page by headings or links.

You can get to the next and previous landmark on the page using the SEMICOLON and SHIFT+SEMICOLON quick navigation keys. In addition, pressing INSERT+CONTROL+SEMICOLON should bring up a dialog box containing a list of landmarks that the screen-reader user can use with his arrow keys to navigate with.

JAWS supports the following landmark roles:

- APPLICATION

- BANNER

- COMPLEMENTARY

- CONTENTINFO

- FORM

- MAIN

- NAVIGATION

- REGION

- SEARCH

Accessible Drag and Drop

JAWS also supports the ARIA drag-and-drop properties `aria-grabbed` and `aria-dropeffect`. These can be added to objects, and the screen reader will be able to announce to the user whether the item is either grabbable, grabbed, or droppable. The keystroke WINDOWS Key+CTRL+EQUALS opens the ARIA Drag and Drop dialog box, which shows a list of droppable objects on the page.

Conclusion

In this chapter, we had a good intro to some accessible JavaScript techniques, as well as the excellent WAI-ARIA specification. We covered some of the basics that you need to be aware of when using scripting in your web sites and applications. More advanced techniques can then be built upon solid accessible foundations. You can build complex scripted interfaces that will work, and I hope this chapter helped to show you that it is as much about your approach as anything else. In the next chapter we will look at how screen-reading technology works, what's going on under the hood in terms of the DOM, accessibility APIs, and the off-screen model (OSM).

CHAPTER 4

Understanding Accessibility APIs, Screen Readers, and the DOM

In this chapter, we'll consider how screen readers work in more detail and take a look at the DOM and accessibility APIs that are used by assistive technology (AT) to access web content. This is important to understand. Although some of this stuff might seem a little abstract or academic and this chapter is not vital for you to build accessible HTML5 content, it will help. By design, it's also short.

▓ **Note** As previously mentioned, although screen readers are not the only technology people with disabilities use to access the Web, they are arguably the most complex. Also, the technical accessibility support requirements found under the hood are probably the most extensive.

Don't worry too much if this chapter seems a little tricky; it's not an easy subject. I've worked with people with disabilities for nearly 10 years, and I've had experience with a broad range of assistive technologies when I worked as an AT specialist. I was fortunate enough to gain a lot of experience in the diverse kinds of AT that exist, as well as the myriad applications for these technologies.

From this experience, I can honestly say that the screen reader is the most complex, both from a development perspective for you, the author of accessible web content and designer of groovy web sites, and from the user perspective. The range or levels of screen reader proficiency varies greatly, from the most basic "Tab around the page" or "Just hit Say All and see what happens" to complex uses of virtual cursors, various kinds of content interrogation, and so on. The advent of a screen reader like VoiceOver, with its support for gestures and the rotor, has made interactions much easier, and we'll see a move toward more gestural interfaces. However, at the moment the keyboard interaction model is overly complex, with far too many custom keyboard combinations for the user to remember. The move to mobile devices will also result in a reduced dependence on the keyboard and a focus on more natural forms of input, such as finger swipes and other gestures.

I look forward to future iterations of these technologies, where the technology mediates the complexity and simplifies the user experience. I still get a buzz out of showing a screen reader user how to do new things with AT, and the low level of digital literacy among AT users still surprises me. AT users sometimes complain about some web site or content being inaccessible, when actually the barrier is the users' inability to use their AT correctly. Users of AT need to be schooled in how to use their technology to the best of their ability. This is a win-win approach in that the user will get more longevity from the technology and the health service provider will have recurring lower costs. Also, paying attention to this chapter will help you to better understand how the screen reader handles the code that you write.

▥ **Note** Assistive technologies can be very, very expensive and, in effect, are a niche technology. This has resulted in a creative, do-it-yourself, kind of punk rock culture, which fuses imaginative use of technology within the often-limited resources available to provide solutions for people with disabilities.

Defining the Elements Under the Hood of Assistive Technologies

When you look at what is happening under the hood with web content and the nuts and bolts of AT interaction, it is complex. This chapter gives you a glimpse of what is happening between the various platform accessibility APIs, and a look at dynamic DOM updating and the correct application of semantics to describe custom controls.

As I mentioned, it took me at least two to three years to get a grip on how a screen reader really works, from both studying the user interaction model and getting familiar with JAWS keystrokes to understanding what's happening under the hood. And that was just from the screen reader side—never mind how data gets Ping-Ponged between various APIs! So don't worry if you feel a little lost at sea. This chapter is my attempt to explain things to you in a way I wish someone had done for me years ago.

What's an API?

An API is an *application programming interface*. This is the framework or set of rules that provide the code, functions, or vocabulary needed to program in any given language. An API can be thought of as a library of code you use to tell software, like a browser or assistive technology, to do something.

For example, the browser converts web content written in HTML5 to a Document Object Model (DOM). This DOM of the webpage is associated with a layout engine that the browser uses. The browser then takes information from both the layout engine and the DOM to support an operating system (OS) platform accessibility API. This API allows an assistive technology to monitor and query any accessibility information that the browser exposes to it.

What's a Layout Engine?

A layout engine is an embedded component in every browser that displays in the browser the HTML, XHTML, XML, or other such content and formatting information such as Cascading Style Sheets (CSS). Different browsers have their own rendering engine, with their own rules for how they should display web content. For example, Firefox uses the Gecko engine, Internet Explorer uses Trident, Safari and Chrome use the Webkit rendering engine, and Opera has its own rendering engine called Presto.

What Are Accessibility APIs?

Accessibility APIs are platform-specific APIs that are used either in the desktop or in the browser to communicate accessibility information in a way that assistive technologies can understand. The HTML5 code that you will write contains elements like headings, buttons, form controls, and so on. Each of these elements then has a role, state, and property set (as well as parent/child relationships to the rest of the document elements) that are defined by the accessibility API platform.

Here are some of the main accessibility APIs:

- MSAA

- UIAutomation

- Apple Accessibility API

- iAccessible2

- AT-SPI

▓ **Note** There are other accessibility APIs. For example, if you're writing a JAVA application and you want to make it accessible, you need to use the JAVA access bridge to provide accessibility mapping. It's not enabled by default in JAVA.

The Off-Screen Model (OSM)

Before we look at APIs themselves in any more detail, we need to backpedal a bit and discuss the first accessibility model: the off-screen model, or OSM. It was developed as a means of making the visual desktop and the first graphical user interfaces (GUIs) accessible to early screen readers and Braille output devices. An awareness of the off-screen model will help you develop a broader understanding of how these related technologies interact and behave.

Early DOS-based systems, or command-line-interface systems, can be quite accessible because they are text based. The information that the user types into the system, as well as the information that the system returns, can be captured easily in the memory buffer and synthesized into speech. This speech output is achieved by using the kind of formant synthesis I talked about in Chapter 2, "Understanding Disability and Assistive Technology." Characters such as text strings and data are stored in a buffer (or memory store) that can be easily accessed directly by the screen reader and then output as speech to the end user.

▓ **Note** This basic speech output is known as TTS, or "Text-to-Speech," synthesis. There is a wide range of both hardware and software TTS engines.

With the advent of the GUI, this all changed. Controls then moved from being input via the command line, or text based, to being grouped as related selectable controls displayed visually on the screen (such as menus and application controls) that could be understood easily by sighted people. In effect, the user interface was converted to graphical pixels on the screen rather than it being more accessible text. As a result, the original text could not be easily accessed. A method was needed, therefore, to access information from drawing calls and windowing information *before* it was converted to pixels and stored in an off-screen data model that could be accessed and read by a screen reader. Getting this to work was a very complex operation. To deal with this complexity and to provide a way for on-screen content to be rendered in an accessible way by a screen reader, the off-screen model was developed and implemented. This was a missing link that was needed to make GUIs accessible.

■ **Note** For a very interesting piece of screen-reader history, I recommend the paper "Making the GUI Talk," by Richard Schwerdtfeger, who is the CTO of the Accessibility Software Group at IBM and a renowned accessibility expert. Rich also worked with the great Dr. Jim Thatcher, who developed one of the first screen readers for DOS as well as the first screen reader for the GUI-based PC. You can get this paper at `ftp://service.boulder.ibm.com/sns/sr-os2/sr2doc/guitalk.txt`.

For GUI-based systems, the off-screen model works by capturing information about the controls that are to be rendered visually on screen and then creating a separate version of the page (the off-screen model—hence, the name). The screen reader then interacts with this OSM and uses its contents as a basis to output speech that the end user can understand.

You can think of the off-screen model as a snapshot of the screen at any given time. What is happening is a technique known as *screen scraping* or hooking graphics calls. These days, for desktop systems, the OS provides vehicles to expose and retrieve this information, but it is the application and its user-interface components that expose the information through the APIs.

Modern programming languages allow for the use of descriptions of objects and elements that the screen reader can latch onto via the accessibility API. The screen reader then outputs these names and properties as speech for the user when they receive focus via the keyboard. As I mentioned, for desktop applications the need to maintain an OSM has lessened, but it's not entirely gone, and it's still useful in cases where developers have been semantically neglectful in labeling controls. So the OSM might still come into play in a support role to provide as much information as possible to the screen reader and therefore facilitate a more complete user experience.

For an operating system, making it accessible certainly presented particular challenges, but they have more or less been conquered because an OS is usually well engineered and is a more closed type of environment. This makes design for an application like a screen reader easier, because good programmatic practices, such as correctly labelled controls and so on, can be incorporated directly into the operating system. So what about the *world wild web*, where anything goes?

■ **Note** Confused? Well, it's a little complicated, so don't worry. In short, the OSM can be thought of as an internal database that the screen reader accesses before content gets rendered to the screen. As a sighted person, you look at the browser and get a picture for what the content of the page is and what the various controls are, including their function and so on. The screen reader just gets this info from the same source that the browser does, but it bypasses the visual rendering and uses the code to both navigate the page content and output it as speech.

How Do Screen Readers Access Information on a WebPage or Application?

These days, not all screen readers primarily use an OSM for interacting with the Web. An OSM is seen as outdated technology. Also, maintaining an OSM is technically difficult and presents challenges for developers. For example, you might find it hard to understand what's going on with the screen reader when you try testing webpages yourself for the first time. You will lose your place on the page or find it difficult to know where the screen reader's focus is at certain times. (It will happen.) It helps to understand that you're not interacting with the browser directly in the first place, but with this *third place*.

■ **Note** When interacting with the Web, in reality that "third place" is a combination of the DOM and accessibility API output—as well as the OSM for some screen readers. It can help, when you are just getting your head around this stuff for the first time, to initially think of them as representing the same thing. They're not the same, but in effect combine to create the "third place." So it's useful as an abstraction—so that your head doesn't explode.

Earlier we talked about the various cursors that a screen reader like JAWS uses when interacting with the Web. The PC *virtual cursor* is what JAWS uses mostly for browsing the Web. That virtual cursor is actually pointing at a database of content—which is really a cache of what is available from a combination of OSMs and API calls—in a virtual buffer. This buffer of what is visualized on the screen allows the AT user to browse the contents of the screen. The virtual cursor, therefore, represents the screen-reader user's *browsing point*, which might not match the focus point when a sighted user visually scans a webpage.

■ **Remember** What a sighted user can see in the browser is just a visual rendering of the contents of the DOM, styled by CSS. Note, this doesn't apply to plugins like Flash content or Java Applets or, indeed, the HTML5 `<canvas>` API.

For this snapshot to work with assistive technologies or for it to be considered accessible, the off-screen model needs to be fed good semantic code, as mentioned previously. This means that the more accessibility-aware developer has marked up page headings, list items, form controls, and graphics in a way that conforms to accessibility best practice. When you do this, the contents of the OSM are structured, being supported by good semantics. So adding your `<h1>`s, your `<li>`s, and your form input `<labels>` isn't just an esoteric exercise, but a vital way of creating an accessibility architecture that provides a structure for assistive technologies to use for navigation and comprehension.

You might remember earlier I talked about a Forms Mode that the screen reader uses. A screen reader like JAWS uses a virtual cursor so that the user can navigate the headings by pressing the H key, G key (for graphics), or the B key (for buttons) or bring up a dialog box of links on the page. This is possible because the virtual cursor has captured the keystrokes to use them as navigational controls. So what about when you want to enter some data on a webpage? You obviously cannot use these kinds of navigational features of the screen reader at the same time.

115

■ **Remember** This is why there is a Forms Mode with a screen reader like JAWS. In Forms Mode, the screen reader switches from using the PC virtual cursor to interacting with the browser directly. This disables the virtual cursor and allows the screen reader user to enter data directly into a form.

This Forms Mode also presents certain challenges for the web developer, because when the developer is working in Forms Mode, important data that would be available via the PC virtual cursor might not be available. This missing data might be instructions on how to fill in the form and so on. Care should be taken with form validation and updating on-screen content when in Forms Mode so that the screen-reader user doesn't miss out on instructions or feedback you need to give them, such as missing input data and so on.

In brief, you've seen an overview of the off-screen model, and some of the cursors that a screen reader like JAWS uses. Next, we'll look at the DOM, and then dive into heuristics.

■ **Tip** Remember that some screen readers don't use an off-screen model at all. These include VoiceOver for the Mac and NVDA for the PC, which is an excellent free, open-source screen reader than can be used with some of the existing voice-synthesis packages on a screen-reader user's system, such as SAPI4 or SAPI5.

What Is the DOM?

DOM stands for *Document Object Model* and represents the semantic structure of a webpage or other kinds of documents, in a kind of tree form. As shown in Figure 4-1, the various HTML elements in the webpage form the leaves on the tree that are the element nodes.

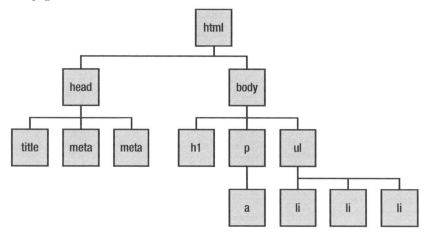

Figure 4-1. Meet the HTML that creates the DOM

The nodes shown in Figure 4-1 represent the various structural parts of the document that the browser or assistive technology will see. The DOM might also provide information about a node's *state*.

As you can see in the diagram, you have a header, which contains the `<title>` of the document, and you have the `<body>`, which contains a node that is a heading (`<h1>`), a node that is a paragraph (`<p>`), which has a child that is an `<a>`, and a node that is an unordered list (`<ul>`) with three little `<li>` children.

▨ **Note** In reality, the user agent, which might be a browser or some assistive technology, has several options when building a picture or model of a web document. It might interact with the DOM directly or use an off-screen model, or it might get information about these various nodes and their states and properties via a platform accessibility API. I mentioned some of these accessibility APIs earlier, such as MSAA, iAccessible2, Apple Accessibility API, and others.

How Do Accessibility APIs Work?

An accessibility API acts as a gateway or bridge between the browser, DOM, and AT. For the contents of the DOM to be understood by the assistive technology, these contents need to be mapped to a corresponding role within the accessibility API. The API is like a filter to help the AT what is happening in the DOM at any given time. The actual API does more than this, because it isn't entirely static. It can facilitate dynamic interaction between the user-interface components and the assistive technology.

▨ **Remember** The accessibility API is like a bridge between both the operating system and the Web for assistive technologies.

An API, such as MSAA or Apple Accessibility API, allows the screen-reader user to know when an item has focus and what its name is. If the item is a control, the API lets the screen reader know what type of control it is. If it is an interactive control like a check box, the API indicates what state it is in—selected or unselected, for example.

Does that sound familiar? It should—this is the kind of thing that WAI-ARIA aims to do when it gives you the ability to add these descriptive name, role, and state properties to widgets that don't have any inherent semantics. It's also what native HTML controls do—they expose their name, role, and so on (at this stage, you should get the picture!) to the accessibility API, and this information gets passed to the AT when the user gives an item focus via the keyboard.

Figure 4-2 gives you an overview of what exactly is going on and shows how the contents of the DOM are output visually to the screen and screen readers.

▨ **Note** The diagram in Figure 4-2 is a slight oversimplification, but it's designed to outline in broad strokes the interaction between the core HTML code and what gets output as speech by the screen reader.

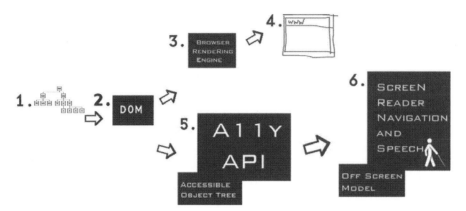

Figure 4-2. Accessible DOM output to both the screen and the Text-to-Speech engine

Here is a description of the items in the preceding illustration:

- **Item 1: HTML elements**—These form the DOM.

- **Item 2: The DOM**—This is the root of what both the assistive technology and the browser use to build a picture of the document to present to the user in the way that the user requires. Note that the same core HTML document can be used by both the visual browser and the nonvisual screen reader. This is pretty amazing and shows that universal access is a technical reality.

- **Item 3: The browser rendering engine**—This is used to determine how the combined HTML and CSS will be presented visually within the browser.

- **Item 4: The browser**—This is a visual screen display that is a combination of the contents of the DOM and CSS declarations put together by the browser's rendering engine. It's usually the main focal point for a sighted person to use when accessing the Web. If the user isn't sighted, however, he still needs to be able to access the same content. In a more accessible webpage, the page is rendered visually in the browser in a layered way—for example, according to the declarations defined by the CSS, the behaviors as defined by the unobtrusive and progressively enhanced JavaScript, and the HTML or WAI-ARIA code that provide the semantics that are vital for assistive technology.

- **Item 5: The accessible object tree and accessibility API**—The accessible object tree is mapped from the DOM. This is where the accessibility API is instantiated.

- **Item 6: The screen reader and off-screen model (OSM)** —The OSM is maintained by the screen reader. There is a constant interaction between the two. As the contents of the DOM are updated, the contents of the OSM also need to be updated. The screen reader drives the Text-to-Speech (TTS) engine, which is an application such as Nuance, ViaVoice, DECTalk, or Microsoft Speech.

That is the initial model for screen-reader navigation and speech output. But is it the whole picture? What about user interaction and so on?

Figure 4-3 provides a more complete picture that encompasses the interaction model and shows interaction and TTS output. (I removed the visual browser from the diagram to make things clearer.)

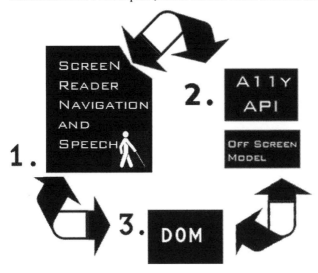

Figure 4-3. Interaction and TTS output—a dynamic, interactive loop

Here is a description of the items in Figure 4-3:

- **Item 1: The user navigating or interacting with the page via the keyboard and the speech output**—The user agent might be either using the DOM directly or using a combination of the OSM, the accessible object tree that is instantiated within the accessibility API, and DOM data. Hence, the bidirectional arrows depict events that can get triggered in the DOM that cause the page to update—in particular, for dynamic web content.

- **Item 2: The accessibility API and OSM**—These are fed via the DOM and, as stated in the previous item, the screen reader can interact either with the DOM directly or with the accessibility API/OSM that now updates every few milliseconds.

- **Item 3: The DOM**—The DOM responds to events that are triggered when the user interacts with web content in the browser.

"Accessibility": The Movie, Co-starring "The Heuristics"

Often screen readers need to call on additional support to make content more accessible to the end user. To do this, screen readers use a combination of the information they get via the DOM, the accessibility

API (whom you just met), and what are called *heuristics*. These evaluations help the user build a better picture of a webpage when there is little information (such as an inaccessible webpage) for it to go on.

For example, if a webpage has been badly authored and contains very little accessibility information (it's poorly coded and so on), there is then little information to be passed on to the screen reader that it can make sense of. What happens then is that the software uses a method of trying to find out as much info as possible by guessing (an educated guess of course) about what certain content might be or is likely to be when found in a given context. This is called *heuristic evaluation*. The software activates a set of rules to try and figure out what is what. This process can involve determining what an image is likely to be by looking at content around the image or guessing what the table headers in a document are likely to be by looking at the first items contained in the top row (which are likely to be headers). This method of relying on heuristics for repair is brittle and prone to error—hence, the importance of semantically correct code.

■ **Note** The term "heuristic" just means "a set of rules."

Changes in the DOM and Dynamic Content

The off-screen model can also be thought of as a *virtual buffer*. This buffer is a temporary memory store that contains a snapshot of the DOM at any given time. When this page doesn't change, this snapshot is pretty static and the screen reader can interrogate page content happily, without the user being too worried about things changing.

■ **Note** I don't mean "interrogate" in the good cop/bad cop way, but rather in the strict sense of a user interacting with web content. You can think of this interaction as a conversation along the lines of the following:

Q: What are you?

A: I'm a check box.

Q: Are you checked or unchecked?

A: I'm checked.

That's not as exciting or dramatic as a good cop/bad cop routine, but what are ya' gonna' do?

This situation is markedly different when the contents of the page are changing dynamically and the buffer needs to be updated (as illustrated previously). It was a distinct problem a few years ago when AJAX came along as a development method, and asynchronous content updating became the norm, courtesy of the XHR object.

■ **Note** AJAX developers will be familiar with the `XMLHttpRequest` or `XHR` object that can facilitate more client-side functionality, by reducing calls to the server, and help to create more dynamic and responsive web applications.

Although client side updating is great and is a real step forward, dynamic content updating found in AJAX or Web 2.0 applications presented challenges to the more accessibility-aware developer. How can a developer let the AT know that parts of the page content have updated? How can this be done in a way that is unobtrusive? This was very tricky before the advent of WAI-ARIA, because the virtual buffer update had to be forced for the user to see any changes in the DOM. It isn't so much of an issue now because the virtual buffer updates automatically every few milliseconds, so DOM changes can be passed on to the user far more reliably and quickly.

■ **Note** For some screen-reader history about this issue, if you fancy nerding out a little, I recommend the following articles by Gez Lemon and Steve Faulkner at `www.Juicystudio.com`. Gez and I also wrote about the subject and presented a paper to a technical conference in Leeds, UK consisting of about five people, and we were two of them. So this subject truly does have a broad appeal, lol!

For more information, go to the JuicyStudio web site and check out `http://juicystudio.com/article/making-ajax-work-with-screen-readers.php` and `http://juicystudio.com/article/improving-ajax-applications-for-jaws-users.php`.

If you do get busy with some heavily scripted webpages or applications, it's important that you develop them to be accessible. These things are possible to do and just require some extra care and attention.

Commonly Used Accessibility APIs

The following sections describe some of the most commonly used accessibility APIs. These are found on different platforms such as Windows, Mac, and Linux. Some are also cross platform.

MSAA

MSAA is the older, big-brother API that has been used on the Windows platform since the mid to late '80s. There is an *accessible object*, which is at the heart of MSAA, as well as the ability to pass vital information about an element's roles, names, state, and other values.

MSAA communicates information by sending small chunks of information about elements of a program to the assistive technology object. The four critical pieces of information on which the AT relies to help users interact with applications are an element's role (what a control does), name (what it is), value (which can be a numerical value or the value of an input field), and state (whether or not a check box is selected).

■ **Note** MSAA has a rather limited set of features that doesn't allow for more sophisticated or advanced user-interface controls, and it is able to give only a relatively small amount of property information to the AT.

Welcome to the Automator!

MSAA was supposed to be partially replaced by UIAutomation with the advent of Windows Vista and newer Windows versions. UIAutomation is a more sophisticated and advanced API that has a richer object model. The idea is that it will expand the capabilities of MSAA but improve on its shortcomings.

UIAutomation shows information about a user-interface component to the assistive technology as a tree, similar to the way the DOM tree is exposed to accessibility APIs allowing AT to consume web content. Any properties associated with the component are also shown to the AT via the API, as well as system events and so on.

The API covers some common control types like drop-down menus, combo boxes, check boxes, and other controls that will prepare the AT for interaction, as well as *control patterns* that show the kind of functionality and interaction they support for the AT. Different functionality is represented by these control types and can be combined to create sophisticated interaction models and controls.

■ **Note** I say "partially replaced" in this introduction to MSAA because it is still widely used as a platform accessibility API, as a way of exposing information to AT. The newer APIs, however, have a lot of potential in supporting new markup languages like HTML5 and WAI-ARIA. Both Web and OS information can be accessed and shared by both APIs.

IAccessible 2

The IAccessible COM method is at the heart of MSAA, and it has the ability to generate the all-important tree structure that you come across again and again.

■ **Remember** Are you starting to see a pattern? It's all about the document tree, and the various leaves or nodes on the tree being exposed to AT, as well as whatever properties, states, and so on these nodes have. That is the core of API accessibility.

Although UIAutomation represents a leap forward with its potential to richly describe a user-interface component and its values and states, IAccessible2 is an alternative API that extends the capabilities of MSAA rather than intending to replace it. It was built into browsers like Mozilla Firefox from version 3 forward, as well as implemented in JAWS, NVDA, ZoomText (a popular screen-magnification program), Window-Eyes, and others.

The support for IAccessible2 for the Firefox browser was a very interesting development, as Firefox became the go-to browser for many who were testing more advanced accessibility features, such as WAI-ARIA when it first came out. Because IAccessible2 builds on MSAA, there was no conflict with the existing APIs and developers could piggyback on the support for current roles, states, and properties to expose vital accessibility information via the API to AT.

■ **Note** Both UIAutomation and IAccessible2 have the ability to be cross-platform APIs. IAccessible2 is also used in the Chrome browser, for example.

Apple Accessibility API

Apple has developed accessibility APIs that are used in both OSX and IOS. This accessibility framework was introduced by Apple in Mac OS X 10.2 and was designed to accommodate the older Carbon and newer Cocoa developer framework. This was done in a rather clever way. It uses an *accessibility object* that passes information about itself (again, its name, state, role properties, and so on) to both Carbon and Cocoa applications in a uniform way, regardless of the framework that was used to develop it. These accessibility objects and a uniform way of passing information about user-interface components remove much of the complexity of software development and reduce the need for code forking and so on.

The standard controls that come with the operating system are already highly accessible. It's only when you design your own custom controls that you have to be very careful and provide the name, role, and (you guessed it) properties to the object.

The Code and Interface Builder applications make it easy to add accessibility information to your custom controls.

This really relates to applications/software. What about the Web?

Webkit Accessibility

Webkit is the rendering engine that powers the Safari browser as well as many others. Safari has support for the excellent screen reader VoiceOver. VoiceOver is a total game-changer from an accessibility perspective. It has excellent, advanced navigation and interaction features, and a blind computer user can now be equally happy using the same screen reader on a multitude of Apple iDevices.

The Webkit engine behind Safari gives it a great deal of support for many HTML5 elements and features (which I'll get in to in the next chapter), such as HTML5 sectioning elements, CSS3 web fonts, Web sockets, HTML5 form validation, HTML5 audio and video, as well as closed captions and the infamous 2D JavaScript rendering engine, Canvas. (I'll say more about this later.)

■ **Note** Apple has the open-sourced Webkit, which is now the rendering engine behind the Chrome browser, as well as ions and Android browsers and others. Even though Webkit has been outsourced, this doesn't mean that VoiceOver will work particularly well with other browsers. It doesn't. It's closely tied to Safari, but then again Safari is a great browser, so it's a win-win situation.

LINUX Accessibility APIs

The main Linux accessibility API you should be aware of is the AT-SPI, or Assistive Technology Service Provider Interface. This was developed by the GNOME Project. This API is used by UBUNTU, which is an excellent flavor of Linux that has a high level of accessibility support out of the box for screen readers such as ORCA.

■ **Note** The UBUNTU operating system also has screen magnification, modifier keys (rather like Sticky keys in Windows), Voice Recognition support, and an interesting app called Dasher, which requires neither a keyboard nor a mouse to work but uses dwell functionality and an eye tracker. It's completely free, so well worth checking out. To see more and download a copy, go to www.ubuntu.com.

HTML5 and Accessibility APIs

For a good snapshot of how HTML5 maps to accessibility APIs, I recommend the document created by Steve Faulkner (of The Paciello Group) and Cynthia Shelly (of Microsoft). It might seem a little abstract looking at this stuff, but it can give you a good overview of how accessible the new HTML5 elements are, because they need to be mapped to an accessibility API for AT to understand what they are, what they do, and how to interact with them.

As stated in the document:

> *"There is not a one to one relationship between all features and platform accessibility APIs. When HTML roles, states and properties do not directly map to an accessibility API, and there is a method in the API to expose a text string, expose the undefined role, states and properties via that method.*
>
> *IAccessible2 and ATK use object attributes to expose semantics that are not directly supported in the APIs. Object attributes are name-value pairs that are loosely specified, and very flexible for exposing things where there is no specific interface in an accessibility API. For example, at this time, the HTML5 header element can be exposed via an object attribute because accessibility APIs have no such role available.*

For accessibility APIs that do not have object attributes per se, it is useful to find a similar mechanism or develop a new interface to expose name/value pairs. Under the Mac OS X Accessibility Protocol, all getters are already simply name-value pairs and it is possible to expose new semantics whenever necessary. Keep in mind, this also requires working with the assistive technology developers to gain support for the new semantics."

■ **Note** The full text and detailed table outlining the HTML5/API mappings is available at
`http://dev.w3.org/html5/html-api-map/overview.html`.

So these things are a work in progress. As you read this, the mappings of the various APIs to HTML5 will certainly have improved.

I am including a screen shot here (Figure 4-4) of the matrix that outlines how HTML5 elements map to accessibility APIs so that you can get an idea of what it's like. More information can be found at the URL just shown.

3. HTML element to Accessibility API Role Mapping Matrix

Notes:

- A ? in a cell indicates the data has yet to be provided.
- A N/A (Not Applicable) means the element does not need to be exposed via an accessibility API. This is usually because the element is not displayed as part of the user interface.

Mappings of HTML elements to platform accessibility APIs: ARIA, MSAA, IAccessible2, UIA, ATK, and AX

HTML element	HTML4	HTML5	WAI-ARIA	MSAA Role	IAccessible2	UIA	AT-SPI Role	Mac Accessibility role AX
a element that represents a hyperlink	yes	yes	link role	ROLE_SYSTEM_LINK. Also, apply special rule to expose STATE_LINKED to link and all its descendants.	ROLE_SYSTEM_LINK. Also, apply special rule to expose STATE_LINKED to link and all its descendants.	HyperLink	ROLE_LINK	AXLink
a element (with no href)	yes	yes	none	ROLE_SYSTEM_TEXT	ROLE_SYSTEM_TEXT	Text	ROLE_TEXT	AXStaticText
abbr element	yes	yes	none	ROLE_SYSTEM_STATICTEXT	IA2_ROLE_TEXT_FRAME + Object attribute role="abbr"	Text	Object attribute role="abbr"	AXStaticText, AXRoleDescription="abbr"
address element	yes	yes	none	ROLE_SYSTEM_GROUPING	Object attribute role="address"	?	Object attribute role="address"	AXGroup, AXRoleDescription="address"
area element that represents a hyperlink	yes	yes	link role	ROLE_SYSTEM_LINK. Also, apply special rule to expose STATE_LINKED to link and all its descendants.	ROLE_SYSTEM_LINK. Also, apply special rule to expose STATE_LINKED to link and all its descendants.	HyperLink	ROLE_LINK	AXLink
area element that has no href attribute	yes	yes	none	ROLE_SYSTEM_TEXT	ROLE_SYSTEM_TEXT	Text	ROLE_TEXT	AXStaticText
article element	no	yes	article role	ROLE_SYSTEM_DOCUMENT + STATE_SYSTEM_READONLY	Object attribute role="article"	Expose as text string "article" in AriaRole	ROLE_DOCUMENT_FRAME + do not expose STATE_EDITABLE	AXGroup, AXRoleDescription="article"
aside element	no	yes	complementary role	ROLE_SYSTEM_GROUPING	Object attribute role="complementary"	Expose as text string "complementary" in AriaRole	Object attribute role="complementary"	AXGroup, AXRoleDescription="complementary"
audio element	no	yes	none	?	?	?	?	?
b element	yes	yes	none	ROLE_SYSTEM_TEXT	ROLE_SYSTEM_TEXT	Text	ROLE_TEXT	AXStaticText
base element	yes	yes	none	N/A	N/A	N/A	N/A	N/A
bdo element	yes	yes	none	ROLE_SYSTEM_TEXT	ROLE_SYSTEM_TEXT	text	ROLE_TEXT	AXStaticText
blockquote element	yes	yes	none	ROLE_SYSTEM_GROUPING	?	?	?	?
body element	yes	yes	document role	ROLE_SYSTEM_DOCUMENT + STATE_SYSTEM_READONLY	ROLE_SYSTEM_DOCUMENT + STATE_SYSTEM_READONLY	Document	ROLE_DOCUMENT_FRAME + STATE_READONLY	AXGroup, AXRoleDescription="document"
br element	yes	yes	none	ROLE_SYSTEM_WHITESPACE	ROLE_SYSTEM_WHITESPACE	?	?	?
button element	yes	yes	button role	ROLE_SYSTEM_PUSHBUTTON	ROLE_SYSTEM_PUSHBUTTON	Button	ROLE_PUSH_BUTTON	AXButton
canvas element	no	yes	none	?	?	?	ROLE_GRAPHIC + STATE_ANIMATED	?

Figure 4-4. Screen shot of HTML5 and API mapping

■ **Tip** If you want to find out what kind of role any HTML5 or ARIA control has, you can use several tools to do this, such as INSPECT32 (Win) or AccProbe (MSAA/IAccessible2 on Windows). When you focus on a widget in the browser, these tools will let you see how they map to the accessibility API.

Conclusion

In this chapter, you learned about accessibility APIs, the DOM, and how screen readers receive information from the DOM via the accessibility API, as well as the older but still used off-screen model. In future chapters, we'll move toward more use of accessibility APIs vs. the OSM. As mentioned earlier, a screen reader is not the only piece of AT in existence, but it is one of the most complex. In the chapters that follow, as we continue to look at HTML5 in more detail, the areas we covered in this chapter will certainly be a great help in giving you a better understanding of how the code is handled by AT. Also, I hope you can better understand why you sometimes might need to provide some extras to support older AT that, for example, doesn't use the more advanced APIs.

The good news is that this is all doable, and with some care and attention you'll be able to build accessible HTML5 applications that can be used easily by the newer browsers and AT that support it, while still being nice to those that don't.

CHAPTER 5

HTML5: The New Semantics and New Approaches to Document Markup

In this chapter, you'll start to look at the HTML5 specification in more detail, especially the aspects of it that most relate to the development of accessible interfaces. There are many new APIs that do background client/server processing and data storage that can be leveraged for rich, responsive applications, but you'll be seeing mostly the aspects of HTML5 that impact accessibility for users.

You'll also see the new HTML5 elements and the semantics used to define document outlines and new structural forms.

HTML5: What's New?

Early versions of HTML were relatively simple document markup languages. They allowed documents to be linked and referenced, and they provided semantics for structuring the content to support a small range of browsers and platforms. This variety of content ranged from the likes of data tables to content providing interaction via simple links (which is really the heart of the Web) to form controls, as well as some very simple media—implemented a la embedded graphics.

But that was really it. These items formed the basis of the abilities of earlier HTML markup languages. Clever people then worked out ways of compressing audio and video by using plugins such as Flash, Silverlight, QuickTime for the Maccies, or RealPlayer for PC heads (and indeed what plugin fun all that was). These technologies enabled the Web to be used as a platform for rich media like animated content and video.

Note Video is now really big business, with Netflix in the US accounting for between 22-35 percent of all Web traffic (depending on who you ask). So the nature of the delivery platform is pretty important. And yes, Netflix was one of the first companies to adopt HTML5 to serve video to its clients.

These early iterations of HTML were expected to go way above the call of duty, as the Web moved far beyond pages being mere documents into the application space and so on.

OK, so what's new in HTML5? Quite a lot. So much that HTML5 totally breaks the model of being merely a declarative document markup language. HTML5 has a host of new features that cover a broad range of new exciting functions. In many ways, much of it might not seem very HTML like, and in truth the language goes way beyond its predecessors. HTML5 really is a disruptive technology.

⬚ **Caution** With any new or game-changing technology, you have to take care and adopt a flexible trial-and-error approach. The way HTML5 adoption works (in part, anyway) is that the specification makes parsing rules that give browser manufacturers a standard they can build their browsers around. Support within the browser often is provided in a piecemeal way. As the spec evolves, a browser vendor might implement certain parts of it only.

From an accessibility perspective, the net result is that what is or isn't supported by the browser or assistive technology (AT) vendor can seem to be a little arbitrary. For example, it took absolutely years for CSS2 to be widely supported in the browser. And when it finally was, it was often only partially supported, and this led to bugs and glitches (such as "box-model rendering inconsistencies"). There are the same peculiarities in the world of AT. For example, the `<scope>` attribute of the `<table>` element made authoring more accessible data tables in HTML4 much quicker than using the better supported `<headers>` and `for/id` methods. However, it was so poorly supported that this easier authoring method, unfortunately, just couldn't be relied upon.

New HTML5 Semantics

HTML is a language that is largely associated with meaning. There are controls that you are familiar with already that have an inherent behavior (such as links being clickable or activated via the keyboard, and so on), but these behaviors are handled by a user agent, such as the browser. The underlying code provides a basic structure that allows the core content (which is usually and mostly text) to be consumed by a broad range of devices. This content layer provides a practical basis for the "author once, and publish to many devices" model that gives a huge edge to electronic communication, enabling interoperability without a great deal of customization between a plethora of devices.

⬚ **Note** The HTML5 spec is quite strict when it comes to elements being used only for their intended purpose.

The preceding observations really make sense when you think of the importance that semantics have on interoperability and, indeed, accessibility. Think of what we have covered already regarding how important structured content is in supporting an accessibility architecture and passing usable information via the accessibility API to the AT. My apologies if your head still hurts, but all this should be a little clearer now.

However, this rule of "the right tool for the right job" that the HTML5 spec is quite explicit about really does break down in the wild. Developers pretty much just do what they want, as long as it "works" for their purposes. It's also worth noting that the concept of "it seems OK, it's working, just don't look too close under the hood" really breaks down when it comes to accessibility.

This is because the stuff that is broken under the hood might only come to light when you do some kind of expert accessibility auditing or user testing with real people. We'll look at this topic in more detail in Chapter 9.

It suffices to say that the advice the new spec gives does focus on software interoperability and not its impact on the end user. In fact, the spec tries to not define the user experience, and there is a double standard at play to some degree. Why? Because certain aspects of the specification do actually outline what the user experience should be in some detail. However, when it comes to accessibility—more often than not—this isn't clearly delineated.

Semantic Ninjas

It is also worth noting that while I was being a little blasé about some developers' attitudes to their code ("It seems OK to me, so it's OK"), this would actually be fine with me if the stuff that developers threw together *did* work for people with disabilities. I guess I have a particular prejudice against web content that doesn't work for people with disabilities and older people. I'm mentioning this because well-formed code, strict validation, or even semantic correctness take second, third, and fourth place behind a positive user experience for people with disabilities who might be using ATs.

Ideally, these should support accessibility, and in many ways they do—but not all the time and in all situations. If well formedness, validation, and semantic correctness were cast-iron guarantees of accessibility, it would be happy days for all, but they're not. So don't think in absolutes; there are many relative considerations when it comes to HTML5 and accessibility.

Just so it's clear when you read this: I'm all for following the rules, but only when they work in a way that doesn't break the user experience for people with disabilities—or without disabilities, actually. I'm less concerned with the rules of well-coded, well formedness, or conformance to normative specification outlines or whatever you want to call it. Having said that, I don't condone sloppy code or designing code in any old way; I am merely acknowledging that there will be times when you have to follow your own intuition or insightful empirical judgment rather than merely what the specification dictates.

There are some people who call themselves knowledgeable about accessibility when actually they are specification zealots, and possibly validation vampires. Conformance to either approach is no guarantee of accessibility, good usability, or a positive user experience. All these development tools really can do is indicate the developer knew what she was doing when it came to writing code that conforms to a formal published grammar, but they don't necessarily factor in the user experience in terms of user-agent support and exactly what works with either the browser or the AT. The only thing that will help developers understand the practical reality is the experience of user testing or becoming proficient with using a screen reader. At that point, the developer's own testing might well help signal when something is or isn't working. This kind of knowledge is very important because it is based on the subjective reality of the user experience.

■ **Note** OK, actually well-formed code is important. Good semantics are really important, *but* real-world accessibility is very nuanced—particularly for new content and element types. However, bear in mind that an un-encoded ampersand (which will throw a validation error) *never* resulted in an inaccessible webpage. Having *some* heading structure, rather than none, on a web document is far more important than merely ensuring the headings are ordered in the correct way.

Semantic No-Gos

The introductory part of the HTML5 specification that deals with new elements warns against both the use of nonconforming content and the use of conforming elements in nonconforming ways. You are advised not to use the nonconforming attribute value ("carpet", in the example) and the nonconforming attribute ("texture" in the example), which are not allowed in HTML5. Use of these is shown here:

```
<label>Carpet: <input type="carpet" name="c" texture="deep pile" /></label>
```

This is certainly good to know—not very useful, but good to know. The spec suggests, however, that the following code example makes more semantic sense and could therefore be *valid* HTML5:

```
<label>Carpet: <input type="text" class="carpet" name="c" data-texture="deep pile" /></label>
```

■ **Note** I'm not joking about the carpet example! You can check it on

`http://dev.w3.org/html5/spec/Overview.html#elements.`

OK, so while the example may seem initially a little silly it isn't without purpose. You can see from it how the semantics do make more sense. The `<input type="text" />` segment is standard input that is given an arbitrary attribute (`class="carpet"`). The `data-texture="deep pile"` segment will be ignored by user agents that don't understand it, which is all of them!

On a more serious note, if you did have a document fragment that could be used to represent the heading of a corporate site, this would also be nonconforming because the second line is not intended to be a heading of a subsection, merely a subheading or subtitle. You might think the semantics are a bit iffy, and you are right. However, there was no way in earlier versions of HTML to define the relationship between grouped headings. You can see that the following is nonconforming:

```
<body>
 <h1>ABC Company</h1>
 <h2>Leading the way in widget design since 1432</h2>
[…]
```

HTML5 brings a `<hgroup>` element to help to define where a heading can have a direct subheading, such as what you find here:

```
<body>
 <hgroup>
  <h1>ABC Company</h1>
  <h2>Leading the way in widget design since 1432</h2>
 </hgroup>
[…]
```

This kind of code is useful when you have a strap line that provides a cool tagline for your site or project. For example, if you have a web site for an animal shelter, you could have the following code:

```
<hgroup>
 <h1>Animal Sanctuary</h1>
 <h2>A lifeline for all creatures great and small</h2>
</hgroup>
 ...
```

Figure 5-1 shows an example of the code in Listing 5-1 in a page, as well as how it might look with a little Cascading Style Sheets (CSS) styling thrown in.

Listing 5-1. Using an <hgroup>

```
body
{
    background-image:url(../Images/gray_white_tile2.png);
}

#hg
{
    margin: 10px;
    padding: 10px;
    border-radius: 15px;
    background-color: #333;
    height: 80px;
    margin: 20px;
    padding: 15px;
}

h1
{
    font-family: Lucida Sans Unicode, Lucida Grande, sans-serif;
    color: #C90;
    background-color: #333;
    margin: 0;
    padding: 0;
    border-radius: 15px;
}

h2
{
    font-family: Century Gothic, sans-serif;
    color: #FFF;
    font-size: 50%;
}
```

Figure 5-1. Use of new <group> example

▧ **Note** The preceding example is the beginning of a new approach to document layout. It's a more sophisticated way of defining content and outlines that uses new elements such as `<section>`, `<article>`, `<header>`, `<footer>`, and so on with HTML5. The HTML5 spec does warn that the use of scripting will change the values of many attributes, text, and indeed the entire structure of the document. You can easily make this happen dynamically so that a user agent must update these semantics of a document in order to represent the current state of the document correctly. It is very important to maintain the semantic integrity of the document so that interoperability and accessibility can also be supported properly. The spec does advise authors "to use declarative alternatives to scripting where possible, as declarative mechanisms are often more maintainable, and many users disable scripting." That is good advice.

Global Attributes in HTML5

The following are common attributes that can be added to any of the native elements:

- `accesskey`
- `class`
- `contenteditable`
- `contextmenu`
- `dir`
- `draggable`
- `dropzone`
- `hidden`
- `id`
- `lang`
- `spellcheck`
- `style`
- `tabindex`
- `title`

You've seen some of these global attributes before, such as `id` (a unique identifier for an element that you can use as a hook for your CSS or JavaScript), `class` (which is the same as `id`, except it's reusable on many elements), `title` (advisory information for an element), `accesskey` (a way of providing author-defined shortcut keys), `tabindex` (for giving sequential keyboard focus to elements), and `style` (adding CSS), to name a few.

■ **Note** With the `accesskey` attribute, the idea was that authors would be able to add quick, shortcut keys to their web content. It seems like a good idea, unless you use AT—because if you do, those keystrokes already do something! As an author, I strongly suggest you avoid using access keys, unless you can find some reserved keys that are not already used by the lion's share of AT out there. Good luck with that, by the way.

There are a load of event-handler attributes that can be also be added to any HTML element:

- onabort
- onblur*
- oncanplay
- oncanplaythrough
- onchange
- onclick
- oncontextmenu
- oncuechange
- ondblclick
- ondrag
- ondragend
- ondragenter
- ondragleave
- ondragover
- ondragstart
- ondrop
- ondurationchange
- onemptied
- onended
- onerror*
- onfocus*
- oninput
- oninvalid
- onkeydown

- onkeypress
- onkeyup
- onload*
- onloadeddata
- onloadedmetadata
- onloadstart
- onmousedown
- onmousemove
- onmouseout
- onmouseover
- onmouseup
- onmousewheel
- onpause
- onplay
- onplaying
- onprogress
- onratechange
- onreset
- onscroll*
- onseeked
- onseeking
- onselect
- onshow
- onstalled
- onsubmit
- onsuspend
- ontimeupdate
- onvolumechange
- onwaiting

■ **Note** The preceding event handlers that are marked with asterisks might change meanings, depending on the context they're used in—in this case, if they are used on a `<body>` element or window object.

Some More ARIA, Sir?

The specification also recommends that for assistive technology products that might need more detail than the current HTML5 spec can provide, a "set of annotations for assistive technology products can be specified (the ARIA role and aria-* attributes)."

We covered a lot of ground on ARIA in an earlier chapter, but it is worth outlining here how ARIA and HTML5 play together because they both have native semantics.

Here's an enlightening quote taken directly from the HTML5 spec:

> *"The following table defines the strong native semantics and corresponding default implicit ARIA semantics that apply to HTML elements. Each HTML language feature (element or attribute) in the first column implies the ARIA semantics (role, states, and/or properties) given in the cell in the second column of the same row. When multiple rows apply to an element, the role from the last row to define a role must be applied, and the states and properties from all the rows must be combined. The following is a list of how this works in detail."*[1]

Table 5-1 outlines strong native semantics and their corresponding default, implicit ARIA semantics.

Table 5-1. Native and ARIA Semantics

Language Feature	Strong Native Semantics and Default Implied ARIA Semantics
`<area>` element that creates a hyperlink	`link` role
`<base>` element	No role
`<datalist>` element	`listbox` role, with the `aria-multiselectable` property set to "false"
`<details>` element	`aria-expanded` state set to "true" if the element's open attribute is present, and set to "false" otherwise
`<head>` element	No role
`<hgroup>` element	`heading` role, with the `aria-level` property set to the

---

[1] http://dev.w3.org/html5/spec/Overview.html#wai-aria

	element's outline depth
`<hr>` element	`separator` role
`<html>` element	No role
`<img>` element whose alt attribute's value is empty	`presentation` role
`<input>` element with a type attribute in the Checkbox state	`aria-checked` state set to "mixed" if the element's indeterminate IDL attribute is true, or "true" if the element's checkedness is true, or "false" otherwise
`<input>` element with a type attribute in the Color state	No role
`<input>` element with a type attribute in the Date state	No role, with the `aria-readonly` property set to "true" if the element has a readonly attribute
`<input>` element with a type attribute in the Date and Time state	No role, with the `aria-readonly` property set to "true" if the element has a readonly attribute
`<input>` element with a type attribute in the Local Date and Time state	No role, with the `aria-readonly` property set to "true" if the element has a readonly attribute
`<input>` element with a type attribute in the E-mail state with no suggestions source element	`textbox` role, with the `aria-readonly` property set to "true" if the element has a readonly attribute
`<input>` element with a type attribute in the File Upload state	No role
`<input>` element with a type attribute in the Hidden state	No role
`<input>` element with a type attribute in the Month state	No role, with the `aria-readonly` property set to "true" if the element has a readonly attribute
`<input>` element with a type attribute in the Number state	`spinbutton` role, with the `aria-readonly` property set to "true" if the element has a readonly attribute, the `aria-valuemax` property set to the element's maximum, the `aria-valuemin` property set to the element's minimum, and, if the result of applying the rules for parsing floating point number values to the element's value is a number, with the `aria-valuenow` property set to that number

`<input>` element with a type attribute in the Password state	textbox role, with the `aria-readonly` property set to "true" if the element has a readonly attribute
`<input>` element with a type attribute in the Radio Button state	aria-checked state set to "true" if the element's checkedness is true, or "false" otherwise
`<input>` element with a type attribute in the Range state	slider role, with the `aria-valuemax` property set to the element's maximum, the `aria-valuemin` property set to the element's minimum, and the `aria-valuenow` property set to the result of applying the rules for parsing floating point number values to the element's value, if that results in a number, or the default value otherwise
`<input>` element with a type attribute in the Reset Button state	button role
`<input>` element with a type attribute in the Search state with no suggestions source element	textbox role, with the `aria-readonly` property set to "true" if the element has a readonly attribute
`<input>` element with a type attribute in the Submit Button state	button role
`<input>` element with a type attribute in the Telephone state with no suggestions source element	textbox role, with the `aria-readonly` property set to "true" if the element has a readonly attribute
`<input>` element with a type attribute in the Text state with no suggestions source element	textbox role, with the `aria-readonly` property set to "true" if the element has a readonly attribute
`<input>` element with a type attribute in the Text, Search, Telephone, URL, or E-mail states with a suggestions source element	combobox role, with the `aria-owns` property set to the same value as the `list` attribute, and the `aria-readonly` property set to "true" if the element has a readonly attribute
`<input>` element with a type attribute in the Time state	No role, with the `aria-readonly` property set to "true" if the element has a readonly attribute
`<input>` element with a type attribute in the URL state with no suggestions source element	textbox role, with the `aria-readonly` property set to "true" if the element has a readonly attribute
`<input>` element with a type attribute in the Week state	No role, with the `aria-readonly` property set to "true" if the element has a readonly attribute

`<input>` element that is required	The `aria-required` state set to "true"
`<keygen>` element	No role
`<label>` element	No role
`<link>` element that creates a hyperlink	`link` role
`<menu>` element with a type attribute in the context menu state	No role
`<menu>` element with a type attribute in the list state	`menu` role
`<menu>` element with a type attribute in the toolbar state	`toolbar` role
`<meta>` element	No role
`<meter>` element	No role
`<nav>` element	`navigation` role
`<noscript>` element	No role
`<optgroup>` element	No role
`<option>` element that is in a list of options or that represents a suggestion in a datalist element	`option` role, with the `aria-selected` state set to "true" if the element's selectedness is true, or "false" otherwise.
`<param>` element	No role
`<progress>` element	`progressbar` role, with, if the progress bar is determinate, the `aria-valuemax` property set to the maximum value of the progress bar, the `aria-valuemin` property set to zero, and the `aria-valuenow` property set to the current value of the progress bar
`<script>` element	No role
`<select>` element with a `multiple` attribute	`listbox` role, with the `aria-multiselectable` property set to "true"

`<select>` element with no `multiple` attribute	`listbox` role, with the `aria-multiselectable` property set to "false"
`<select>` element with a `required` attribute	The `aria-required` state set to "true"
`<source>` element	No role
`<style>` element	No role
`<summary>` element	No role
`<textarea>` element	`textbox` role, with the `aria-multiline` property set to "true", and the `aria-readonly` property set to "true" if the element has a readonly attribute
`<textarea>` element with a `required` attribute	The `aria-required` state set to "true"
`<title>` element	No role
An element that defines a command, whose type facet is "checkbox", and that is a descendant of a menu element whose type attribute in the "list" state	`menuitemcheckbox` role, with the `aria-checked` state set to "true" if the command's Checked State facet is true, and "false" otherwise
An element that defines a command, whose Type facet is "command", and that is a descendant of a menu element whose type attribute is in the "list" state	`menuitem` role
An element that defines a command, whose type facet is "radio", and that is a descendant of a menu element whose type attribute in the "list" state	`menuitemradio` role, with the `aria-checked` state set to "true" if the command's Checked State facet is true, and "false" otherwise
Element that is disabled	The `aria-disabled` state set to "true"
Element with a hidden attribute	The `aria-hidden` state set to "true"
Element that is a candidate for constraint validation but that does not satisfy its constraints	The `aria-invalid` state set to "true"

139

■ **Note** Where ARIA is added to a native HTML5 element, in general, the added ARIA semantics will trump the HTML and override the default semantics. However, in some cases this doesn't happen and there are some restrictions that apply. Also note that any element can be given the presentation role, regardless of the restrictions shown in Table 5-2.

Table 5-2. List of ARIA/HTML5 Restrictions

Language Feature	Default Implied ARIA Semantics	Restrictions
a element, which creates a hyperlink	link role	Role must be either link, button, checkbox, menuitem, menuitemcheckbox, menuitemradio, tab, or treeitem
address element	No role	If specified, role must be contentinfo
article element	article role	Role must be either article, document, application, or main
aside element	note role	Role must be either note, complementary, or search
audio element	No role	If specified, role must be application
button element	button role	Role must be either button, link, menuitem, menuitemcheckbox, menuitemradio, radio
details element	group role	Role must be a role that supports aria-expanded
embed element	No role	If specified, role must be either application, document, or img
footer element	No role	If specified, role must be contentinfo
h1 element that does not have an hgroup ancestor	heading role, with the aria-level property set to the element's outline depth	Role must be either heading or tab
h2 element that does not have an hgroup	heading role, with the aria-level property set	Role must be either heading or tab

ancestor	to the element's outline depth	
h3 element that does not have an hgroup ancestor	heading role, with the aria-level property set to the element's outline depth	Role must be either heading or tab
h4 element that does not have an hgroup ancestor	heading role, with the aria-level property set to the element's outline depth	Role must be either heading or tab
h5 element that does not have an hgroup ancestor	heading role, with the aria-level property set to the element's outline depth	Role must be either heading or tab
h6 element that does not have an hgroup ancestor	heading role, with the aria-level property set to the element's outline depth	Role must be either heading or tab
header element	No role	If specified, role must be banner
iframe element	No role	If specified, role must be either application, document, or img
img element whose alt attribute's value is absent	img role	No restrictions
img element whose alt attribute's value is present and not empty	img role	No restrictions
input element with a type attribute in the "button" state	button role	Role must be either button, link, menuitem, menuitemcheckbox, menuitemradio, radio
input element with a type attribute in the "checkbox" state	checkbox role	Role must be either checkbox or menuitemcheckbox
input element with a type attribute in the	button role	Role must be either button, link, menuitem, menuitemcheckbox, menuitemradio, radio

"image button" state		
input element with a type attribute in the "radio button" state	radio role	Role must be either radio or menuitemradio
li element whose parent is an ol or ul element	listitem role	Role must be either listitem, menuitemcheckbox, menuitemradio, option, tab, or treeitem
object element	No role	If specified, role must be either application, document, or img
ol element	list role	Role must be either directory, list, listbox, menu, menubar, tablist, toolbar, tree
output element	status role	No restrictions
section element	region role	Role must be either alert, alertdialog, application, contentinfo, dialog, document, log, main, marquee, region, search, or status
ul element	list role	Role must be either directory, list, listbox, menu, menubar, tablist, toolbar, tree
video element	No role	If specified, role must be application
body element	document role	Role must be either document or application

Copyright © 2011 W3C® (MIT, ERCIM, Keio),

Some of this must seem rather complex and gnarly, and at first glance it kind of is. However, it's best to be aware of how the semantic interplay between HTML5 and added languages like WAI-ARIA work. As you saw earlier, there are many similarities between the two.

Content Models

The new HTML5 elements are defined in a way that includes information about the following:

- The Category that an element belongs in
- The Context that the element can be used in

- The Content Model that outlines the children of the elements that should be included
- The DOM interface that the element should implement

▓ **Note** Attributes can have any string value, including an empty sting. There are some restrictions, but these general rules apply.

The Content Model outlines what an element is expected to contain. This makes sense when you think about it, because it helps clearly outline how content should behave and what the browser should do when it encounters certain items. This is also made more relevant when you consider how nested items should behave. In general, usage of an element must follow its Content Model.

▓ **Note** This can get a little murky when dealing with strong vs. weak semantics, or "what trumps what" determinations in certain contexts, such as those you can see in Table 5-1 and Table 5-2. I mentioned categories of HTML content that group elements, and here is a list of them:

Metadata content

Flow content

Sectioning content

Heading content

Phrasing content

Embedded content

Interactive content

There is a nice interactive SVG diagram in the spec that visually illustrates how these categories relate to each other. For more information, go to http://dev.w3.org/html5/spec/Overview.html#kinds-of-content.

Metadata Content

Metadata content is content that outlines the behavior or presentation of page content. What you will be used to using is typical metadata content such as JavaScript and or CSS, using the following elements:

- <base>

- <command>
- <link>
- <meta>
- <noscript>
- <script>
- <style>
- <title>

Metadata content can also provide information about how documents relate to each other.

■ **Note** noscript is still valid HTML5 content. It is a less than elegant way of presenting content to a user who doesn't have JavaScript available for whatever reason.

Flow Content

These are the main elements used in the body of a HTML document. There are rather a lot, and you will recognize most of them:

- <a>
- <abbr>
- <address>
- <area> (if it is a descendant of a map element)
- <article>
- <aside>
- <audio>
- <b>
- <bdi>
- <bdo>
- <blockquote>
-
- <button>
- <canvas>
- <cite>

- `<code>`
- `<command>`
- `<data>`
- `<datalist>`
- `<del>`
- `<details>`
- `<dfn>`
- `<div>`
- `<dl>`
- `<em>`
- `<embed>`
- `<fieldset>`
- `<figure>`
- `<footer>`
- `<form>`
- `<h1>`
- `<h2>`
- `<h3>`
- `<h4>`
- `<h5>`
- `<h6>`
- `<header>`
- `<hgroup>`
- `<hr>`
- `<i>`
- `<iframe>`
- `<img>`
- `<input>`
- `<ins>`
- `<kbd>`

- `<keygen>`
- `<label>`
- `<map>`
- `<mark>`
- `<math>`
- `<menu>`
- `<meter>`
- `<nav>`
- `<noscript>`
- `<object>`
- `<ol>`
- `<output>`
- `<p>`
- `<pre>`
- `<progress>`
- `<q>`
- `<ruby>`
- `<s>`
- `<samp>`
- `<script>`
- `<section>`
- `<select>`
- `<small>`
- `<span>`
- `<strong>`
- `<style>` (if the scoped attribute is present)
- `<sub>`
- `<sup>`
- `<svg>`
- `<table>`

- `<textarea>`

- `<u>`

- `<ul>`

- `<var>`

- `<video>`

- `<wbr>`

- `<text>`

Sectioning Content

This is content that is related and can be grouped together. The following new elements can be used to define new sections of thematically grouped content:

- `<article>`

- `<aside>`

- `<nav>`

- `<section>`

Heading Content

This kind of content is used when defining the headings of a document that are traditionally used to structure page content. There are some usual suspects here that we'll revisit later in the chapter:

- `<h1>`

- `<h2>`

- `<h3>`

- `<h4>`

- `<h5>`

- `<h6>`

- `<hgroup>`

You will be familiar with these headings and their usage from your previous web projects. They are invaluable in creating accessible content. The `<hgroup>` element is the new kid on the block.

Phrasing Content

This is the main body of text in a document and the inline elements used to mark up that content:

- <a> (if it contains only phrasing content)
- <abbr area> (if it is a descendant of a map element)
- <audio>
- <b>
- <bdi>
- <bdo>
-
- <button>
- <canvas>
- <cite>
- <code>
- <command>
- <data>
- <datalist>
- <del> (if it contains only phrasing content)
- <dfn>
- <em>
- <embed>
- <i>
- <iframe>
- <img>
- <input>
- <ins> (if it contains only phrasing content)
- <kbd>
- <keygen>
- <label>
- <map> (if it contains only phrasing content)
- <mark>
- <math>
- <meter>

- `<noscript>`
- `<object>`
- `<output>`
- `<progress>`
- `<q>`
- `<ruby>`
- `<s>`
- `<samp>`
- `<script>`
- `<select>`
- `<small>`
- `<span>`
- `<strong>`
- `<sub>`
- `<sup>`
- `<svg>`
- `<textarea>`
- `<u>`
- `<var>`
- `<video>`
- `<wbr>`
- `<text>`

Generally, the specification states that elements that allow phrasing content need to have some kind of embedded content, or what is known as *interelement whitespace*. The term "interelement whitespace" sounds like it belongs in quantum physics or string theory, but all it means is "empty space" or "empty text nodes."

In general, what is classed by the HTML5 spec as *phrasing content* should contain only other phrasing content. This defines largely how valid content can be created.

■ **Note** You might have noticed that some of the phrasing content is also flow content (quite a lot are actually). This overlap should make validation errors a little easier to avoid as you mix and match.

Embedded Content

This is content that is, well, embedded or that *imports* another resource into the document:

- <audio>
- <canvas>
- <embed>
- <iframe>
- <img>
- <math>
- <object>
- <svg>
- <video>

Some of these elements are designed to have *fallback content*—content that is a functional replacement or equivalent when any of the preceding elements aren't supported by the browser or other user agent, such as a screen reader. The accessibility, at the time of this writing, of <canvas>, for example, means that you really have to consider how users of screen readers will experience your content. (Note that <canvas> is also currently problematic for screen-magnification users because there is currently no way to expose where the focus of the canvas is to a screen magnifier.)

The following snippet illustrates fallback content for the <canvas> element:

```
<html>
<canvas id="Groovy_anim_with_fallback" width="300" height="150">
<p> Some fallback instruction for the user..or links to other more accessible resources</p>
</canvas>
</html>
```

An older browser or user agent will ignore the <canvas> because it won't understand it; however, it will be able to parse the markup that is contained within. User agents that do understand the <canvas> element will just render that and ignore the embedded content.

■ **Note** You can use some conditional functions such as if(), which contain your <canvas> drawing methods. If they are not supported, an image can be shown instead.

```
<html>
<canvas id="Groovy_anim_with_fallback" width="300" height="150">
<h1>Oops..your browser won't show our groovy Canvas Animation</h1>
<img scr="myserver/usful_andgroovy_image.png" alt="Visit the 'overview' section of the website
which has a more accessible content">
</canvas>
</html>
```

In the preceding example, rather than describe a groovy graphic to a screen-reader user, I gave the image alternate text that provides some kind of useful instruction. This might not be totally valid HTML, but it provides something useful, which to me is more important.

If the image is purely decorative and the embedded content heading is sufficient to inform the user of what she can do to access a more accessible version of the content, or whether it's just a heads-up that she can ignore it, then giving the image a null alt value (alt="") will result in the image being treated as presentational and ignored by most screen readers.

You also can give the canvas the ARIA role of presentational, as shown here:

```
<html>
<canvas id="Groovy_anim_with_fallback" width="300" height="150"role='presentational'>
<h1>Oops..your browser won't show our groovy Canvas Animation</h1>
<img scr="myserver/usful_andgroovy_image.png" alt="Visit the 'overview' section of the website
which has a more accessible content">
</canvas>
</html>
```

Using role="presentational" should hide the canvas from the newer screen readers that support ARIA.

We will discuss <canvas> in a later chapter. How fallback content should be handled is supposed to be outlined in an element's definition. However, I feel this is underspecified in terms of what the fallback should be. Ideally, fallback content is a functional replacement or sometimes just a heads-up for a user that something just might not work. In reality, fallback implementations can also be disruptive to the user experience. No one wants to go back to the days of "you don't have a groovy browser—how dare you!" type of messages, but without a clear idea of what the fallback should be, what is the developer to do? The spec is clear enough that <canvas> content, for example, should not be used where there is a more suitable HTML5 design pattern that has inherent semantics. However, we all know the world doesn't work like that and that the *street* finds its own uses for things.

In an ideal world, something like <canvas> would be ready for prime time, with a fully accessible architecture—it ain't.

※ **Note** What <canvas> is ready for is mostly visual users, but it will still present challenges for screen-magnification users because there is currently no way for the screen magnifier to follow critical changes in <canvas> content.

Interactive Content

This is content that is for user interaction:

- <a>
- <audio> (if the controls attribute is present)
- <button>
- <details>
- <embed>

- `<iframe>`

- `<img>` (if the usemap attribute is present)

- `<input>` (if the type attribute is not in the hidden state)

- `<keygen>`

- `<label>`

- `<menu>` (if the type attribute is in the toolbar state)

- `<object>` (if the usemap attribute is present)

- `<select>`

- `<textarea>`

- `<video>` (if the controls attribute is present)

The preceding list of HTML elements represents the framework for building established user-interaction design patterns. The controls have inherent *activation behaviors* that fire particular events.

▪ **Note** The spec also outlines that flow content and phrasing content should contain *palpable content*. This really means "stuff that the end user can perceive and isn't hidden."

Paragraphs

The <p> element is one that will be very familiar to you. It represents phrasing content. That is "a block of text with one or more sentences that discuss a particular topic."

Some older elements such as <ins> and <del> are still a part of HTML5. You might not have used them much, but they are useful for showing content that has been inserted into a paragraph or deleted from a paragraph, respectively. The following example details their use:

```
<section>
  <h1>Example of paragraphs using <pre>ins</pre> and <pre>del</pre></h1>
<p>This is a chunk of content that was <del>deleted</del> <ins>and then updated</ins>.</p>
  <p>This is another paragraph where nothing was inserted or deleted.</p>
</section>
```

What is new is how the <paragraph> element can be used with some of the new HTML5 sectioning elements, such as <aside>, <section>, and so on.

HTML Document Metadata

HTML5 has the following elements that provide document metadata, usually in the head of the HTML file.

The <head> Element

This provides some simple metadata for the document. It can take the following general form:

```
<!DOCTYPE HTML>
<html>
 <head>
  <title>What kinda of page am I?</title>
 </head>
 <body>
```

OK, so far so good. Nothing really new there. The following element is really important for screen-reader accessibility, so pay attention!

The <title> Element

There is nothing new about the <title> element in HTML5, and its purpose is reveal the document's title or name to the user agent. The spec advises this:

> *"Authors should use titles that identify their documents even when they are used out of context, for example in a user's history or bookmarks, or in search results."* [2]

This is really good advice and not just because of its potential use as a way to identify the contents of a page in your bookmarks menu (though that is great). It's also because the <title> element is the first item read by a screen reader when an HTML document loads. This makes it a very important piece of information to help a screen-reader user know where they are within a web site.

You can see from Figure 5-2 how the <title> element shows the user the identity of the site.

---

[2] http://dev.w3.org/html5/spec/Overview.html#the-title-element

Figure 5-2. *Use of the Animal Sanctuary <title> element*

Some More Elemental Cleverness

Clever use of the `<title>` element can help to guide users through a process, like buying something using an online shopping function. For example, say the entire buying process has three or four stages. In this case, you should use the `<title>` element to re-enforce to the user what stage he is in at any given time. You can do this with prompts such as "Select your product," "Enter a Shipping Address," and "Enter your Credit Card Information."

For each of the pages, the `<header>` might look something like the code example in Listing 5-2.

Listing 5-2. *Using the <title> Element*

```
Stage 1:
<!DOCTYPE HTML>
<html>
 <head>
  <title>Select your product</title>
 </head>
```

```
  <body>

Stage 2:
<!DOCTYPE HTML>
<html>
 <head>
  <title>Enter a Shipping Address</title>
 </head>
 <body>

Stage 3:
<!DOCTYPE HTML>
<html>
 <head>
  <title>Enter your Credit Card Information</title>
 </head>
 <body>
```

The page content that follows support the user in each of the steps, and it obviously allows the user to complete the transaction. So the <title> element is really useful for all users, because it appears in the heading of your browser as well as in the tab name (in Safari). See Figure 5-3.

Figure 5-3. How the <title> element is displayed in Safari

The <base> Element

This is an element used to define what's called a *document base URL*. Why would you want to do this? I hear you ask, "Are URLs not defined relative to the HTML document root or index.html file?" Well, good question, and yes they are. You might want to provide more of a context for the current document, for better SEO perhaps if you have a subsection of a web site that contains collections of related documents. It is a void element, so it doesn't take any kind of content, and it sits in the header of the document. Also, in HTML5 you can now add a *target* attribute to the base URL, which you couldn't do in earlier versions of HTML. Listing 5-3 details use of the <base> element.

Listing 5-3. Use of the <base> Element

```
<!DOCTYPE HTML>
<html>
    <head>
        <title>&lt;Base&gt; element sample</title>
        <base href=http://www.mysiteandsubsite.com/repository/index.html />
    </head>
    <body>
        <p>Visit the <a href="collectionoflinks.html">Here is a collection of interesting
documents</a>.</p>
        <p>Visit the <a href="collectionofworddocuments.html">Here is a collection of
interesting Word documents</a>.</p>
```

```
       <p>Visit the <a href="collectionofimages.html">Here is a collection of interesting
images</a>.</p>
    </body>
</html> ³
```

The <link> element

The <link> element is that useful piece of header metadata that helps you define where you keep your scripts and your CSS. It is also used to indicate other resources in the header of your HTML documents. A <link> element must have a rel attribute, as shown in the following snippet:

```
<head>
<link rel="stylesheet" type="text/css" href="generalstyle.css" />
</head>
```

■ **Note** When the <link> element has a rel attribute, it applies to the whole of the document. However, when it's used on the <a> or <area> element, it refers to a link where the context is given by its location within the document.

There are various content attributes associated with the <link> element:

- href
- rel
- media
- hreflang
- type
- sizes

The title attribute is also a member of this list. The href attribute is one you are familiar with, and we just talked about the rel attribute. The type attribute is used with the icon keyword to link elements in order to create an external resource link. The icons can be auditory icons, visual icons, and so on. The sizes attribute gives the sizes of icons, as described. The hreflang can be used to provide the language of a linked resource.

---

³ All of these links would resolve to "www.mysiteandsubsite.com/repository."

■ **Note** If you want a screen reader to pick up on a change of language within a document, you are better off using the `lang` attribute. In general, the language of the document can be provided by `lang="en"` for English, `lang="fr"` for French, or `lang="de"` for German, respectively. I found the example in Listing 5-4 on Roger Johanssons' web site (the excellent www.456bereastreet.com), and he got it from Wikipedia. The listing uses `lang` attributes and attaches them to a `<div>` element. When a screen reader comes across these attributes, they switch synthesis modules in order to output the language correctly.

Listing 5-4. Using the Lang Attribute

```
<div lang="sv">
    <h2>Svenska</h2>
    <p>Välkommen till Wikipedia, den fria encyklopedin som alla kan redigera.</p>
</div>

<div lang="de">
    <h2>Deutsch</h2>
    <p>Wikipedia ist ein Projekt zum Aufbau einer Enzyklopädie aus freien Inhalten in allen
Sprachen der Welt.</p>
</div>

<div lang="fr">
    <h2>Français</h2>
    <p>Bienvenue sur Wikipédia, le projet d'encyclopédie libre que vous pouvez améliorer.</p>
</div>

<div lang="es">
    <h2>Español</h2>
    <p>Bienvenidos a Wikipedia, la enciclopedia de contenido libre que todos pueden
editar.</p>
</div>
```

The heads-up that the `lang` attribute gives to the screen reader, enabling it to shift into an appropriate mode to output the language in a way that suits the natural prosody and so on, certainly helps the legibility. It also means the screen reader doesn't talk like a tourist.

The `media` attribute is usually left blank, meaning that links within the document apply to all different types of media. The type attribute is important because it can be used to indicate the MIME or content type for all kinds of content, including rich media or HTML documents. Choosing the correct MIME type will determine how your content is parsed, for example. The `title` attribute gives extra advisory info to the user agent, apart from when it's used as a way to define alternative style sheets.

To define alternative style sheets, you might code something like what's shown in Listing 5-5.

Listing 5-5. *Use of Alternate Style Sheets*

```
<!–if you need to define a persistent style sheet->
<link rel="stylesheet" href="main.css" />

<!–if you have an alternate style sheet->
<link rel="stylesheet" href="main_pref.css" title="More accessible styles" />

<!-- some alternate style sheets->
<link rel="alternate stylesheet" href="b_w_y.css" title="Black White and Yello Layout" />
<link rel="alternate stylesheet" href="large.css" title="16 Point Layout" />
<link rel="alternate stylesheet" href="fluid.css" title="Fluid Layout" />
```

The <meta> Element

The <meta> element, shown in Listing 5-6, is used in the header of the HTML document to describe content that is defined by some of the previously mentioned header elements. It has name, http-equiv, content, and charset attributes. It can be used to specify a document's character encoding, to specify an application type (if the webpage represents a particular application), and so on. Originally, the description and keywords were designed to be served to search engines, but they have been largely abused by authors over the years. However, in principle they should probably still be used, even if your favorite search engine page-ranking algorithm chooses to ignore it. There are other technologies that might find them useful, such as for use within a large CMS-powered web sites or Semantic Web applications.

Listing 5-6. *Example of Meta Content*

```
<!DOCTYPE HTML>
<html>
 <head>
 <meta charset="UTF-8" />
<meta name="description" content="This site outlines how the smartest guys in the room are
amoral strawmen who would sell their grandmothers into slavery to enhance their profit and
prestige. They may also gain tenure at Columbia for doing so." />
 <meta name="keywords" content="Money, Gold, Economics, Greed, Folly, House of Cards, Pyramid
Scam, Ponzi Scheme" />
  <title>A website about Economics</title>
 </head>
 <body>
[…]
```

■ **Note** Maybe ignore the last few keywords…at your own peril! (lol)

More examples of <meta> usage can be found at http://dev.w3.org/html5/spec-author-view/the-meta-element.html#the-meta-element.

The <style> Element and scoped Attribute

The <style> element is nothing new in HTML5, but the scoped attribute is. The scoped attribute allows you to define some inline styles for a section of your webpage. It allows you to define the range of elements that the style is applied to. If the scoped attribute is present in your HTML content, only the section that has the <style> element with the scope attribute will be affected by the CSS declaration. This could be useful for content syndication in order to maintain a particular brand or design style of an article.

Existing document styles can be defined as usual within the header of the document as shown in Listing 5-7 (inline styling is used here for illustration).

Listing 5-7. Sample CSS

```
<!DOCTYPE HTML>
<html>
 <head>
 <meta charset="UTF-8" />

<!--document css styles declared in the normal way-->

<style type="text/css">

h1{
    color: #ff0;
    background-color: #999;
    border-radius: 15px;
    padding: 15px;

}

p{
    color: #fff;
    background-color: #999;
    border-radius: 15px;
    padding: 15px;

}


</style>
</head>

<body>
<article>
<h1>Really interesting news article that you'll soon find in other online Papers</h1>
<p>Here is some really interesting news that just has to go around the world</p>
</article>

</body>
</html>
```

Then these can be combined with some inline styling using the scoped attribute if, say, you had a page with several articles, the first article is syndicated content, and you want the styles to be preserved. (See Listing 5-8.)

Listing 5-8. *Sample CSS and Use of the Scoped Attribute*

```
<!DOCTYPE HTML>
<html>
 <head>
 <meta charset="UTF-8" />

<!--document css styles declared in the normal way-->

<style type="text/css">
h1{
    color:#ff0;
    background-color:#999;
    border-radius: 15px;
    padding: 15px;

}

p{
    color:#fff;
    background-color:#999;
    border-radius: 15px;
    padding: 15px;

}

</style>
</head>

<body>
<article>
<style scoped>

h1{
    color: #ff0;
    background-color: #999;
    border-radius: 15px;
    padding: 15px;

}

p{
    color: #fff;
    background-color: #999;
    border-radius: 15px;
    padding: 15px;

}
```

```
</style>

<h1>Really interesting document that contains nicely styled news articles that you&apos;ll
find in other online Papers</h1>
<p>Here is some really interesting news that just has to go around the world</p>
</article>


<article>
<h2>Second really interesting article that just has to go around the world, that you&apos;ll
also find in other online Papers</h2>
<p>Here is some really interesting news that just has to go around the world</p>
</article>

<article>
<h2>Third really interesting article that just has to go around the world, that you&apos;ll
also find in other online Papers</h2>
<p>Here is some really interesting news that just has to go around the world</p>
</article>

</body>
</html>
```

░ **Note** If all the articles were to be syndicated, you could add the `scoped` style attribute inline to each of the preceding articles with whatever CSS declarations were appropriate.

New HTML5 Sectioning Elements

You met some of the new HTML5 sectioning elements in some previous examples, such as when the article element was used. These new sectioning elements are just that, a way of providing useful semantics for describing frequently used parts of a web document.

- body

- section

- nav

- article

- aside

- h1 h6

- hgroup

- header

- footer

- address

You saw the new <hgroup> element earlier, and you are familiar with the <body>, <h1>, <h2>, <h3>, <h4>, <h5>, and <h6> elements.

Before we look at some of the newer section elements in more detail, we'll take another look at headings—what they are and how to use them to make your web content more accessible.

Don't just increase the font size and bold it! Headings in HTML have a special significance, particularly for people using assistive technology (AT). There is more going on than just the visual presentation of the heading. So it isn't enough for you to increase the font size or just change the typeface to convey structure. Yes, for a sighted person this might be enough, but semantics are more than just skin deep. To make your content more accessible, the use of heading elements is vital. So here is a brief "Headings 101" tutorial.

A sighted user can pretty much just glance at a page and quickly be able to visually distinguish what the various section headings are. This ability, in turn, allows the reader to quickly internalize and grow the document structure. The sighted person can also tell where each section of the pages' content begins and ends, and what section a group of paragraphs actually belongs in. She can then quickly make some judgment call on what parts of the document are of interest to her and what parts she can ignore. She can then visually jump to read the sections of interest.

■ **Note** While the use of HTML is largely about structuring content to let users access it, it is just as important for the end user to sometimes ignore and bypass content or functionality that isn't of interest.

I did mention in an earlier chapter how a screen-reader user might navigate web content using only headings, but it's important and worth going over again. Screen-reader users often browse a webpage by using their AT to pick different types of content, depending on what's available in the page. It might be links—or, in this case, headings—that are a little difficult to understand if you have never seen a screen reader being used.

■ **Note** There are many online demos of screen readers in action. I recommend you head over to YouTube after you've read this chapter and have a look.

This is how it works.

The screen reader user uses a particular keystroke combination for whatever application he is using. JAWS, for example, uses Insert + F6, or the user can press the H key. For Window-Eyes, the user presses the number keys and H. Then a dialog window appears that contains all of the headings available to it from the document. If he is using VoiceOver, the user can open up the rotor and choose headings to navigate with. When he swipes forward or back, the screen reader jumps to the next or previous heading in the document. The screen reader will also often tell the user how many headings there are.

The screen-reader user can quickly bounce through the document, getting an overview of it and then choosing the heading that sounds like his topic of interest. Good descriptive headings are therefore really useful.

As mentioned, this is vital as an aid to comprehension and navigation for a nonsighted person. Why? Because a sighted user can very quickly visually scan a long or complex document and see what parts are of interest to them. Being able to visually scan acts as a natural navigation mechanism allowing the user to jump over unrelated or uninteresting content. A blind user cannot do this. So that person's screen reader provides the navigational mechanism.

If there are no structured HTML headings in the document at all, the blind user must go through line after line of content until she gets what she wants. If the document is very long, having to do this can be very annoying and tedious, and it can get old pretty fast.

■ **Note** As previously mentioned, with any project you need to think about its information architecture and how it is structured. However, it isn't so important that the headings are even strictly in the right semantic order (though it's advisable to structure them that way). What is more important is that they are actually there in the first place, because they are vital for accessible navigation, as well as overall document structure.

Screen readers are linear output devices. This means they output the items that have focus, as speech, one at a time. So you do have to consider things like source order for elements within the DOM, the order in which headings appear, and the quality of the descriptive text you use in your headings. Make it useful.

A Quick Recap on How and Why to Use Heading Elements

■ **Note** There are lots of ways of doing the same thing with HTML. My advice on headings that follows is just that, my advice. There might be better ways of doing things, and the spec might also differ from me on some matters, but as far as the latter goes, this wouldn't be the first time.

HTML5 headings still have six levels of semantic importance, so there's not much different from the way things were done in earlier versions of the markup language. Table 5-3 is an example of how these various headings might be applied to a webpage about musical instruments—in this case guitars—and it would be equally applicable to HTML4 or earlier.

Table 5-3. *Heading Outline*

Heading 1 <h1>	Grooviest Guitar Gallery Listing
Heading 2 <h2>	**Favorite Fender Guitars**
Heading 3 <h3>	Some classic Fender history
Heading 4<h4>	History of the Strat

Heading 4 <h4>	History of the Telecaster
Heading 4 <h4>	History of the Jaguar
Heading 2 <h2>	**Favorite Gibson Guitars**
Heading 3 <h3>	Some classic Gibson history
Heading 4 <h4>	History of Les Paul
Heading 4 <h4>	History of the ES Range
Heading 4 <h4>	The new Firebird X range
Heading 2 <h2>	**Favorite Acoustic Guitars**
Heading 3 <h3>	Some classic Acoustic history
Heading 4 <h4>	History of the Nylon Guitar
Heading 4 <h4>	History of the Semi Solid
Heading 2 <h2>	**Acoustic folk [...]**

Table 5-4 gives an example of a possible way to use headings in a web document.

Table 5-4. Heading Use Possibilities

Heading 1 <h1>	You will pretty much use this only once per page, to provide a heading title for your main content.
Heading 2 <h2>	Use this as often as you need to break the document up into suitable major sections.
Heading 3 <h3>	Use this as often as you need for subheadings of a document and to generally assist flow within the document.
Lower-level headings (h4, h5, h6)	Use these as needed in long articles, where you might need a deeper hierarchy.

In the Guitars overview, I didn't really use the lower level headings, but then I felt I didn't need to. For example, if you have a very long article with detailed subheadings that are buried deep down within it, you might need to call up <h4> and <h5> or <h6> and use them as required.

As in the preceding example when those subheadings are finished and you want to mark up the start of a new section, you can again start with your <h2> headings. In the preceding example, note that I bolded text where the higher level <h2> headings are used to show you when the higher-level headings come back into use after a chunk of related content is finished.

■ **Note** It's not advisable to bounce from headings too dramatically for no good reason, because they are used to show how content relates to other content. So try to follow a logical order within a document. However, it is true that HTML5 allows blocks of content to be structured in such a way that it can seem *modular* and get plugged into different webpages a la syndication.

Some general HTML5 headings rules (mine) would be

- There should only ever be one <h1> (think of Highlander).

- The rest of the headings can be used as often as needed to provide a document outline.

- Headings should ideally follow a logical order.

As I mentioned earlier, from an accessibility perspective, don't worry too much about whether the page structure is absolutely correct all the time. In my experience, most screen-reader users will be happy that the headings are there at all and will not quibble about the order.

■ **Note** If you get the "Highlander" reference, I'm showing my age. If not, go see the movie. You'll like it, I promise.

Meet the New divs on the Block

OK, so that was the old school, and that was about as far is it went in terms of being able to describe content or sections of content. You are used to wrapping all of your blocks of web content (I nearly said "block level elements…") in <divs> and then just getting on with marking up your content. Well, that's going to change somewhat because the new HTML5 elements provide a new semantic scaffold. You will still markup your content in much the same way and provide a much-needed accessibility structure for your documents, as outlined previously. Doing this *old school* will help to provide a level of backward compatibility with older browsers and AT.

HTML5 provides these new sectioning elements as a way of providing a markup structure for the layout of your web content. This is new, and it makes great sense. A common page format would be something like the following Groovy Times site that we looked at earlier.

Let's remind ourselves, visually. See Figure 5-4.

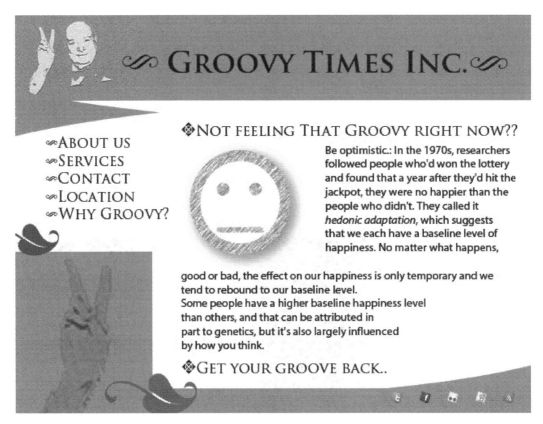

Figure 5-4. *The glorious Groovy Times web site*

And we can say that has the general semantic layout we looked at earlier, which goes along the lines you see in Figure 5-5.

166

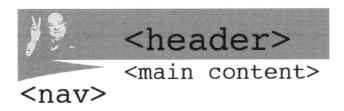

Figure 5-5. *Semantic grooviness*

OK, so the eagle-eyed among you—and I am sure that there are many—will notice that I changed the *semantic outline* that you saw the last time you looked at Groovy Times. There was a <banner> at the top. I removed this because that is an ARIA role. What is outlined is a general document overview of how you might structure a generic page by adding these ids to the <div> element.

So a webpage pre-HTML5 might have had a structure like the one shown in Listing 5-9.

Listing 5-9. *Pre-HTML5 Structure*

```
<html>
<body>

<div id="header">
[…]
</div>

<div id="nav">
[…]
</div>

<div id="main content">
[…]
</div>

<div id="footer">
[…]
</div>

</body>
</html>
```

The […] represents any content and son, and I'll leave it to your imagination as to how you would use CSS to style it.

Now, in HTML5, you can stop using the semantically useless <div> all the time, where you try to give them common sense ids so that you could remember what hooks to use in your CSS declarations and flip the code to actually describe a section's role/purpose. So we have something like that shown in Listing 5-10.

Listing 5-10. Groovy Times HTML Example

```
<!DOCTYPE HTML>
<html>
 <head>
 <meta charset="UTF-8" />
<title> Groovy HTML5 outline example</title>
</head>
<body>

<header>
<h1> Groovy Times</h1>
</header>

<nav>
<ul>
<li>About us</li>
<li>Services</li>
<li>Contact</li>
<li>Location</li>
<li>Why Groovy?</li>
</ul>
</nav>

<div id="main content">
<h2>Not feeling that groovy right now?</h2>
<p>Be optimistic:in the 1970s, […] </p>
</div>

<footer>
 […]
</footer>
</body>
</html>
```

▨ **Note** There is no *content* or *main* content role in HTML5. So you can see in the preceding example how I just used a regular <div> and gave it an id name that described it.

The preceding example is a very basic one that uses some of the new sectioning elements to provide a semantic outline of the document. In practice, your webpages will have a lot more content. This is where the likes of section, article, and aside come in.

▓ **Note** There is a peculiar bug in earlier versions of JAWS 10/11, where it doesn't like the `<header>` element and using it can be problematic (and basically won't work with very early versions of Firefox, such as Firefox 4 and earlier. Terrill Thompson wrote about it on his blog at `http://terrillthompson.com/blog/37`. It affects only JAWS and Firefox, not VoiceOver, NVDA, or WinEyes and others, and it seems to be related to the use of head in `<header>`.

Getting Sectioned

The `<section>` element is just that—an element for sections of content. It represents the section of a document that is around a general theme and often comes with a specific heading. A common use would be a chapter of a book, but online you probably won't be writing that much! It will more likely be used to divide page content into related chunks, like an Introduction, followed by some background info on the topic and so on.

It is not to be thought of as "here is a section I want to style visually, so I'll mark it up as a section." If you want to do that, just use a div. You will probably use all of these elements in conjunction with generic div's for visual styling and presentation. However, elements like `<section>` are to be used for structuring your webpage content, as shown in Listing 5-11.

Listing 5-11. Structuring Your HTML5 Page

```
<article>
 <hgroup>
  <h1>The Guitar Gallery</h1>
  <h2>Lots of groovy guitars</h2>
 </hgroup>

<section>
<h2> Fenders</h2>
 <p>Are you a Fender guy or a Gibson gal? Well if it's good enough for Jimi, it's good enough
for me!</p>
<p>[…]</p>
<h3> The first Fender Guitars</h3>
<p>[…]</p>

 </section>

<section>
  <h2>Gibson</h2>
 <p>I want an SG but don't want to take out a mortgage, Dear Anne.. got a problem</p>
 <p> More about my feelings of deprivation due to lack of antique Gibson guitars[…]</p>
 </section>
```

```
<section>
 <h2>Acoustic Dreams</h2>
  <p>For the softer moments we have nylon acoustic guitarts</p>
 <p> Well, I really like John Fahey and Leo Kottke, […]</p>
<h3>What kind of guitar did Robbie Basho play??</h3>
 </section>
</article>
```

■ **Note** The <p> […] </p> bits, just represent where you would put your content.

In this example, we have several sections that are about different kinds of guitars. I hope you can see that it's pretty straightforward using it to define related, well, sections! You can see that they are wrapped up in an <article> element, which we will look at now.

Self-Contained Article

The new <article> element is a more self-contained, independent type creature. It is used to outline a self-contained composition that can be spread around the net if required, and it won't need to pack a spare pair of pajamas because it has everything it needs already.

■ **Note** The <article> element can also represent a widget, and not just a blog entry or comment, but a composition and so on.

So if a blog post was added to our Guitar Gallery example using the <article> element, we might find it looking something like Listing 5-12.

Listing 5-12. Using <article> to Add a Blog Post

```
<article id="MyGuitarBlog">
 <header>
  <h1>Your first high end Guitar</h1>
<p> Taking the plunge, and why you should do it </p>
</header>
<p>Buying your first really high end axe is up there with moving house, doing a driving test
or getting married in terms of being really important but the good news is it's nothing like
as stressful as any of those are!</p>
 <p>[…] </p>
 <footer>
  <p>Some comments from interested humans </p>
 </footer>
</article>
```

If some comments were actually added, they might look like Listing 5-13.

Listing 5-13. Comments in Blog Post Wrapped in <article> Elements

```
<article id="MyGuitarBlog">
 <header>
  <h1>Your first high end Guitar</h1>
<p> Taking the plunge, and why you should do it </p>
</header>
<p>Buying your first really high end axe is up there with moving house, doing a driving test
or getting married in terms of being really important but the good news is it's nothing like
as stressful as any of those are!</p>
 <p>[…] </p>

 <section>
  <h1>My Guitar Blog Comments</h1>
  <article id="comment_1">
   <link href="#comment_1">
   <footer>
    <p>Comment by: <span ="name">Not George Harrison</span>
    </p>
   </footer>
   <p>My guitar doesn't Gently Weep anymore.. can anyone help?</p>
  </article>

<article id="comment_2">
   <link href="#comment_2">
   <footer>
    <p>Comment by: <span ="name">Jimi Jimi<span>
    </p>
   </footer>
   <p>I don't know George, but I just hurt my Little Wing, when was I walking along the
Watchtower, these days everything is just a haze, a kinda purpley one weird</p>
  </article>

<article id="comment_3">
   <link href="#comment_3">
   <footer>
    <p>Comment by: <span ="name">Mini JPage</span>
    </p>
   </footer>
   <p>Sounds weird Not George Harrison, does the song not remain the same?</p>
  </article>
 </section>
</article>
```

The idea is that they are kind self-contained so that they can be referenced or syndicated elsewhere if needed. You can also think of an article as a *small unit.*

The Sectioning Bug

There is a sectioning bug that was outlined very well by Jason Kiss of Accessible Culture. If you use nested headings in HTML5 sectioning elements, as opposed to using exclusively <h1> elements, the hierarchy might be misrepresented to the user for browsers and AT that don't recognize the *outline algorithm*. Thanks to Jason for letting me illustrate the bug here.

First, HTML5 defines what's called an *outline algorithm* that allows you to nest multiple <h1>headings in sectioning content (to support content syndication for example). Usually, however, there can only be one (remember Highlander!) right?

■ **Note** You can read more about the outline algorithm at

http://dev.w3.org/html5/spec/sections.html#outlines.

So according to this algorithm, Listing 5-14 and Listing 5-15 are practically identical. The first uses only <h1> heading elements.

Listing 5-14. HTML5 Example Outlining Headers Algorithm

```
<h1>Level 1</h1>
<nav>
   <h1>Level 2</h1>
</nav>
<section>
   <h1>Level 2</h1>
   <article>
      <h1>Level 3</h1>
      <aside>
         <h1>Level 4</h1>
      </aside>
   </article>
</section>
```

The second uses an explicit semantic to show the different heading levels.

Listing 5-15. HTML5 Example Outlining Headers Algorithm with Explicit Semantics

```
<h1>Level 1</h1>
<nav>
   <h2>Level 2</h2>
</nav>
<section>
   <h2>Level 2</h2>
   <article>
      <h3>Level 3</h3>
      <aside>
         <h4>Level 4</h4>
      </aside>
```

```
    </article>
</section>
```

At the time of this writing, support for the new HTML5 outline algorithm isn't great. So a user agent that doesn't support the algorithm will output the content as multiple <h1> elements. Depending on the context of use, this might mean you are better off sticking with the second example, if content isn't to be syndicated. If your page does only use <h1> elements, while it won't really give the user an overview of the correct hierarchical structure, it's not a show-stopper and won't result in totally inaccessible content. Having said that, it's not ideal. However, if content is to be syndicated, use method one, because every nested article might likely end up in another site; if content is more static or to be consumed *on page*, stick with the second method for now.

■ **Note** For more on the Sectioning Bug, visit AccessibleCulture.org at
www.accessibleculture.org/articles/2011/10/jaws-ie-and-headings-in-html5.

As an Aside, Did You Hear the One About the Vicar and the [...]

HTML5 also has a new <aside> element. It is also a sectioning element and is used to provide content that is *tangentially related* to the main article or a parent section. You might be wondering what to do with it? This is natural. An aside is normal in human speech and interaction, but it might be unusual in a markup language. There are some things that I think it could be good for, such as marking up a pull quote, which could be used on a web site where there were client testimonials. For example, take a look at Listing 5-16.

Listing 5-16. HTML5 <aside> Element Example

```
<p>Some our our services include, taking animals into our shelter who are mistreated and
abused. Many people come and visit us also to look for an animal to care for, like this
testimonial from a happy family who brought home a puppy shows.</p>

<aside>
 <q> We are so glad we visited the Animal Sanctuary, and brought home little Puddles, he is
such a good puppy! </q>
</aside>

<p>Without the help and support of people like that we would never be able to do what we
do</p>
```

Other uses for it include marking up content from other sources, such as Twitter feeds or Facebook updates.

Conclusion

You had a good look at the new sectioning elements. In HTML5, much of the grouping content elements are the same with some additions, and the text level semantics are pretty similar. We'll cover them when relevant. In the next chapter, we will take a departure and look at some of the new rich media elements, such as <video>, <audio>, and the infamous <canvas>.

CHAPTER 6

Images, Rich Media, Audio, and Video in HTML5

In this chapter, you'll see how to make images and other rich media accessible using HTML5. This chapter will cover some tried and trusted ways of making graphical content accessible, as well as some new techniques you might not be familiar with. I'll cover other elements used to handle rich media, such as <audio> and <video>, and discuss how the new elements can be used to present audio and visual content in a way that is accessible.

In terms of "new" features in HTML5, nothing is quite as conspicuous as the new <canvas> element. <canvas> is a 2D drawing API that can be used to create some very sophisticated, graphically rich animations natively within the browser. However, <canvas> content does have some particular accessibility challenges. I'll discuss these later on.

■ **Note** While <canvas> has the advantage of bringing graphically rich content natively to the browser, without the need for third-party plugins á la Flash. Flash content isn't going away as it still has uses that might make it more suitable, from an accessibility perspective, than <canvas>.

Making Images Accessible

The Web is primarily a visual medium. Although this is true, you have seen that the Web is also a surprising and diverse medium where many users, regardless of ability, can access the same content and have similar experiences online. It is universal in the scope of its reach in that it supports multiple modes of access regardless of ability.

This is great. Sometimes, however, you need to pay attention to the limitations that some users experience and do your best by correctly applying markup and principles of good design.

Making images accessible is generally one of the first things a web developer will learn how to do when trying to make content accessible. It is pretty easy to learn how to do it, so as an introductory accessibility technique, it has a rather low barrier to entry. However, it is often very easy either to do it incorrectly or to misunderstand what it is you are trying to achieve in the first place.

Meet the Poster Child of Accessible Web Design: The alt Attribute

The alt attribute (or @alt) of the <image> element is what you will mostly use to provide a text alternative to graphical content. This takes the following general form:

```
<img src="someimage.png" alt="Some text that provides an equivalent description or functional
replacement for the image" />
```

So in terms of an overall structure, it's pretty simple. You have the `<img>` element, followed by its source attribute and the @alt. The order of attributes doesn't really matter—you can have the @alt first and then the src, if you prefer. The @alt is explicitly associated with the image using the preceding method, and it represents a complete *structure*. Adding the alternate text in the method shown also has absolutely no impact on the visual presentation of the image.

■ **Note** The `<img>` element also has a `title` (@title) attribute; however, using the @alt attribute is generally a more robust and bulletproof way of providing alternate text. For longer descriptions, there is also the @longdesc attribute. I'll say more about these later.

How Screen Readers Handle @alt Text

When a screen reader gives focus to an `<img>` element in a webpage, the screen reader firstly announces to the user that it has encountered an image. It does this often literally by speaking the word "image." If the image has an @alt value it will announce whatever text string the author has included within it. That's it.

■ **Note** @alt is really well supported in most graphical and text browsers, as well as in most commonly used screen-reading technology out there.

If there isn't an @alt description, the screen reader will look to see if there is a `title` attribute and might (I say might for a reason) announce that. If neither are present, the screen reader will then try to look for any other supporting information it can find, usually by announcing the contents of the src attribute, which might give the user some indication of the type of image or the purpose of the image.

■ **Note** When the image isn't available or couldn't be loaded, most browsers display a bounding box where the image should be and also display the alternate text. Text-only browsers, such as Lynx, read the alternate text by default. For details, see http://en.wikipedia.org/wiki/Lynx_(web_browser).

For example, consider an image that is a button and has no alternate text or @title information. If the file is called *button.png* or some other name that describes its function, such as *logon.png* or *logout.png*, this can help the screen-reader user to get an idea of what the purpose of the button actually is, even though the @alt text is missing.

■ **Note** In general, the situation I describe where there is no `@alt` or `@title` will trigger what's called *heuristic evaluation*. A *heuristic* is rule of thumb or method of evaluation. Heuristics are at the heart of all sorts of things, from basic logic you might learn when studying computer science, to more advanced algorithm design. Don't be put off by the term, just think of "a set of rules." Sometimes screen readers also look at surrounding HTML content in the webpage when heuristic evaluation is triggered.

On the other hand, if your image has what I call a scary URL, which is one that goes along the lines of some random string that a Content Management System (CMS) might use (*12090_IMG.jpg* or something equally opaque), the screen reader will not be able to make any sense of it. This will cause problems for the end user because when a missing `@alt` triggers screen-reader heuristics, the software just won't be able to make any sense of the content. It will output the name of the file, but if that is a long, random text string, it's no use.

■ **Remember** A good default behavior is to give your images descriptive names, even if you are actually applying alternate text descriptions.

@alt Drawbacks

So it seems as though the `@alt` attribute is pretty robust and bulletproof and all that good stuff. Are there any drawbacks? Well, an argument has been made that the alternative text might be useful to "everyone" and should be available to users beyond those who are either using text-only browsers or have vision impairments and are using screen readers. Although this sounds plausible and inclusive, I don't really agree with this view. There are cases where alternate text descriptions can aid comprehension, for sure, but in general I feel that for what it does and the groups it serves, it does well. This discussion is a long and nuanced one that I don't need to go into here. It suffices to say, in the HTML5 working group the argument goes along the lines of "You are discriminating against sighted people by not giving them access to the `@alt` values." To me, this kind of thinking is spurious at best. A markup language that serves the needs of 80 percent of its users well is better than one that serves 100 percent of its users poorly.

Another potential issue is the limitation on the size of the `@alt` text. Technically, it's around 100 characters, but in general, it's hard to get a definitive answer on just how long "too long" is. If you know from the start that your image will need a longer description, there are other methods (such as `@longest` and WAI-ARIA `aria-labeledby`) that can be used instead.

What Should I Describe?

One of the big challenges a developer faces when trying to provide alternate textual descriptions for images is the question of exactly what to describe. This is a big question and one that, unfortunately, is usually moot. In truth, the area is a little fuzzy. This might not be very reassuring, but there you are. Some screen-reader users do want everything to be described, as much as possible, and others are happy as long as they get the information they need at any given time. More importantly, when a site has a specific function, many users are happy just to be able to complete the task they set out to do. They don't care if the graphics are described as long as they aren't missing any core functionality.

What I'll do here is outline some things I've learned over the years from doing user testing and expert evaluation of web sites. This has often involved working with blind screen-reader users, as well as users of other assistive technology (AT) devices. I will present the current thinking on accessibility best practices when it comes to HTML5, images, and other rich media. Then I'll leave you to make up your own mind!

Describing Content: Don't Overdo It

One of the first pieces of wisdom I'd like to impart to you is "Don't overdo it." Sometimes less really is more, and most of the time, enough is actually enough. Initially, you might feel the need to describe, well, everything! This is often very impractical and time consuming. Learning to keep your text descriptions relevant and concise is an art that will take some time for you to master. With experience, you'll discover what sorts of details are unimportant and better left out of textual descriptions of images.

Leave It Out (Part 1)

If you can truly put yourself in an AT user's shoes, you might find there are situations in which you actually don't want an image (or images) explained. In fact, for the best AT user experience, you might want the images to be completely hidden, or ignored. So before I go any further, I should answer the questions I think I hear you asking: "How do I leave an image out? And how do I not include it in what the screen reader outputs?" You can do this in a couple of different ways, and they are pretty easy to grasp.

When a webpage loads, all of the HTML items in the document are loaded into the DOM. Obviously, this includes all of the graphics and other rich media. If you want a graphic to be presented visually but you want the screen reader to ignore it, one of the most tried and tested ways is to give the image a null @alt value. This takes the following form:

```
<img src="someimage.png" alt="" />
```

■ **Note** The @alt has no blank space between the quotes.

This acts as a flag to the screen reader, telling it to ignore the image. The screen reader will act as if the image isn't there at all and will not inform the user about its presence.

"Why would I want to do that?" you might be wondering. Well, if an image is purely presentational, such as an inline graphic that you use to style a button, you will want to hide it from the screen reader because it adds nothing to the AT user's experience. When you think about it, there are many images you really don't need to describe at all because they add no value. So the null @alt is a powerful friend. Use it wisely, and you'll find that it really helps to remove unnecessary clutter from your pages.

Leave It Out (Part 2)

Another way to hide images that have no informational value for a screen-reader user is to use Cascading Style Sheets (CSS). This declaration takes the following form:

```
p {background-image:url('some_bullet.png');}
```

In the example, you can replace the element name of p with whatever element you want to apply the image to. The URL, part points to where you've stored the image you want to use. By default, this property also repeats, so you might want to set a no-repeat as shown here:

```
p {background-image:url('some_bullet.png');
background-repeat: no-repeat;
}
```

If you want the image to repeat vertically on the X access, your code will take the following form:

```
body

{background-image:url('some_repeatinggraphic.png');
background-image: repeat-x;
}
```

To repeat the image horizontally on the Y access, use this:

```
Body
{background-image:url('some_repeatinggraphic.png');
background-image: repeat-y;
}
```

You might find that you want to use some inline CSS to present your images, so you will probably use some <div> or inline <span> elements to act as a hook for the image.

Leave It Out (Part 3)

Another way to hide an image from the screen reader is to use the WAI-ARIA role, role="presentation". This take the form shown here:

```
<img src="some_prettybutsemanticallyuselessgraphic.jpg" role="presentation" />
```

However, I really don't recommend doing this—partly because the previous two approaches are better supported by current and older user agents, and partly because using role="presentation" has other accessibility-related uses in user agents that support it (which most of the latest screen readers and browsers do). For example, the technique is really useful where you want the parent element semantics to be ignored by the screen reader, but not the children. For example, you might need to use a table to contain a widget and control layout. Using role="presentation" allows the screen reader to ignore the table that is used to contain the widget controls, but it allows the screen reader to access the child semantics (the contents of the widget). A neat trick.

Also, please don't shoot me or send winged monkeys to attack my home—using tables for layout is not *that* much of an accessibility no-no.

Different Kinds of Images

I've just outlined some useful techniques for hiding content from screen readers.

So how do you write good alternate text? Where do you start? Well, first, there are a few different kinds of images to consider:

- **A visually rich image:** Generally speaking, photos, drawings, and paintings are very rich in visual content. For example, consider a pretty natural landscape or a family photo. It can be hard to truly capture these kinds of images or the spirit of them.

- **Graphs and Charts:** These can be wide and varied but can contain quite detailed information, as well as illustrating relationships between various kinds of data.

- **An image of text:** This can be an image that contains useful information that is important the user doesn't miss, or that just contains styled text.

- **A functional Image:** This is an image that has a specific function, such as a graphic used for a button.

- **A decorative image:** An image that has no real functional aspect but is useful only as a purely visual embellishment, such as a nicely styled bullet list.

- **Icons:** An image that is used as a *visual clue* and is part of a link.

As you can see, the use cases for alternate descriptions are numerous and varied, and this list isn't even exhaustive! Before we go any further, we'll take a look at some of the new elements in HTML5 that can be used in conjunction with @alt and other methods for describing images.

What's New in HTML5 for Describing Images?

The two new kids on the block for describing or annotating a wide range of diagrams, photos, and illustrations are <figure> and <figcaption>. They are used in such a way as to create a *single unit* that can be pointed to or referenced from another part of the webpage. It's like pointing to an ID within your CSS.

The figure acts as a container for some image, graph, illustration, or photo, and it takes this basic form:

```
<figure>
<img src="someimage.jpg" />
</figure>
```

OK, so that's how it looks without any clothes on. To dress it up and make it suitable for going out, you have to complete the structure by adding a <figcaption>. This is basically a caption for the figure.

The basic structure for adding a <figcaption> to a <figure> is shown here:

```
<figure>
<img src="someimage.jpg">
<figcaption>Some useful description of the image</figcaption>
</figure>
```

So the <figcaption> is just that: a caption for contents of the <figure>.

More detailed examples will follow. I just want to outline the basic structure and get across the point that the use of <figure> in HTML5 has an interesting advantage over the use of @alt because it represents a complete structured unit that can be referenced on a page.

Describing an Image with ARIA-describedby

Using the aria-describedby attribute is another method of referencing an element within the page that provides a suitable description of the image.

This can be a very useful method because there are often times when there is existing text in a page that would perfectly describe an image. Rather than duplicate this text, the idea is that you reference the ID of the image programmatically. You thereby create an explicit connection between the image and the textual description.

For example, consider the following images. The first (Figure 6-1) is a photo of my father-in-law, Fiachra, and myself on top of Ireland's highest mountain, Carrauntoohil, in County Kerry. The photo was taken during the summer of 2011.

Figure 6-1. Josh (right) with his father-in-law, Fiachra (left), atop Mount Carrauntoohil, County Kerry

If this photo were to be embedded within a HTML5 blog that talks about our climb, the code for the blog post before adding the image and the description would look something like that shown in Listing 6-1.

Listing 6-1. An HTML5 Blog Post

```
<!DOCTYPE HTML>
<html>
<head>
<meta Charset="UTF-8">
<head>
<title> my big climb this summer (2011)</title>
</head>
<body>
<article>
<section>
<h1>Climbing the three highest mountains in Ireland</h1>
<p>During the summer of 2011, Fiachra, Dara and I climbed the three highest mountains in
Ireland. This was a stupendous day where the challenge of summiting the three peaks of
Carrauntoohil, Beenkeragh & Caher was too much to resist!</p>
</section>
<section>
<h2> The Coomloughra Horseshoe</h2>
<p>The three peaks are ringed within in a large horseshoe shaped valley and present a very
challenging climb even for experienced hill walkers. We also had fantastic views of the
MacGillycuddy Reeks from Beenkeragh's high, exposed summit. The weather was also very
beautiful and we totally lucked out as we couldn't have asked for a clearer day to see the
spectacular views. We walked over Beenkeragh Ridge with its yawning drops and navigated the
equally spectacular Caher Ridge, with the Black Valley far below, before descending from Caher
into Coomloughra Glen.</p>
</section>
<section>
<h2>Remember to bring water</h2>
<p>It was a very hot day and after 4 hours or so we ran out of water! Fortunately we came
across some fresh mountain streams in the Coomloughra Glen and could top up our water bottles
[…]</p>
</section>
</article>
</body>
</html>
```

If I was to then include the image in the first paragraph and I wanted to point to the paragraph as a textual description, I could do so by coding it as shown in Listing 6-2.

Listing 6-2. Including an Image in the Post

```
<!DOCTYPE HTML>
<html>
<head>
<meta Charset="UTF-8">
<title> My big climb this summer (2011)</title>
</head>
```

```
<body>
<article>
<section>
<h1>Climbing the three highest mountains in Ireland</h1>
<p id="text1"> <img src="fiachra_josh_kerry2011.jpg" aria-describedby="text2" />During the
summer of 2011, Fiachra, Dara and I climbed the three highest mountains in Ireland. This was a
stupendous day where the challenge of summiting the three peaks of Carrauntoohil, Beenkeragh &
Caher was too much to resist!</p>
</section>
<section>
<h2> The Coomloughra Horseshoe</h2>
<p id="text2">The three peaks are ringed within in a large horseshoe shaped valley and present
a very challenging climb even for experienced hill walkers. We had fantastic views of the
MacGillycuddy Reeks from Beenkeragh's high, exposed summit. The weather was also very
beautiful and we totally lucked out as we couldn't have asked for a clearer day to see the
spectacular views. We walked over Beenkeragh Ridge with its yawning drops and navigated the
equally spectacular Caher Ridge, with the Black Valley far below, before descending from Caher
into Coomloughra Glen.</p>
</section>
<section><h2>Remember to bring water</h2>
<p id="text3">It was a very hot day and after 4 hours or so we ran out of water! Fortunately
we came across some fresh mountain streams in the Coomloughra Glen and could top up our water
bottles […]</p>
</section>
</article>
</body>
</html>
```

So what's happening in the code just shown? I'm using the inline text of the blog post to describe the image by pointing to the content of block via their IDs. In this case, I gave each of the <p> elements an ID of text1, text2, and text3, respectively. For user agents that support aria-describedby (and as mentioned in the earlier chapter, many of the new screen readers do, and those that don't will just ignore it), creating a programmatic connection between the image and the description means that the description is announced as soon as the image has focus. Additionally, there are ways you can enhance this basic behavior—for example, by adding an @alt textual description to the image and combining it with the aria-describedby code. This would look something like the code in Listing 6-3. (I'm leaving out the first and last part of the blog post code.)

Listing 6-3. Enhancing the Image Description

```
<section>
<h1>Climbing the three highest mountains in Ireland</h1>
<p id="text1"> <img src="fiachra_josh_kerry2011.jpg" alt="Photo of Fiachra and Josh
standing under the huge cross (over three men high) at the top of Carrauntoohil" aria-
describedby="text2" />During the summer of 2011, Fiachra, Dara and I climbed the three
highest mountains in Ireland. This was a stupendous day where the challenge of summiting the
three peaks of Carrauntoohil, Beenkeragh & Caher was too much to resist!</p>
</section>
<section>
<h2> The Coomloughra Horseshoe</h2>
<p id="text2">This three peaks are ringed within in a large horseshoe shaped valley and
present a very challenging climb even for experienced hill walkers. We had fantastic views of
```

the MacGillycuddy Reeks from Beenkeragh's high, exposed summit. The weather was also very
beautiful and we totally lucked out as we couldn't have asked for a clearer day to see the
spectacular views. We walked over Beenkeragh Ridge with its yawning drops and navigated the
equally spectacular Caher Ridge, with the Black Valley far below, before descending from Caher
into Coomloughra Glen.</p>
</section>

What's interesting about this approach is that it introduces an element of backward compatibility
for older screen readers that don't support `aria-describedby` but will understand the contents of the
`@alt`. Approaching your markup like this is generally a good idea because it covers both user agents that
support a new feature as well as those that don't.

Screen readers that do support both will actually get a rich textual equivalent via the contents of the
`@alt` and `aria-describedby` elements; however, realize that the `aria-describedby` technique currently
can be used only for *in-page* descriptions. So you cannot reference a description on a different webpage.

■ **Note** When a screen-reader user tires of the description or has heard enough, he can just tab away from the
item being described and move to the next one, or he can use his screen reader's navigation features. So it's not
like the user has to listen to stuff he doesn't want to—the output from the screen reader will end as soon as the
user moves to a new HTML element.

Which Method Should I Use?

In general, this decision comes down to context of use and what the best kind of description would be.
The mechanics might vary as you are looking at various ways to provide the description, but there are
factors you need to consider carefully before you storm ahead. To take the examples or types of images
you looked at earlier a little further, we are talking about situations (in order of the items listed
previously) where we have the following:

- **A visually rich image:** When an image such as a photo, drawing, or painting has a
  lot of visual information, `@alt` or `<figcaption>` can be used as a label that briefly
  describes the image or gives an overview of it.

- **Graphs and charts:** When the image is a graph or chart that is rich in informative
  data, `@alt` can be used as a descriptive label that gives a brief overview of the
  thrust of the graph. Graphs and charts are perfect situations where other methods
  such as `aria-describedby` can be really useful.

- **An image of text:** A graphic designer might have used a groovy font that is not
  found on the user's machine (common in web design, and referred to as *image
  replacement techniques*), and the `@alt` is used as a replacement for the image. The
  `@alt` should clearly state what the styled text is.

- **A functional image:** An image might have a function, so you use the `@alt` to
  describe what it does and not what it looks like.

- **A decorative image:** An image might be totally decorative and not need an
  alternate description, and it would need to be hidden from AT.

- **Icons:** An image might be used as a visual clue or icon and be a part of a link.

The following are some examples to support the preceding use cases.

Type 1: Describing a Visually Rich Image

Images often contain a lot of visually rich information. It can be very difficult to describe them in a clinical or exact manner. Although you know the old maxim "A picture says more than a thousand words," is the opposite also true? Do you need a thousand words to describe the picture? There might be some truth in that.

Although WCAG 2.0 suggests that the text you provide for an image should be an equivalent or should replace the image, in practice this often isn't possible. At least not in the sense that the description can really do the picture justice. Imagine trying to provide a textual description for a painting such as the "Mona Lisa."

You could say, "Here is a graceful-looking lady with a faint smile," but you could also say, "Here is a graceful-looking lady with a faint frown." Depending on who you ask, both are correct, and both are on the terse end of the descriptive spectrum.

So often, even when an image is rather rich, you might be better off not trying to capture every detail, but instead trying to capture the spirit of an image by using @alt or <figcaption> in a fun way. For example, consider the photo shown in Figure 6-2, which I think is funny because the subjects could be brothers, except one of them is purple.

Figure 6-2. *My little boy and his owl buddy*

This is a photo of my son, Ruairí, and his rather large (and bright purple) owl friend, Minerva. If I used <figure> and <figcaption> with a combination of @alt, the following might be suitable as an alternate description that goes some way toward what I'm talking about:

```
<figure>
<img src="Ruairi.jpg alt="Ruairi smiling and playing on the couch at home with his large
purple Owl friend Minerva. There is a likeness in their big Moon heads!" />
<figcaption> Two friends together, Ruairi and Minerva</figcaption>
</figure>
```

What I have done here is use the @alt as a way of providing a longer kind of description and the <figcaption> as just that—a caption for the image. They can be used to support each other and provide various types of informational descriptions of the image.

The point I'm making it that sometimes it's just plain hard to write a useful textual description of an image. You might be better off linking to a separate description of the image or using aria-describedby, as discussed previously, to point to a description in the document itself.

OK, so the preceding photo is pretty simple (though very cute!). Let's consider some more complex images and how you might go about providing textual descriptions using HTML5.

Consider the following couple of images from my past life as an artist. (I mean a past life in the "I used to do this" sense, not in the "previous incarnations" sense—but that's a discussion for another day I guess!)

Figure 6-3 is a black-and-white, pen-and-ink drawing called "Creation" that I did many years ago.

Figure 6-3. *"Creation"*

If I included that in an online gallery and wanted to describe it by giving it an alternate textual description, would I be able to do it effectively? Technically, I can give it a text description, but how do I convey its full visual impact or meaning?

I could try by doing something relatively simple, such as the following:

```
<figure>
<img src="josh_drawing_creation.png" alt="A large bright flaming triangle straddled by a Sun
and Moon. In the centre sits a strange symbol, and there are stars." />
<figcaption>Pen and Ink Drawing called 'Creation' by Joshue O Connor</figcaption>
</figure>
```

My @alt content very nearly reached the 100-character limit that was mentioned previously, and—let's face it—the description doesn't really do it.

I could decide to take a more verbose approach and use the aria-describedby method, as shown here:

```
<figure><img src="josh_drawing_creation.png" alt="A large colourful pen and ink drawing with a
cosmic theme of creation" aria-describedby="creation" /><figcaption>'Creation by Joshue O
Connor (1993)</figcaption></figure>
```

And then further within my webpage, I might include the following paragraph, to which I can assign id="creation" to. The whole thing would then look something like Listing 6-4.

Listing 6-4. Image Description Using aria-describedby

```
<!DOCTYPE HTML>
<html>
<head>
<meta Charset="UTF-8">
<title>Some Cosmic Artwork by Josh(2011)</title>
</head>
<body>
<article>
<section>
<h1>Sample of Pen and Ink Drawings</h1>
<p id="creation">
<figure>
<img src="josh_drawing_creation.png" alt="A large colourful pen and ink drawing with a cosmic
theme of creation" aria-describedby="creation" />
<figcaption>'Creation' by Joshue O Connor (1993)</figcaption>
In a past life Josh was far more interested in playing guitars, painting, and in general
larking about than he was with computers.</p>
</section>
<section>
<p> Here is some more background about his artwork for those interested […]
</p>
<p id="creation"> This drawing illustrates the mystery of creation. It shows a large flaming
triangle that holds a bright radiating sun at its apex, and a stylised smiling moon sits at
its base in opposition. At the heart of the triangle there sits an exploding planet with the
ancient Vedic symbol of creation the AUM at its heart. The image sits on a background framed
of stars and small spaceships fly by randomly in the distance.
</p>
```

```
</figure>
</section>
</article>

</body>
</html>
```

The example of a longer description that is found inside the HTML document is a little better. This method really does give the author a little more space to breathe, and hopefully do the image justice. Is it a suitable description, and does it convey the same visual richness of the image? You be the judge. It suffices to say, where images are more functional, it gets a little easier and providing suitable alternate text is a little less fuzzy.

Finally, my point is that you often just can't fully replace what is a visual medium with a textual description. However, you can make the user experience for a screen-reader user better. Making the experience better can also be read as "less terrible." If you find that you just can't get your head around how to describe something, break the image down to its component parts, or find a gestalt view or overview that might help. If all fails, just give the image a null @alt value and it won't intrude on the user experience. This is a last resort, but it's better than not doing anything and triggering screen-reader heuristics, in my opinion.

Before we move to the less murky water of more functional code equivalents, just to illustrate how difficult it can be to provide meaningful descriptions, I've provided another of my drawings in Figure 6-4, "The Seed of Creation." How would you describe this? Also, apologies to those who know some Vedic ontology—Lord Brahma should have four heads. And yes, I did have a lot of free time on my hands.

Figure 6-4. *The "Seed of Creation"*

▓ **Note** If you don't want to use either the figure or `aria-describedby` methods to describe the image and there is a larger textual description on the page, you can also simply use a named anchor saying, "For more on this image, go to" and link to the section of the page or, indeed, another webpage where the description can be found. This is a simple alternative.

You might be wondering if you can still use @longdesc to describe complex images. At the time of writing, the longdesc attribute (or @longdesc) is obsolete and no longer part of the HTML5 specification. The @longdesc attribute was a way of providing a longer textual description of an image if needed, and it has been superseded by better techniques, such as those I previously outlined.

Use of @longdesc takes the following general form:

```
<p><imp src="some_complexgraphic.gif" alt="a complex image"
longdesc="complex_image_description.html" /></p>
```

As you can see, @longdesc was a mechanism for linking to a longer description on the current page or another page. To say it was poorly supported by browsers and AT might be overdoing it, but support certainly wasn't great. It was also little-used outside of academia. For those who did find it useful, it was useful—and I don't have a problem with retaining or improving element functionality or keeping an element in the specification if it serves a use case well, even if its application isn't entirely universal. But that's me.

It did have some advantages, however, and although ARIA is great and HTML5 has made advances in many areas, neither currently provides a fully-functional replacement for @longdesc. @longdesc has a trump card in that it can be used to reference an off-page URI, and also to provide structured content as a textual description. Unfortunately, its implementation in the browser and the resulting user experience often left a lot to be desired. However, that might have had more to do with its implementation than not needing a mechanism for a longer description. This is a hot topic in the HTML working group, and you might well find it resurfacing.

Type 2: Graphs and Charts

When the image is a graph or chart that is rich in informative data that would be difficult to get across in a simple @alt description, @alt again can be used as a kind of descriptive label. This label should give a brief overview of what the graph is aiming to portray.

■ **Remember** Graphs and charts are perfect situations where methods such as using aria-describedby can be really useful, especially where the page might likely contain a more detailed overview that could be already linked with the image.

For example, consider Figure 6-5. It is a graph that I used when researching my MSc thesis on the various kinds of user testing and evaluation methodologies that professional practitioners of inclusive design use.

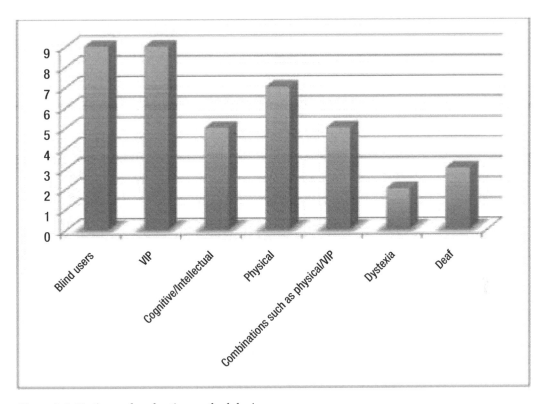

Figure 6-5. *Testing and evaluation methodologies*

To provide a textual description of the graph, I'd give an overview of what the graph conveys visually. Something like this:

```
<img src="disability_types.png" alt="Most user testing is done with blind and vision impaired
people, and the least with Deaf users and people with Dyslexia" />
```

Consider Figure 6-6, a chart that shows the main benefits of user testing. There is a lot of visual information to convey. In this case, using aria-describedby is certainly a better solution.

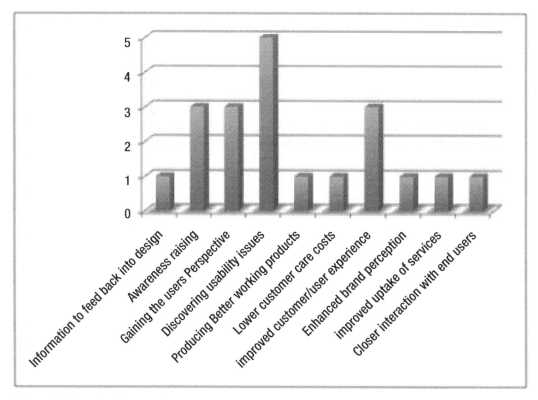

Figure 6-6. Benefits of user testing

You might find it easier to link to the description in the body of the webpage that outlines the findings in a more verbose way. Here I've used a combination of @alt (as a short label) and aria-describedby for the longer description:

```
<img src="benefits_of_usertesting.png" alt="Graph outlining the benefits of user testing"
aria-describedby="benefit_test" />
```

And then deeper in a HTML file, I could have a paragraph that provides a richer description, as well as some commentary:

```
<p id="benefit_test"> From this research we can see that practitioners feel some of the main
benefit of user testing with people with disabilities is discovering usability issues with the
interface, navigation, structure, functionality and so on. User testing as an awareness
raising exercise for developers in order to first hand experience the diverse needs of people
with disabilities and therefore gaining a greater understanding of how things work from the
users perspective, is also an outcome of the research"</p>
```

For Figure 6-7, which looks at user test sizes, is a little easier to describe.

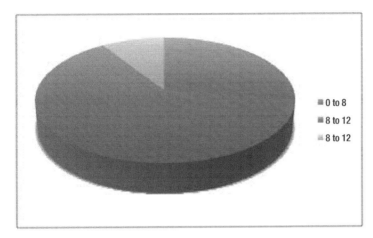

Figure 6-7. Test group sizes

```
<img src="test_sizes"alt="The majority of test group sizes are between 8 12 users." />
```

This is a terse text description, but it perfectly captures the visual information in the chart. Sometimes less is more!

Type 3: An Image of Text

Now we'll deal with the situation mentioned earlier in the chapter: a graphic designer might have used a groovy font not found on the user's machine, and where the @alt is used as a replacement text for the image. In this case, the @alt should clearly state what the styled text is.

For example, Figure 6-8 could be used as a graphical header for a light-box gallery or collection of images related to guitars, where a designer has a particularly stylized font that she wants to use.

Figure 6-8. A graphical header

To ensure that the image is accessible, you could mark it up as shown here:

```
<h1><img src="guitar_gallery.png" alt="The Guitar Gallery" /></h1>
```

▧ **Note** In most cases like this, you would just mirror the text in the image in the alternate text. The next example illustrates why this approach is important.

Figure 6-9 is an example of a "special offer" graphic you might see on a web site. The graphic is designed to be eye-catching and to inform the user about special offers.

Figure 6-9. Text in a graphic

You could mark up the image as follows:

```
<img src="guitar_special_offers.png" alt="Special Offers on all guitars. Ends this Weds" />
```

Without the alternate text, a nonsighted person would have no idea that the shop was having a cool sale on its guitars, or that it was only a limited time offer. There are also instances where a logo might contain some text or represent a company identity. You should then add the company name to the logo image as alternate text, rather than describing what it looks like. Suppose that Figure 6-10 were linked to the HTML5 specification.

Figure 6-10. The HTML5 logo

Rather than giving the image an alternate description along the lines of "New HTML5 logo that looks like a large orange shield, with a big 5 in the middle," you could say something like the following:

```
<a><img src="html5_logo.png" alt="For more on HTML5 specification, visit the W3C website" /></a>
```

This leads us nicely to the next type of image, which I touched on in the last example: the functional ones.

Type 4: A Functional Image

When an image has a specific function, you should use the @alt to describe what it does and not what it looks like.

Imagine if you saw the image in Figure 6-11 on your favourite guitar emporium web site, and the only way to access it was via a link on the image itself.

Figure 6-11. Want to win a classic guitar? Make it accessible and everyone has a chance!

To make this accessible you could mark it up as follows:

```
<a href="competition.html"> <img src="win_a_gibson.png" alt="Win a Classic Guitar..Click here
to enter" /></a>
```

■ **Note** I have seen these kinds of images on some web sites, and literally the only way to enter the competition was by clicking on the link. So where there is some purpose to the link, you can describe its purpose and not what it looks like! Nothing illustrates this better than the following example.

Figure 6-12. Graphic for a link to purchase a guitar

Figure 6-12 illustrates a button that the customer will use to buy a guitar. So there is no need to provide a description along the lines of

```
<a><img src="buy_this_guitar.png" alt="Here is a nice graphic of a Gibson Guitar stylized with some creative Photoshop filters, and using a groovy font called Rosewood /></a>
```

No! You just say what its function is—literally, "Buy this Guitar."

```
<img src="buy_this_guitar.png"alt="Buy this Guitar" />
```

There, that's better! So stick with what the button is doing. You don't even need to include text like "Click here" because that isn't necessary. The screen reader will announce to the user that the graphic is a link, and the user will know how to activate it.

Type 5: A Purely Decorative Image

An image might be totally decorative and not need an alternate description. It would need to be hidden from AT in order to not trigger screen-reader heuristics and also because it doesn't add anything to the user experience.

You do this by adding the null @alt value, which takes the form alt="" (with no space between the ""), such as in the following example:

```
<img src="agroovy_but_semantically_useless_graphic" alt="">
```

I've made this point a few times in the chapter, but I'll make it again: judicious use of the null @alt can add to the user experience because it can be used to remove a lot of webpage clutter. Even many sighted people will agree, when asked, that the graphic design of many web sites is functionally poor with superfluous clutter, or it includes little to give them the functions they need to do what they actually want! Images are often just there, occupying space and, in some cases, actually getting in the way.

In the accessibility community, there are endless discussions about which images should be described and which ones shouldn't. One person's decorative image is another person's art. It also depends on a screen-reader user's preference. Some might want a lot of extras described; others (I'd argue the majority) are happy with much of the clutter being left out.

Type 6: Icons

An image might be used as a visual clue or icon and be a part of a link. The image shouldn't actually be the active link itself, and therefore a null @alt should be used on the image, and the real URL can be used instead.

In Figure 6-13 and its companion Listing 6-5, inline images are used as icons that sit beside a real URL.

 Home

 Contact

 Our Location

Figure 6-13. Inline images used as icons

Listing 6-5. Code for Inline Icons

```
<ul>
<li>
<a href="home.html">
<img src="home_icon.png" alt="" />Home</a>
</li>
<li>
<a href="contact_us.html">
<img src="contactus_icon.png" alt="" />Contact</a>
</li>
<li>
<a href="our_location.html">
<img src="_location_icon.png" alt="" />Our Location</a>
</li>
</ul>
```

When the screen reader gives focus to any of the listed links just shown, the image is ignored and the contents of the <a> elements are announced.

Sometimes you find a duplication of link functions where both the icon and the real link text are clickable. Try to avoid doing this, because it can be a pain for screen-reader users. As they move through a menu, they will get a duplication of the link. For a sighted person, if the icon and the URL beside it are active clickable links, the user can easily choose one or the other. The icon has the effect of visually re-enforcing the purpose of the controls or aiding comprehension in some way. This visual reinforcement is just that—visual.

■ **Tip** You can find more examples of how to make images accessible using the new techniques that have been outlined here by pointing your browser at "HTML5: Techniques for providing useful text alternatives" at http://dev.w3.org/html5/alt-techniques.

Image Color Contrast

In addition to providing meaningful and well-managed descriptions, ensuring that your images—particularly those that are images of text —have sufficient color contrast is very important. There are great tools available that will help you to do that, such as the WAT-C Colour Contrast Analyser. You can get it at www.paciellogroup.com/resources/contrast-analyser.html.

HTML5 and Accessible <video> and <audio>

One of the biggest advances in HTML5 is the ability to now play both audio and video within the browser without the need for any third-party plugins such as Flash, QuickTime, and so on. HTML5 video is a very hot topic. What impact will this have on you as a designer, and what will it mean for the user experience?

HTML5 <video>, <audio>, and You

As a designer, the new HTML5 <video> element has a lot of advantages over how we used to do video back in the day. No more fiddly code and worrying about whether to use <embed> or <object> and, I hope, a more cohesive experience as a designer. Having said that, in the technology domain "progress" often means you replace once set of fiddly with a whole new set of fiddly. Unfortunately, although HTML5 <video> is really great and offers a rich and accessible (when done right) user experience, it's still fiddly.

You still have to deal with the wide range of codecs supported by different browsers, for a start. There hasn't been a consensus on what the officially supported HTML5 codec is, so you are left with several to choose from, and you'll have to do some feature detection and clever coding to ensure that you're serving the right content to the right browser. It would be great if there were only one or two, but all browsers are jockeying for position, and each manufacturer supports (or doesn't support) its own various, preferred formats in an effort to achieve the global dominance that they crave.

■ **Note** The whole "Apple doesn't support Flash" stance was/is a format war.

HTML5 <video> and Your Users

HTML5 video has the ability to create nice accessible players. This is great news. You can use the native controls or script your own. I will show you shortly how to build your own accessible <video> player.

You can also, with a little preparation and legwork, create your own audio descriptions, captions, and subtitles for your movies. We'll also look at how to do that.

What's Wrong With Flash?

Nothing is really wrong with Flash. From an accessibility perspective, it has a lot going for it, including a rich API and the ability to semantically describe most objects easily within the authoring environment. The more database-driven platform, Flex, has the ability to create some fine accessible rich Internet applications that can be used by people with vision impairments, screen-reader users, and so on. However, many developers simply don't make their Flash content accessible. The Flex application space is a little different, with many Flex components having a degree of accessibility out of the box.

The plugin is a third-party solution. It's not native to the browser, and it's proprietary. However, it doesn't look like it's going away. HTML5 isn't the only technology moving into the gaming space; Adobe has such plans for Flash via the Unreal Engine (UE3). Now you can have rich 3D gaming in the Flash environment. So the focus certainly will shift from a platform for video to a platform for rich, immersive gaming.

Accessibility Problems in Flash

With a little effort on the part of developers, a lot of Flash—in particular, Flex content—can be quite accessible if you are using a newer screen reader. However, there are some practical problems with Flash (that might be a result of it not being a "native to the browser" technology) from an accessibility perspective. Most notably is the issue of not being able to easily tab into Flash video content by using the keyboard, and also the rather perverse problem of then not being able to tab out (even if you did manage to get in). Ironically, this wasn't an issue in Internet Explorer, but it does affect most other browsers. The workaround is fiddly, because you have to bump the user back out using scripting.

Building an Accessible Player

Building an accessible <audio> or <video> player in HTML5 is a mixed bag. There are some aspects of building them that are really easy, and then others that might require a pretty good knowledge of scripting and some CSS. (The level of scripting that's needed might put some people off, but I say hang in there.) It's a pity in some ways that it is still a little tricky.

However, in many ways it isn't as daunting as it sounds. How you approach it, what you want it to do, and so on are important factors to consider and will determine the amount of effort you need to put into it to get a workable result.

First Things First: What's New in Embedded Content?

When you want to embed video in your HTML5 pages, you add the <video> element. "Is that all?" I hear you cry. "Yup," is the reply.

The simple code shown in Listing 6-6 invokes the <video> element in the browser. Figures 6-14, 6-15, and 6-16 show the results.

Listing 6-6. *Invoking the <video> Element*

```
<!DOCTYPE HTML>
<html>
<head>
<meta Charset="UTF-8">
<title>Sample native browser controls</title>
</head>
<body>
<video controls>
</video>
</body>
</html>
```

Figure 6-14. *Firefox native video controls*

Figure 6-15. *Opera native video controls*

Figure 6-16. *Safari native video controls*

The <video> element has a few attributes you can access via the Media Elements API (coming up), but that's pretty much it.

<video> Fallback Content

Any content you include inside the <video> element is considered *fallback content*. This is content that is to be seen by user agents that don't support video. You should think carefully about what you include in there so that it's at least useful and not rude (in the sense of "Your browser doesn't support this," or similarly unhelpful messages). The fallback content can be some text and a link to an alternate accessible version, or even a list of links to different file formats. It is always good to give the user a choice, but don't overwhelm them with too much information.

▓ **Note** What we are covering here about fallback content equally applies in principle to the <audio> element contents. Check out http://camendesign.com/code/video_for_everybody for a way to use Flash video as fallback content.

The Media Elements API

So you want to have some video in your HTML5 page—you do that by adding the <video> element to the page. The common attributes of the <video> element are src, preload, autoplay, mediagroup, loop, muted, and controls, crossorigin, and poster. All of these attributes pretty much do what you would expect them to. Here are the specifics:

- **src attribute:** The src attribute is the source of the video or audio file. These days, media can be spread far and wide on many different servers, using the crossorigin content attribute. This attribute relates to resource sharing among different servers, and it's a way to reduce security concerns and issues with dispersed content.

- **preload attribute:** The preload attribute has various keywords or states associated with it. These are none, metadata, and auto. The preload attribute determines how a browser will load (or not) the source material in the background on a page load.

- **poster attribute:** The poster attribute is really useful to display a suitable image while awaiting some input from the user so that the user isn't looking at a blank screen, before she hits play. It literally is a kind of poster of what is to come.

- **mediagroup attribute:** The mediagroup attribute is used to group several audio or video elements or tracks together, which is useful for a playlist of video and audio.

- `controls` **attribute:** This is a Boolean. It tells the browser to display the native controls that is needed to control the media, such as play, stop, and so on. Without this attribute, you must provide your own scripted controls.

- `autoplay`, `loop,` and `muted` **attributes:** They do exactly what they say on the tin.

■ **Note** The controls that the browser provides are often not accessible out of the box, apart from when you use the Opera browser. Opera, out of the box, provides a level of keyboard accessibility that is excellent, so you can play, pause, and vary the volume of the video or audio. Unfortunately, by most other standards, Opera is not a very screen-reader-friendly browser, but in terms of native keyboard access for HTML5 `<video>` and `<audio>` it should take a bow.

Getting Started with <video>

Getting started with the `<video>` element is easy, and you can quickly start to see some results in your browser and define some basic properties using the Media Elements API attributes that I just introduced. Initial steps might resemble Listing 6-7.

Listing 6-7. Using <video>

```
<video width="700" height="500" preload controls poster="../images/mayer_cc_poster.jpg">
<source src="http://mirrors.creativecommons.org/movingimages/webm/MayerandBettle_480p.webm"
type="video/webm" />
<source src="http://blip.tv/file/get/Commonscreative-MayerAndBettle980.ogv" type="video/ogg"
/>
<source src="http://blip.tv/file/get/Commonscreative-MayerAndBettle715.mov"
type="video/quicktime" />
// Fallback content here

<h1>Can't access this video content?</h1><p>Please <a
href='http://creativecommons.org/videos/mayer-and-bettle'>visit the Creative Commons website
for a format that suits you</a>, or if you are happy with Flash content, <a
href="http://blip.tv/play/gpxS60o5g9ky" type="application/x-shockwave-flash">visit the Flash
version of the Mayer and Bettle creative Commons video</a>
</p>
</video>
```

You can see from the code in Listing 6-7 that you have called on three of the API attributes to perform some magic in the browser:

- `preload`, which preloads the content but does not play it.

- `controls`, which asks the browser to display the native browser controls.

- `poster`, which shows an image until the video is played. This is useful because, depending on your browser, you might have a blank or transparent space and you might not even see the video player controls clearly.

We also defined the dimensions of the video and asked the browser to display the native browser controls.

The sample has four different sources or types of video, depending on what browser is being used to access the content. Serving the right codec to each browser can be rather fiddly, and you need to have some video-conversion tools on hand to be able to produce the versions you need. It's relatively trivial to do this, but it can be time consuming. You arrange the different video formats and their source URL, one after the other; when the browser hits something it understands, it preloads it and plays it. If the browser doesn't understand any of the formats you provide, this triggers the display of the fallback content that is embedded between the `<video>` and `</video>` elements.

Some Encoding Tools

Here is a list of some tools you might find useful to encode your audio/video media:

- **Audacity:** An excellent, free, open-source audio recorder. Get it at `www.audacity.sourceforge.net`.

- **Firefogg:** A video and audio encoding application for Firefox. Get it at `www.firefogg.org`.

- **FFmpeg2theora:** A convertor for OggTheora files, which is available at `http://v2v.cc/~j/ffmpeg2theora/`.

- **HandBrake**: An open-source video transcoder. Get it at `www.handbrake.fr`.

Are You My Type?

The MIME type tells the browser what kind of media a URL refers to. Adding the correct MIME type to the end of the source attribute is very important. (You can see the MIME types in Listing 6-7.) Some browsers are rather strict about playing only media that is served with it, such as (Firefox and Opera).

Some of the most-used audio file formats and their corresponding MIME types are the following:

- **MP3:** audio/mpeg

- **OGG:** audio/ogg video/ogg

- **MP4:** audio/mp4 video/mp4

- **WebM:** audio/webm video/webm

- **WAV:** audio/wav

- **AAC:** audio/3gpp, audio/3gpp2, audio/mp4, audio/MP4A-LATM, audio/mpeg4-generic

Table 6-1 is an overview of the audio formats that are supported by the major browsers.

Table 6-1. *Overview of Browser and Audio Codec Support*

Browser Name/Number	MP3	OGG	WAV	AAC
IE 9	X		X	
Firefox 4 +		X	X	
Opera 10 +	X	X		
Safari 5 +	X			X
Chrome 6 +	X	X	X	X

▓ **Note** While the codec represents the compression/decompression algorithm used to deliver media, it also represents the container for the codec.

Table 6-2 covers the video codecs, and which browsers support each.

Table 6-2. *Browser and <video> Codec Support*

Browser Name/Number	Ogg Theora	MP4 (H.264)	VP8 (WebM)
IE 9		X	
Firefox 8	X		X
Chrome 15	X	X	X
Safari 5		X	
Opera 11.5	X		X

Certain containers can take more than one file format. (Remember, the codec is both the algorithm and the *wrapper*, or container that holds it.) You can get a good overview of containers and comparisons of them at http://en.wikipedia.org/wiki/Comparison_of_container_formats.

■ **Tip** For your content to hit the most browsers with the minimum number of format creation and decoding on your part, you should serve your audio in at least two formats, such as MP4 and Ogg, and serve your video in at least the three most commonly-used formats: MP4, WebM, and Ogg.

Making Your Controls Accessible

■ **Note** Some special thanks are due to my friend Gez Lemon, and to Mark Boas and Sylvia Pfeiffer for their generous help, comments, and advice when I was putting together this section.

In some ways, you have looked at the easy bit. What you will look at next is adding your own controls and making them both keyboard accessible and accessible to screen-reader users. We'll also look at how to make jump forward and jump back features, as well as a control to mute the audio. Unfortunately, out of the box, there isn't currently a way to easily do this, so you have to script and create your own.

■ **Note** The awkward bit is really the scripting, but if you keep it simple you can achieve a lot and not lose your mind in the process. Well, that might not entirely be true. Also, you can just use native HTML input controls such as buttons, and then add the scripts. This gives you a lot more accessibility out of the box, but you are a little limited in your styling options. With hand-rolled controls, you have a lot more scope to style them as you want.

There are lots of ways you can approach the development of controls, so we will look at a couple. Obviously, it is very important that you ensure that your player is accessible, and all of the following is presented with an eye on accessibility. Here, I created my own graphics to represent the controls and then applied the necessary JavaScript. You can also use CSS to create and style the buttons. Either way, the JavaScript will be very similar.

Figure 6-17 is a screen shot of the controls I created in Photoshop that I'll use to control my video. They are Play, Stop, Mute, and Jump forward/Jump back, respectively.

Figure 6-17. A group of hand-rolled controls for the video player

To get started, I wrapped each of the controls in a <div> element and then named it appropriately. Within each of the <div> elements, there was an image element and a suitable @alt text value to describe the control. For example, here are the button controls:

```
<div id="play">
<a href="#" onclick="return false();">
<img src="player/play_button.png" alt="Play Button" /></a>
</div>
```

In some browsers, these controls are all accessible from the keyboard, and when the screen reader gives focus to the preceding control, "Play Button" is announced. You will have to test what works and what doesn't, however.

▪ **Note** In this first example, I used a # to make the controls focusable via the keyboard. Use of # was traditionally to give JavaScript a focus, but as DOM scripting has progressed and toolkits like jQuery gain ground, it's not always necessary. If you do use this method, be sure to add the "return false();" statement after it because this stops the "#" URL from firing.

Listing 6-8 shows the code for all of the controls. Just to get started, you will deal with the Play, Stop, and Mute Audio buttons.

Listing 6-8. Implementing Video Controls

```
<div id="player_controls">
<div id="play">
<a href="#" onclick="return false();">
<img src="player/play_button.png" alt="Play Button" /></a>
</div>

<div id="stop">
<a href="#" onclick="return false();">
<img src="player/stop_button.png" alt="Stop Button" /></a>
</div>

<div id="mute">
<a href="#" onclick="return false();">
<img src="player/mute_button.png" alt="Mute/Unmute button" /></a>
</div>
```

The JavaScript you needed to make the controls focusable and to attach the methods such as Play, Stop, and Mute/Unmute is pretty straightforward. I left out the Forward and Backward controls just for the moment; we'll look at those later. Study Listing 6-9 and see if you can make sense of it.

Listing 6-9. JavaScript for Video Control Focus

```
<script type="text/javascript">

window.onload=function(){

var video = document.getElementById('access_video');
var play = document.getElementById('play');
```

```
var stop = document.getElementById('stop');
var mute = document.getElementById('mute');

// Script needed to attach the onclick events with the functional buttons
// **Remember** even though the event is called onclick it still works from //
// the keyboard

play.onclick = playVideo;
stop.onclick = stopVideo;
mute.onclick = muteVideo;

// function to play, pause, mute etc

function playVideo() {
video.play();
}
function stopVideo() {
video.pause();
}

// This function allows the button to be used as control to
// toggle the audio on or off

    function muteVideo(objEvent) {
       if (objEvent.type == keydown')
       {
               var iKeyCode = objEvent.keyCode;
               if (iKeyCode != 13 && iKeyCode !=32) {
                       return true;
               }
       }
       video.muted = !video.muted;
}
```

───

▓ **Note** The use of the iKeyCodes for ensuring the muteVideo function is triggered by the Enter key or spacebar only.

───

There are also some simple CSS declarations involved to put the whole thing together:

```
<style>
#player_controls {
color:#999;
margin: 10px;
border:10px;
float:left;
}
</style>
```

Accessible HTML5 Video Player Version 1

Listing 6-10 gives the code in toto, including the code needed for the Jump Forward and Jump Back buttons.

Listing 6-10. Accessible Player V.1

```
<!DOCTYPE HTML>
<html>
<head>
<meta Charset="UTF-8">
<title>Working HTML 5 video player</title>
<script type="text/javascript">
window.onload=function() {

 var video = document.getElementById('access_video');
var play = document.getElementById('play');
var stop = document.getElementById('stop');
var mute = document.getElementById('mute');
var forward = document.getElementById('forward');
var back = document.getElementById('back');

// Script needed to attach the onclick events with the functional buttons.
  // **Remember** even though the event is called onclick it still works from the
  // keyboard.

    play.onclick = playVideo;
    stop.onclick = stopVideo;
    mute.onclick = muteVideo;
    forward.onclick = jumpForward;
    back.onclick = jumpBack;

    // Duplicate onkeydown events for keyboard a11y

    play.onkeydown = playVideo;
    stop.onkeydown = stopVideo;
    mute.onkeydown = muteVideo;
    forward.onkeydown = jumpForward;
    back.onkeydown = jumpBack;

// New function for play

    function playVideo(objEvent) {
     if (objEvent.type == keydown')
     {
            var iKeyCode = objEvent.keyCode;
            if (iKeyCode != 13 && iKeyCode !=32) {
                   return true;
            }
     }
     video.play();
}
```

207

```
// New function for pause

      function stopVideo(objEvent) {
      if (objEvent.type == keydown')
      {
              var iKeyCode = objEvent.keyCode;
              if (iKeyCode != 13 && iKeyCode !=32) {
                      return true;
              }
      }
      video.pause();
}

    // This function allows the button to be used as a control to
    // toggle the audio on or off.

      function muteVideo(objEvent) {
      if (objEvent.type == keydown')
      {
              var iKeyCode = objEvent.keyCode;
              if (iKeyCode != 13 && iKeyCode !=32) {
                      return true;
              }
      }
      video.muted = !video.muted;
}

// Jump forward, Jump Back

    forward.onclick = jumpForward;
    function jumpForward(objEvent) {
       if (objEvent.type == keydown')
       {
              var iKeyCode = objEvent.keyCode;
              if (iKeyCode != 13 && iKeyCode !=32) {
                      return true;
              }
       }
    video.currentTime = video.currentTime + 15;
    video.play();
    return false;
    }

    back.onclick = jumpBack;
    function jumpBack(objEvent) {
       if (objEvent.type == keydown')
       {
              var iKeyCode = objEvent.keyCode;
              if (iKeyCode != 13 && iKeyCode !=32) {
                      return true;
              }
```

```
        }
    video.currentTime = video.currentTime 15;
    video.play();
    return false;
    }

};

</script>


<style>
#access_video {
color:#999;
margin: 30px;
border:30px;
}
#player_controls {
color:#999;
margin: 10px;
border:10px;
float:left;
}
</style>

</head>
<body>
<video id="access_video" width="500" height="300" preload="none"
poster="../images/mayer_cc_poster.jpg">
<source src="http://mirrors.creativecommons.org/movingimages/webm/MayerandBettle_480p.webm"
type="video/webm" />
<source src="http://blip.tv/file/get/Commonscreative-MayerAndBettle980.ogv" type="video/ogg"
/>
<source src="http://blip.tv/file/get/Commonscreative-MayerAndBettle715.mov"
type="video/quicktime" />
<h1>Oops cannot access this video content? Never fear!</h1>
<p>Please <a href="http://creativecommons.org/videos/mayer-and-bettle">visit the Creative
Commons website for a format that suits you</a>
</p>
</video>


<div id="player_controls">
<div id="play">
<a href="#" onclick="return false();">
<img src="player/play_button.png" alt="Play" /></a>
</div>
<div id="stop">
<a href="#" onclick="return false();">
<img src="player/stop_button.png" alt="Stop" /></a>
</div>
<div id="mute">
```

```
<a href="#" onclick="return false();">
<img src="player/mute_button.png" alt="Mute/Unmute" /></a>
</div>
<div id="forward">
<a href="#" onclick="return false();">
<img src="player/forward_button.png" alt="Jump Forward" />
</a>
</div>
<div id="back" role="button" tabindex="0">
<a href="#" onclick="return false();">
<img src="player/back_button.png" alt="Jump Back" /></a>
</div>
</div>
</body>
</html>
```

Figure 6-18 shows a screen shot of your first version of the accessible player.

Figure 6-18. The accessible video player

OK, it's not very exciting, but it works. There are things you can do to improve things on all fronts, however.

Accessible HTML5 Video Player Version 2

There are some issues with the code in the last example. First, what happens if JavaScript is off or unavailable; is using the # a good idea? Well, in the case of explicit controls, the point is a little moot. This is because even if you want to create an unobtrusive control, doing so begs the question of what you can point to as an alternative, because the purpose of the control is to play some video. In the preceding example, there is some good provision for fallback content. If HTML5 isn't supported, the user can point his browser at the site and download content there.

There are some things you can do to improve the player. First, you can remove the empty URLs with "#", changing them to <divs>, making them focusable from the keyboard, and adding some ARIA role attributes.

▓ **Note** For now the JavaScript stays the same. You will look at adding the script for the Forward and Backward functions as well as some other controls later.

So let's look at the new code:

```
<div id="play" tabindex="0">
<img src="player/play_button.png" alt="Play Button" role="button" />
</div>
```

The main changes here are the addition of the ARIA role="button" attribute, which tells screen readers and browsers what the purpose of the <div> is. You have also made the <div> accessible from the keyboard by adding the tabindex="0" value. So that's a win on two fronts!

Both attributes should be applied to all controls. I also added the following code to make sure that the controls will highlight on focus from the keyboard:

```
*[tabindex]:focus {
outline:none;
border:
solid yellow 2px;
}
```

▓ **Note** Regarding using the URL # as a way of focusing on the control or a <div> with tabindex="0", you will need to test both methods in as many different browsers as possible. Some developers like the # methods and others like the <div> with the tabindex, although the latter is now pretty well supported.

The JavaScript code for this example (which actually uses both a # and the tabindexed <div>) is pretty simple, but then it all seems simple when it finally works!

See if you can figure out what's going on in Listing 6-11.

Listing 6-11. Code to Add the Play, Stop, Mute, Forward, and Back Functions

```
window.onload=function(){


    var video = document.getElementById('access_video');
    var play = document.getElementById('play');
    var stop = document.getElementById('stop');
    var mute = document.getElementById('mute');
var forward = document.getElementById('forward');
var back = document.getElementById('back');



    // Script needed to attach the onclick events with the functional buttons.
```

```
// **Remember** even though the event is called onclick it still works from the
// keyboard.

play.onclick = playVideo;
stop.onclick = stopVideo;
mute.onclick = muteVideo;
forward.onclick = jumpForward;
back.onclick = jumpBack;

// Duplicate onkeydown events for keyboard a11y

play.onkeydown = playVideo;
stop.onkeydown = stopVideo;
mute.onkeydown = muteVideo;
forward.onkeydown = jumpForward;
back.onkeydown = jumpBack;


// New function for play

  function playVideo(objEvent) {
   if (objEvent.type == keydown')
   {
          var iKeyCode = objEvent.keyCode;
          if (iKeyCode != 13 && iKeyCode !=32) {
                 return true;
          }
   }
   video.play();
}

// New function for pause

    function stopVideo(objEvent) {
   if (objEvent.type == keydown')
   {
          var iKeyCode = objEvent.keyCode;
          if (iKeyCode != 13 && iKeyCode !=32) {
                 return true;
          }
   }
   video.pause();
}

// This function allows the button to be used as a control to
// toggle the audio on or off.

    function muteVideo(objEvent) {
   if (objEvent.type == keydown')
   {
          var iKeyCode = objEvent.keyCode;
          if (iKeyCode != 13 && iKeyCode !=32) {
```

```
                          return true;
                  }
        }
      video.muted = !video.muted;
}

    // Jump forward, Jump Back

    forward.onclick = jumpForward;
    function jumpForward(objEvent) {
        if (objEvent.type == keydown')
      {
              var iKeyCode = objEvent.keyCode;
              if (iKeyCode != 13 && iKeyCode !=32) {
                      return true;
              }
        }
    video.currentTime = video.currentTime + 15;
    video.play();
    return false;
    }

    back.onclick = jumpBack;
    function jumpBack(objEvent) {
        if (objEvent.type == keydown')
      {
              var iKeyCode = objEvent.keyCode;
              if (iKeyCode != 13 && iKeyCode !=32) {
                      return true;
              }
        }
    video.currentTime = video.currentTime 15;
    video.play();
    return false;
    }


};


</script>
```

The code for the controls themselves is shown in Listing 6-12.

Listing 6-12. Attaching Functions to the Customized Controls Using tabindex="0" to Focus on a <div>
Instead of Using #

```
<div id="player_controls">

<div id="play" tabindex="0"><img src="player/play_button.png" role="button" title="Press to
activate" alt="Play" />
</div>
```

```
<div id="stop" tabindex="0"><img src="player/stop_button.png" role="button" title="Press to
activate" alt="Stop" />
</div>

<div id="mute" tabindex="0"><img src="player/mute_button.png" role="button" title="Press to
activate" alt="Mute/Unmute" />
</div>

<div id="forward" tabindex="0"><img src="player/forward_button.png" role="button" title="Press
to activate" alt="Jump Forward" />

</div>

<div id="back" tabindex="0"><img src="player/back_button.png" role="button" alt="Jump Back" />

</div>
```

You can see a working version of the player at
http://techrecord.net/html5/HTML5_video_player_no_captions_final.html.
Next, we'll look at how to add captions to the video.

■ **Note** If all that is too much, there are out-of-the-box video players you can use, such as jPlayer and jQuery UI
for video. You can access them at http://jplayer.org and https://github.com/azatoth/jquery-video,
respectively.

Audio Description and Captioning with the <track> Element

If you want to do various kinds of audio descriptions or captioning of your video files, HTML5 has a new
element called the <track> element. Table 6-3 outlines what you can do with the new element.

Table 6-3. Media Elements Overview[1]

Keyword	State	Brief Description
subtitles	Subtitles	Transcription or translation of the dialog, suitable for when the sound is available but not understood (for example, because the user does not understand the language of the media resource's audio track). Overlaid on the video.
captions	Captions	Transcription or translation of the dialog, sound effects,

---

[1] http://dev.w3.org/html5/spec-author-view/the-track-element.html

		relevant musical cues, and other relevant audio information, suitable for when sound is unavailable or not clearly audible (for example, because it is muted, because it is drowned-out by ambient noise, or because the user is deaf). Overlaid on the video; labeled as appropriate for the hard-of-hearing.
descriptions	Descriptions	Textual descriptions of the video component of the media resource, intended for audio synthesis when the visual component is obscured, unavailable, or not usable (for example, because the user is interacting with the application without a screen while driving or because the user is blind). Synthesized as audio.
chapters	Chapters	Chapter titles, intended to be used for navigating the media resource. Displayed as an interactive (potentially nested) list in the user agent's interface.
metadata	Metadata	Tracks intended for use from script. Not displayed by the user agent.

To use the Captions, Subtitle, or Chapter info in your video content, you add them via the kind attribute. The src attribute points to where the text is stored, the srclang attribute defines what language it is in, and the label attribute gives a title. Listing 6-13 details the correct usage.

Listing 6-13. Adding Subtitles and Captions to the <track> Element

```
<video src="brave.webm">
 <track kind="subtitles src=brave.en.vtt" srclang="en" label="English">
 <track kind="captions src=brave.en.hoh.vtt" srclang="en"label="English for the Hard of
Hearing">
 <track kind="subtitles src=brave.fr.vtt" srclang="fr"lang="fr" label="Français">
 <track kind="subtitles src=brave.de.vtt"srclang="de" lang="de" label="Deutsch">
</video>²
```

In principle, adding audio descriptions and/or captions is pretty straightforward, right? Well, it would be if this stuff was supported in your favourite browser, and it currently isn't (at the time of this writing), but that will change. To get this to work, I used the open-source JavaScript library Captionator and found that it worked really well.

---

[2] From http://dev.w3.org/html5/spec-author-view/the-track-element.html

> ▓ **Note** You can download the JavaScript library and get more information about Captionator at https://github.com/cgiffard/Captionator.

Adding it to your video is as simple as adding the following script to your page:

```
<script type="text/javascript" src="js/captionator.js"></script>
<script type="text/javascript">
    window.addEventListener("load",function(eventData) {
        captionator.captionify();
    });
</script>
```

Then enable it by adding the following:

```
captionator.captionify(document.getElementByID("video"));
```

That's it. I could go on about creating the captions themselves using Text Wrangler to write a .vtt file. The .vtt file format is easy to use—just open your favourite editor, and save the file that you create with the extension *.vtt*.

Cue Settings

There are a lot of different cue settings for you to use. They are detailed in Table 6-4.

Table 6-4. *Cue Settings for <track> Element*[3]

Vertical text	D:vertical (vertical growing left) D:vertical-lr (vertical growing right)
Line position	A specific position relative to the video frame:•L:[a number]%, where [a number] is a positive integer. A line number:•L:[a number], where [a number] is a positive or negative integer.
Text position	T:[a number]%, where [a number] is a positive integer.
Text size	S:[a number]%, where [a number] is a positive integer.
Text alignment	A:start or A:middle or A:end

---

[3] From www.delphiki.com/webvtt/#cue-settings

It is quite easy to get started. Figure 6-19 shows my caption file for my video. You define the start and end time for a caption or subtitle to appear, and then use the cue settings to tell the browser the size, alignment, and so on. Have a look at the following screen shot from my .vtt file that I used to caption a video. And do experiment. It's strangely compelling work, and quite time consuming but also fun.

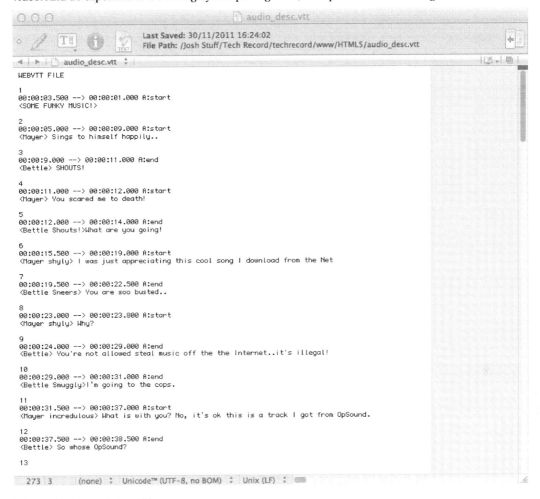

Figure 6-19. Sample VTT file

▓ **Note** For more information on VTT and a nice article, have a look at Ian Devlin's useful overview at

http://www.iandevlin.com/blog/2011/05/html5/webvtt-and-video-subtitles.

You can see a screen shot of the video player with captioned video in Figure 6-20, and go online to try it out at http://techrecord.net/html5/HTML5_video_player_captions_final.html.

Figure 6-20. *Screen shot of captioned video in accessible player*

■ **Note** For more information on HTML5 video with a good accessibility angle, see the new book by Silvia Pfeiffer, *The Definitive Guide to HTML5 Video* (Apress, 2010).

Creating an <audio> Player

This is just a quick note to say that creating an audio player is a little easier, and the things you have learned about making the <video> player (in terms of creating your own controls and so on) apply also to an audio player.

<canvas> Accessibility

The 2D drawing API that renders dynamic bitmap graphics on the fly can be used to create some very nice visual animations (and more) right in the browser without the need for any plugins. There are examples of many groovy test cases and web sites that use <canvas> in whole or in part very successfully. However, from an accessibility perspective (to make life easier for everyone), don't use <canvas> for anything more than pretty pictures. At the time of this writing, it cannot be considered accessible. There is plenty of work going on behind the scenes in the Worldwide Web Consortium (W3C) and efforts to make it so. However, from what I can see, if there is another way of developing content you can use that is more suitable, you should use it instead. In fact, the specification recommends this, as follows:

"Authors should not use the canvas element in a document when a more suitable element is available. For example, it is inappropriate to use a canvas element to render a page heading: if the desired presentation of the heading is graphically intense, it should be marked up using appropriate elements (typically h1) and then styled using CSS and supporting technologies such as XBL."

"When authors use the canvas element, they must also provide content that, when presented to the user, conveys essentially the same function or purpose as the bitmap canvas. This content might be placed as content of the canvas element. The contents of the canvas element, if any, are the element's fallback content." [4]

There have been all sorts of things developed using `<canvas>` that really shouldn't have been. The text editor Bespin comes to mind as a tool that looks good but isn't and, indeed, might never be accessible.

▒ **Note** You can check out Bespin at `http://benzilla.galbraiths.org/2009/02/17/bespin-and-canvas`. In many ways, it is impressive, but I think it uses the wrong tool as its foundation.

As an aside, some other uses for `<canvas>` that I think are really clever (leaving aside accessibility concerns) are these:

- **SoundManager 2 / 360° Player Demo:** Available at `www.schillmania.com/projects/soundmanager2/demo/360-player/`. This is great, and these nice people also give you a look at the source code.

- **9elements:** Available at `http://9elements.com/io/projects/html5/canvas/`. It has nice mouse interactions and groovy tune interactions!

- **Cufón:** A font generator and a possible sIFR replacement. Available at `http://cufon.shoqolate.com/generate/`. Roger Johannes writes about Cufón and screen readers at `www.456bereastreet.com/archive/200905/cufon_and_screen_readers/`.

- There is a good list of the games, widgets, and so on that have been built using `<canvas>` that's available from `www.w3.org/html/wg/wiki/AddedElementCanvas`. Here you will also find lots of links to discussions on `<canvas>` and the challenges faced when trying to make this drawing API more accessible.

Having said that, `<canvas>` is in its infancy and has big challenges ahead from an accessibility perspective. It has no DOM, for example, so how is a screen reader to generate an overview of the document? If you keep your use of `<canvas>` to eye candy, you'll be fine. HTML5 has many great tools to build stuff that is accessible and provides a rich user experience for many user groups with diverse abilities. So when you need a spoon, use a spoon. Although some would say, "There is no spoon."

---

[4] `www.w3.org/TR/html5/the-canvas-element.html#the-canvas-element`

■ **Note** If you want a nice reference for creating your own `<canvas>` eye candy, I recommend Nihilogics HTML5 `<canvas>` cheat sheet, which is available at
`www.nihilogic.dk/labs/canvas_sheet/HTML5_Canvas_Cheat_Sheet.pdf`.

Conclusion

In this chapter, we looked at many of the new ways you can make HTML5 rich media more accessible. There are many best practices based on how you used to do things with HTML 4 that you can still apply, but there are also some new tricks that I hope this chapter has turned you on to. In the next chapter, we'll look at how to approach making data tables accessible using HTML5.

CHAPTER 7

HTML5 and Accessible Data Tables

In this chapter, you'll learn all you need to know about creating both simple and more complex accessible data tables using HTML5.

Data tables are commonly used as ways of visually presenting tabular data. This data can be about anything of interest to the author. The table layout allows authors to present information so that web site users can easily associate data in any given cell with various categories or relationships, which are usually defined at the start of every column or row.

This is usually done in a layout that is common to many of us, the individual data cells are related to different columns and rows. The user of the web site can look at the individual data cells and quickly scan to see what columns and rows they relate to. They can then quickly grasp what the data in each cell means.

The Trouble with Tables

For a sighted person, figuring out these relationships is straightforward and often happens very quickly. If a table is well designed and therefore makes understanding these relationships easier in the first place, most sighted users have no problems figuring them out. They start with focusing on what the table data is—in other words, what topic it relates to—and then determining what the information contained within the table actually means.

For a nonsighted person to finish both of these steps successfully takes more work on the part of the developer. There are several reasons for this, but primarily it's because when a table is shown in a browser, a sighted user often just quickly *gets* these relationships. A nonsighted user will be accessing the data in a table in a very different way—in a linear fashion, one item after another.

Before a nonsighted person even starts to investigate or *interrogate* (I love using this term as it relates to data tables and accessibility) the data table, she first needs a way to easily understand what the purpose of the table is. This boils down to the user asking, "What is this table for?", quickly followed by "What does it mean?"

Screen Readers and Data Tables

Creating a table that a sighted person can easily understand is rather easy (as long as the initial data you are trying to represent is straightforward). You create some headings for each column, perhaps add boldface styling to them, and then add rows, and perhaps add boldface styling to the first item in each row. Pretty simple. If this was a paper document, that would be fine.

However, to make a data table accessible in HTML5 you must think of a way to define the relationships between the data cells and their corresponding columns and rows *programmatically*. Doing so helps user agents like assistive technologies (AT) understand the relationships between the data cells and their corresponding columns and rows, and therefore it enable AT to inform the nonsighted user in a way the user can understand.

For users of screen readers, the HTML5 language has ways of defining these relationships and therefore making data tables easy first to understand second to navigate, and then, if the table isn't relevant to the user's needs, to bypass.

▪ **Note** A screen reader is a *linear output* device. This means it outputs information to the user one piece at a time. For a nonsighted user to have a gestalt view of HTML content, you need to use appropriate code to help that person. This is often done by writing text overviews of the content and programmatically associating it with the table so that it will be announced when a table has focus. I'll say more on how to do this later in the chapter.

Common Patterns for Data Tables

Most data tables you are likely to author will be simple and follow a well-worn path in terms of their form. I can hear you cry in outrage, "Are you suggesting I won't be creating complex, multicolumn irregular data tables?" Yes, I am. The tables you create might have more or less columns or rows, but they will be mostly a basic grid with headers at the top of your columns and corresponding rows.

They might take the form shown in Table 7-1.

Table 7-1. General Form of Most Data Tables

<Some Heading #1>	<Some Heading #2>	<Some Heading #3>
Data of some sort relating to Heading #1	Data of some sort relating to Heading #2	Data of some sort relating to Heading #3
Data of some sort relating to Heading #1	Data of some sort relating to Heading #2	Data of some sort relating to Heading #3

The table might be square or rectangular, and although it will not always be the case, by and large your tables will take the form shown in Table 7-1. So the techniques we'll look at to make the table accessible will apply equally to the simple table just shown and to one with a large number of columns and rows. In this case, size doesn't matter.

You need to be able to do two things. First, for sighted visual users, you need to create the table so that they can look at the information at the top of the table (the header info) and then, more often than not, at the first column in each row. Then they can look across the table to make the necessary associations for each data cell. By doing this, they can see what the data in each cell relates to.

Second, for the tables to be accessible to a screen-reader user, you need to use HTML5 to associate the data in each cell with its corresponding column header and row so that the screen reader itself can announce to the user which header relates to each data cell.

Using HTML5 to mark up your data cells correctly accomplishes two practical functions. First, it informs the screen-reader user of the column and row combination each cell relates to when it has focus; second, it allows the user to understand where he is within the table as he navigates through it.

Screen-reader users can navigate between data cells easily using cursor keys. What I show you in the remainder of this chapter will help you make your tables really accessible in simple steps.

TMI?

Before we look at how to approach making your data tables accessible, I suggest that you do the following:

1. Try to make the data table as simple as possible in the first place. If the table is complex and busy, the code will be too. Although it is possible to create complex tables that are accessible, it will help if you can simplify the architecture of the table in the first place.

2. Try not to span multiple cells/rows. Again, a more simple, well-presented table is often much easier to make accessible.

3. Finally, consider the following question: Can the information you are trying to present be included in the body text of your site? In other words, do you really need a table at all?

How to Create Accessible Tables

Figure 7-1, which you'll see later in the chapter, shows a table that expands on the "animal sanctuary" theme presented in some of the other examples in this book. The table outlines the upcoming workshops that are taking place in our animal sanctuary.

Ok, first things first. As mentioned earlier, a sighted person can look at the table and tell what it is pretty much from the get-go. How can you do this for a nonsighted person? The answer is, by adding a `<caption>` element.

The `<caption>` element is a way of giving both the sighted user and the screen-reader user a way of understanding the purpose of the table. The HTML5 specification describes the `<caption>` element as providing a title for the table. This isn't a bad way of thinking of it. Adding the `<caption>` element is easy, and whatever text string you add to the `<caption>` element is *programmatically associated* with the table. As soon as the table receives focus from a screen, it will be announced to the user without any more interaction required. This is very useful and is the first important step in making your data table accessible. It's also good for sighted users as it is presented visually and can be styled using CSS.

Adding the `<caption>` element to a data table takes the following form:

```
<section>
<h1>Animal Sanctuary workshops</h1>
<table>
<caption>An overview of upcoming animal sanctuary workshops in 2012</caption>

[…]
</table>
```

Using the `<caption>` element or title for the table is useful for helping the screen reader understand what a table is. Adding `<caption>` in this way really comes into its own if you consider a webpage with five or six (or even more) data tables on it. A sighted person can quickly scan the page and figure out what all of these tables are. As mentioned previously, screen-reader users can use their AT to navigate a webpage by selecting various HTML elements—such as headings, and links. They can do the same thing using any `<table>` elements that are present on a page. For example, pressing the T key in JAWS causes the AT to bounce the user from the first table to the last one (and back again). If there is no suitable `<caption>` on each table, the screen reader just announces "Table," "Table," and lets the user know how many rows, columns, and so on the table has, but it won't be able to tell the user what the table is for. Adding `<caption>` fills in the gaps. A data table with a suitable `<caption>` announces the contents on focus. So if all tables on my suggested page with six tables have <caption> elements, the screen-reader user can easily find what she is looking for—because when each table is given focus, the contents of the <caption> element are announced. Neat!

■ **Tip** When a table is more complex, you can add a summary attribute (@summary) to the table element. This attribute is designed to provide an overview for a screen-reader user of more complex data tables, but it's now obsolete in HTML5, unfortunately. I still think @summary is very useful because it is announced to the screen-reader user as soon as he focuses on a table. I often use @summary in my projects to provide supplementary information if I think it can help the user understand the table or, in general, have a better user experience. This is slightly out of scope for what it is designed to do, but it works well in my experience. For many simple data tables, @summary isn't really required because a useful <caption> is enough. @summary is hidden from sighted users, but it will be picked up by the screen reader.

I think @summary should be retained and used, but the HTML5 working group made the decision to make it obsolete. Along with other friends and colleagues in the accessibility community, I repeatedly made the case to retain it—but to no avail. If you want to know the grizzly details, you can have a look at the logs in the working group's "Issue Tracker" at www.w3.org/html/wg/tracker/issues/32 or visit the W3C ESW wiki at www.w3.org/html/wg/wiki/SummaryForTABLE.

Doing these things covers informing the screen-reader user of what a table is about. What about navigating the table itself and understanding what data cell relates to what column and row?

Creating Programmatic Associations Between Data Cells, Table Headers, and Rows

There are a couple of common ways of marking up HTML5 tables to make them accessible and also more backward-compatible with older AT (for which there are many users!). The first method involves the use of header/ID combinations to identify the contents of each table cell. The second method uses header/scope combinations.

Accessible Tables Method 1: Use of Header/ID Combinations

The first method that we'll look at is a little more time consuming, but I consider it more bulletproof. We're going to create associations between the header and ID elements of the table's HTML. This is a way of associating the contents of a data cell with its appropriate header. Doing so causes the screen reader to announce what column the data cell is in *before* the contents of the cell are announced to the user.

To create header/ID associations, you first deal with the headers and then with the table body.

Start by giving each header a unique ID; it is perfectly fine to give a header the same ID as the contents. For my table about upcoming workshops in my animal sanctuary, my header IDs are as follows:

- Header #1 = "Course"

- Header #2 = "Start"

- Header #3 = "End"

- Header #4 = "Cost"

- Header #5 = "Extras"

In HTML code, the headings look like this:

```
<th id="Course">Course</th>
<th id="Start">Start Date</th>
<th id="End">End Date</th>
<th id="Cost">Cost</th>
```

<th id="Extras">Included Extras</th>It can just as easily be the following or something similar to the following:

```
<th id="header1">Course</th>
<th id="header2">Start Date</th>
<th id="header3">End Date</th>
<th id="header4">Cost</th>
<th id="header5">Included Extras</th>
```

If you have any naming convention you are happy with, you can certainly use it. The point is that the header IDs are *unique* because they are used to create a programmatic association with your table data (as you shall see). It seems more natural to me that for them to be related, but it doesn't really matter. Now that you have suitable header IDs, you can go ahead and map the cell contents of each row in the table body to an appropriate header, as shown in Listing 7-1.

Listing 7-1. Mapping the Cell Contents

```
<th id="Course">Course</th>
<th id="Start">Start Date</th>
<th id="End">End Date</th>
<th id="Cost">Cost</th>
<th id="Extras">Included Extras</th>
<tr>
<td headers="Course">How do you start an Animal Sanctuary</td>
<td headers="Start">June 10</td>
<td headers="End">June 16</td>
<td headers="Cost">650 Euros</td>
<td headers="Extras">includes lunches, one dinner and extensive materials.</td>
</tr>
<tr>
<td headers="Course">Working with Dogs: A beginners workshop</td>
<td headers="Start">April 12</td>
<td headers="End">April 16</td>
<td headers="Cost">300 Euros</td>
```

```
<td headers="Extras">includes lunches, and materials.</td>
</tr>
```

[…]

Final Accessible Table Using Header/ID Combinations

By looking at the example in Listing 7-1 to get started, can you see how the associations between headers and the contents of the data cells are made?

Figure 7-1 is a screen shot of the final table.

Animal Santuary workshops

An overview of upcoming Animal Sanctuary workshops in 2012

Course	Start Date	End Date	Cost	Included Extras
How do you start an Animal Sanctuary	June 10	June 16	650 Euros	includes lunches, one dinner and extensive materials.
Working with Dogs: A beginners workshop	April 12	April 16	300 Euros	includes lunches, and materials.
Massage for You & Your Animals	September 29	October 4	400 Euros. A Half day session is 220 Euros.	includes lunch, and book.
Yoga with Animals	May 18	May 21	300 Euros.	includes lunch, dinner and book.
A Creative Artistic workshop and Retreat	June 18	June 23	500 Euros	includes lunch, dinner and art supplies.
Why Compassion for Animals matter: Philosophy and Animals	July 12	July 14	200 Euros.	includes lunch, and materials
Sanctuary Basics	September 22	September 24	275 Euros.	includes lunch, and class materials

Figure 7-1. Accessible data table example

Listing 7-2 shows the final fully coded sample (with a suitable `<caption>` element also).

Listing 7-2. Final Table Code for Accessible Tables Method 1

```
<section>
<h1>Animal Sanctuary workshops</h1>
<table>
<caption>An overview of upcoming Animal Sanctuary workshops in 2012</caption>
```

```
<th id="Course">Course</th>
<th id="Start">Start Date</th>
<th id="End">End Date</th>
<th id="Cost">Cost</th>
<th id="Extras">Included Extras</th>
<tr>
<td headers="Course">How do you start an Animal Sanctuary</td>
<td headers="Start">June 10</td>
<td headers="End">June 16</td>
<td headers="Cost">650 Euros</td>
<td headers="Extras">includes lunches, one dinner and extensive materials.</td>
</tr>
<tr>
<td headers="Course">Working with Dogs: A beginners workshop</td>
<td headers="Start">April 12</td>
<td headers="End">April 16</td>
<td headers="Cost">300 Euros</td>
<td headers="Extras">includes lunches, and materials.</td>
</tr>
<tr>
<td headers="Course">Massage for You & Your Animals</td>
<td headers="Start">September 29</td>
<td headers="End">October 4</td>
<td headers="Cost">400 Euros. A Half day session is 220 Euros.</td>
<td headers="Extras">includes lunch, and book.</td>
</tr>
<tr>
<td headers="Course">Yoga with Animals</td>
<td headers="Start">May 18</td>
<td headers="End">May 21</td>
<td headers="Cost">300 Euros</td>
<td headers="Extras">includes lunch, dinner and book.</td>
</tr>
<tr>
<td headers="Course">A Creative Artistic workshop and Retreat</td>
<td headers="Start">June 18</td>
<td headers="End">June 23</td>
<td headers="Cost">500 Euros</td>
<td headers="Extras">includes lunch, dinner and art supplies.</td>
</tr>
<tr>
<td headers="Course">Why Compassion for Animals matter: Philosophy and Animals</td>
<td headers="Start">July 12</td>
<td headers="End">July 14</td>
<td headers="Cost">200 Euros</td>
<td headers="Extras">includes lunch, and materials</td>
</tr>
<tr>
<td headers="Course">Sanctuary Basics</td>
<td headers="Start">September 22</td>
<td headers="End">September 24</td>
<td headers="Cost">275 Euros.</td>
```

```
<td headers="Extras">includes lunch, and class materials</td>
</tr>
</table>
</section>
```

Accessible Tables Method 2: Use of Header/Scope Combinations

Another method of marking up the same table is to use the table headers in conjunction with the scope attribute (@scope). The HTML5 specification says this about building data tables using header/scope combinations:

- The headers in the first row all apply directly down to the rows in their column.

- The headers with the explicit scope attributes apply to all the cells in their row group.

- The remaining headers apply just to the cells to the right of them.

This means that you can have irregular tables that would still be considered simple, but they might have headers that should not be included in a particular row, or they might have a row that covers several columns.

The specification gives the example shown in Listing 7-3. Note that, in this case, the headers with the explicit scope attributes apply to all the cells in their row group other than the cells in the first column. See also the new HTML5 syntax of using no closing elements for the <th>, <td>, or <tr> elements or, indeed, no *quotes* for any of the cell values. You can still code in the older way if you prefer. You can also see the new <thead> (table header) and <tbody> (table body) elements that pretty much do what their names indicate, allowing you to denote blocks of content in your tables. There is also a <tfoot> (table footer) element, which is not shown here.

Listing 7-3. Using the Scope Attribute

```
<table>
 <thead>
  <tr> <th> ID <th> Measurement <th> Average <th> Maximum
 <tbody>
  <tr> <td> <th scope=rowgroup> Cats <td> <td>
  <tr> <td> 93 <th scope=row> Legs <td> 3.5 <td> 4
  <tr> <td> 10 <th scope=row> Tails <td> 1 <td> 1
 <tbody>
  <tr> <td> <th scope=rowgroup> English speakers <td> <td>
  <tr> <td> 32 <th scope=row> Legs <td> 2.67 <td> 4
  <tr> <td> 35 <th scope=row> Tails <td> 0.33 <td> 1
</table>
```

The code in Listing 7-3 produces the table in Figure 7-2, which is slightly more complex.

ID	Measurement	Average	Maximum
	Cats		
93	Legs	3.5	4
10	Tails	1	1
	English speakers		
32	Legs	2.67	4
35	Tails	0.33	1

Figure 7-2. HTML5 specification data table example

The th element can have a scope content attribute specified. The scope attribute has the following five states (with particular keywords):

- The row keyword, which maps to the row state. The row state means the header cell applies to some of the subsequent cells in the same row(s).

- The col keyword, which maps to the column state. The column state means the header cell applies to some of the subsequent cells in the same column(s).

- The rowgroup keyword, which maps to the row group state. The row group state means the header cell applies to all the remaining cells in the row group.

- The colgroup keyword, which maps to the column group state. The column group state means the header cell applies to all the remaining cells in the column group.

- The auto state. The auto state makes the header cell apply to a set of cells selected based on context.

Figure 7-3 is from the HTML5 specification. It visually demonstrates how the algorithm works.

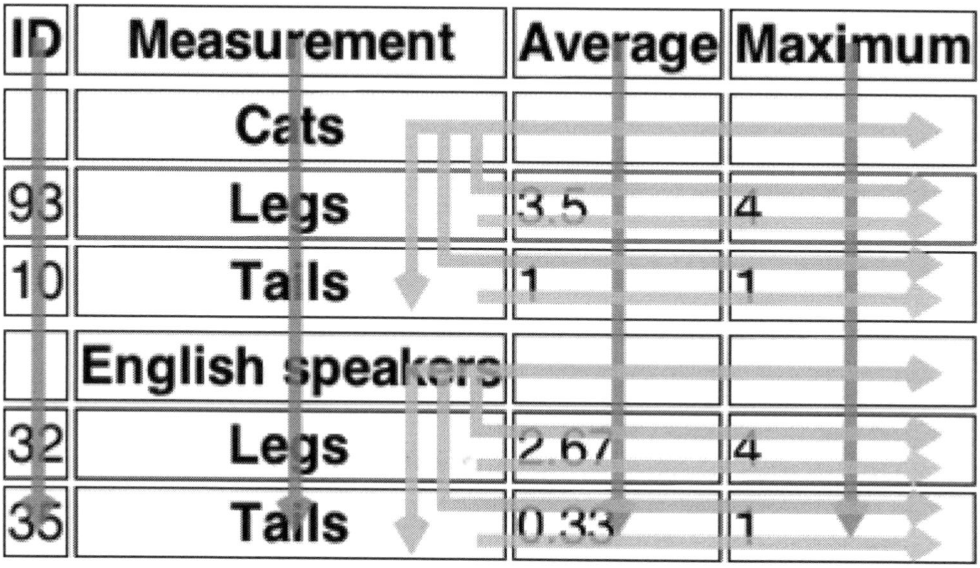

ID	Measurement	Average	Maximum
	Cats		
93	Legs	3.5	4
10	Tails	1	1
	English speakers		
32	Legs	2.67	4
35	Tails	0.33	1

Figure 7-3. Visualization of HTML5 scope algorithm[1]

The four arrows that point straight down from the top represent the table headers—"ID," "Measurement," and so on—and show that they are associated with all of the contents of their corresponding rows. The presence of a table header (<th>) and this association with all of the data cells in their related rows is very well supported by most browsers and AT, even older AT. This basis programmatic association goes a long way toward making your tables accessible. How it works for a screen-reader user is as follows: when that user encounters a table with appropriate headers, she uses her cursor keys to navigate around the data cells, the AT first announces what the table header is, and then it announces the contents of the data cell.

The other arrows show how the @scope element, as applied in the preceding example, relates to the remaining cell in its row, as well as how the cells apply to the cell to their right.

An Example Using Header/Scope Combinations

If you applied the header/scope method to our table, the markup would resemble that shown in Listing 7-4.

---

[1] www.w3.org/TR/html5/tabular-data.html#attr-th-scope

■ **Note** In HTML5, the scope attribute on the td element is obsolete. You used to be able to add it to a `<td>` cell in HTML 4, but you cannot do so any more if you want valid HTML. (I'll talk about validation in Chapter 10, "Tools, Tips, and Tricks: Assessing Your Accessible HTML5 Project.") For HTML5 data tables, use the scope attribute on a th element instead.

Listing 7-4. Using the Header/Scope Method

```
<section>
<h1>Animal Sanctuary workshops</h1>
<table>
<caption>An overview of upcoming Animal Sanctuary workshops in 2012</caption>
<th scope="col">Course</th>
<th scope="col">Start Date</th>
<th scope="col">End Date</th>
<th scope="col">Cost</th>
<th scope="col">Included Extras</th>
<tr>
<th scope="row">How do you start an Animal Sanctuary</th>
<td>June 10</td>
<td>June 16</td>
<td>650 Euros</td>
<td>includes lunches, one dinner and extensive materials.</td>
</tr>
<tr>
<th scope="row">Working with Dogs: A beginners workshop</th>
<td>April 12</td>
<td>April 16</td>
<td>300 Euros</td>
<td>includes lunches, and materials.</td>
</tr>
<tr>
<th scope="row">Massage for You & Your Animals</th>
<td>September 29</td>
<td>October 4</td>
<td>400 Euros. A Half day session is 220 Euros.</td>
<td>includes lunch, and book.</td>
</tr>
<tr>
<th scope="row">Yoga with Animals</th>
<td>May 18</td>
<td>May 21</td>
<td>300 Euros.</td>
<td>includes lunch, dinner and book.</td>
</tr>
<tr>
```

```
<th scope="row">A Creative Artistic workshop and Retreat</th>
<td>June 18</td>
<td>June 23</td>
<td>500 Euros</td>
<td>includes lunch, dinner and art supplies.</td>
</tr>
<tr>
<th scope="row">Why Compassion for Animals matter: Philosophy and Animals</th>
<td>July 12</td>
<td>July 14</td>
<td>200 Euros.</td>
<td>includes lunch, and materials</td>
</tr>
<tr>
<th scope="row">Sanctuary Basics</th>
<td>September 22</td>
<td>September 24</td>
<td>275 Euros.</td>
<th>includes lunch, and class materials</td>
</tr>
</table>
</section>
```

"So which is best?" I hear you cry. The second method using headers/@scope is a little less time consuming and easier to author, as you can see from Listing 7-4. The net result for users of screen readers is pretty much the same with both examples, with one exception. The @scope attribute is not very well supported by older screen readers, so for my money the header/ID combination method is more robust and better for backward compatibility.

More Complex Tables

Here is an example of a more advanced version of the preceding table, coded using the headers/@scope method as well as the newer HTML5 syntax. The idea is to display information for both introductory and advanced classes with the name of each course coded to act like a heading and spanning several columns.

Visually, the table looks like the one shown in Figure 7-4.

Animal Santuary workshops

An overview of upcoming Animal Sanctuary workshops in 2012

Course Number	Course	Start Date	End Date	Cost	Included Extras
	How do you start an Animal Sanctuary				
#001	Introduction	June 10	June 16	250 Euros	includes lunches, and one dinner.
#002	Advanced	August 10	August 16	550 Euros	includes lunches, one dinner and extensive materials.
	Working with Dogs: A beginners workshop				
#003	Introduction	April 12	April 16	100 Euros	includes lunches, and materials.
#004	Advanced	May 16	May 20	300 Euros	includes lunches, and materials.
	Massage for You & Your Animals				
#005	Introduction	September 29	October 4	200 Euros. A Half day session is 110 Euros.	includes lunch.
#006	Advanced	November 29	December 4	400 Euros. A Half day session is 220 Euros.	includes lunch.
	Yoga with Animals				
#007	Introduction	May 18	May 21	100 Euros.	includes lunch.
#008	Advanced	June 18	June 21	200 Euros.	includes lunch, dinner and book.
	A Creative Artistic workshop and Retreat				
#009	Introduction	June 18	June 23	250 Euros	includes lunch.
#010	Advanced	June 18	June 23	500 Euros	includes lunch, dinner and art supplies.
	Why Compassion for Animals matter: Philosophy and Animals				
#011	Introduction	July 12	July 14	200 Euros.	includes lunch.
#012	Advanced	August 12	August 14	400 Euros.	includes lunch, and materials.
	Sanctuary Basics				
#013	Introduction	September 22	September 24	275 Euros.	includes lunch.
#014	Advanced	September 22	September 24	275 Euros.	includes lunch, and class materials

Figure 7-4. A more advanced table using HTML5 syntax and the headers/@scope method

The code to build it using HTML5 syntax is shown in Listing 7-5.

Listing 7-5. Using the Headers/@scope Method to Create a More Advanced Table

```
<section>
<h1>Animal Sanctuary workshops</h1>
<table>
<caption>An overview of upcoming Animal Sanctuary workshops in 2012</caption>
<thead>
<tr>
<th>Course Number
<th>Course
<th>Start Date
<th>End Date
<th>Cost
<th>Included Extras
<tbody>
<tr>
<td><th scope=row group>How do you start an Animal Sanctuary<td><td><td><td>
<tr>
<td>#001
<td>Introduction
<td>June 10
<td>June 16
<td>250 Euros
```

```
<td>includes lunches, and one dinner.
<tr>
<td>#002
<td>Advanced
<td>August 10
<td>August 16
<td>550 Euros
<td>includes lunches, one dinner and extensive materials.
<tbody>
<tr>
<td><th scope=rowgroup>Working with Dogs: A beginners workshop<td><td><td><td>
<tr>
<td>#003
<td>Introduction
<td>April 12
<td>April 16
<td>100 Euros
<td>includes lunches, and materials.
<tr>
<td>#004
<td>Advanced
<td>May 16
<td>May 20
<td>300 Euros
<td>includes lunches, and materials.
<tbody>
<tr>
<td><th scope=rowgroup>Massage for You & Your Animals<td><td><td><td>
<tbody>
<tr>
<td>#005
<td>Introduction
<td>September 29
<td>October 4
<td>200 Euros. A Half-day session is 110 Euros.
<td>includes lunch.
<tr>
<td>#006
<td>Advanced
<td>November 29
<td>December 4
<td>400 Euros. A Half-day session is 220 Euros.
<td>includes lunch.
<tbody>
<tr>
<td>
<th scope=rowgroup>Yoga with Animals<td><td><td><td>
<tr>
<td>#007
<td>Introduction
<td>May 18
<td>May 21
```

```
<td>100 Euros.
<td>includes lunch.
<tr>
<td>#008
<td>Advanced
<td>June 18
<td>June 21
<td>200 Euros.
<td>includes lunch, dinner and book.
<tbody>
<tr>
<td>
<th scope=rowgroup>A Creative Artistic workshop and Retreat<td><td><td><td>
<tr>
<td>#009
<td>Introduction
<td>June 18
<td>June 23
<td>250 Euros
<td>includes lunch.
<tr>
<td>#010
<td>Advanced
<td>June 18
<td>June 23
<td>500 Euros
<td>includes lunch, dinner and art supplies.
<tbody>
<tr>
<td>
<th scope=rowgroup>Why Compassion for Animals matter: Philosophy and Animals<td><td><td><td>
<tr>
<td>#011
<td>Introduction
<td>July 12
<td>July 14
<td>200 Euros.
<td>includes lunch.
<tr>
<td>#012
<td>Advanced
<td>August 12
<td>August 14
<td>400 Euros.
<td>includes lunch, and materials.
<tbody>
<tr>
<td>
<th scope=rowgroup>Sanctuary Basics<td><td><td><td>
<tr>
<td>#013
<td>Introduction
```

```
<td>September 22
<td>September 24
<td>275 Euros.
<td>includes lunch.
<tr>
<td>#014
<td>Advanced
<td>September 22
<td>September 24
<td>275 Euros.
<td>includes lunch, and class materials
</table>
</section>
```

You can also see the headers in the table itself by using a tool like Webaim's WAVE Toolbar (which we'll look at in depth in Chapter 10) to see the headers at both the top of the data table as well as the headers that are contained deeper in the data table. Figure 7-5 shows an overview of the WAVE Toolbar interface.

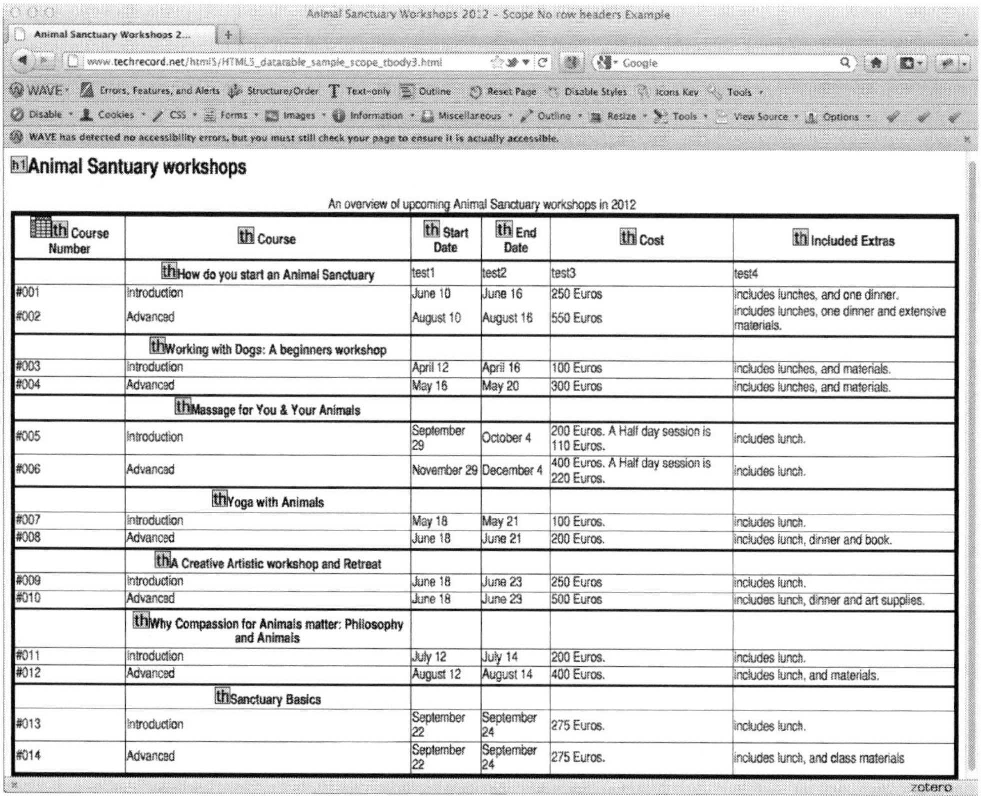

Figure 7-5. *Visual view of the <th> elements in a data table*

What about more complex tables? Ultimately, for more complex tables—for example, cells span multiple rows and there are headings nested deeper in the table—you are a little limited in the markup you can apply that will really work (from an accessibility perspective). I seriously suggest always trying to simplify your data table design wherever possible and making sure that you use more bulletproof methods like header/ID combinations. Adding a <caption> element to a table is a big help, and although the use of @summary is currently frowned upon in HTML5, adding one still works with many AT. If that is a bridge too far, you can add aria-describedby to provide more instruction; however, using that method means that the instruction needs to be an *on-page* description. I would break the law and still add @summary to describe the complex table to a blind user (it is hidden visually). Then again, I think I just have problems with authority.

Should you build complex tables at all? Well, you can certainly have headers for data cells that span more than one column or row, but you really need to ensure that you embed headers in your more tricky tables (see Figure 7-5) and use appropriate IDs to create programmatic associations between these headers and data cells.

Although there are more advanced HTML markup methods that promise to be easier to author or just be 'better' as technology advances, in practice the simple methods outlined here are what you should stick to. For more complex tables—where the use of @scope would be ideal –bear in mind that it is still poorly supported. So even though a markup method may be 'good' (from a pure coding perspective) and make sense semantically, you still have to be careful and test, test, test. The rub is that the AT vendors need to play catch up with what authors are doing and what the spec is suggesting. Actually, there is little new in @scope. It has been around for years.

▪ **Note** Regarding the new HTML5 Table Syntax, I must admit that initially I had mixed feelings about it. However, when I was coding the preceding example, I found the leaner syntax easier to write first of all, and then quite good when I was reviewing the code. I like the way it lends itself to thinking in the grid. You can lay out the code in your editor of choice, pretty much as you would–visually–the table cells in your data table. Sure, you can also do this with HTML 4, but the newer syntax is much less cluttered and makes visually parsing the code a little easier. Although I was initially reluctant, I found myself pleasantly surprised.

Use of Scope and AT Support

Although technically the scope attribute is supposedly supported by some screen readers today, in practice it is really rather limited. Support for header/ID combinations (as mentioned earlier), on the other hand, is excellent. The AT vendors might claim to support @scope, but when you build data tables using it, you might notice very little (if any) difference between a table that uses @scope and one that doesn't.

In time, this needs to change for a couple of reasons. First, authoring accessible data tables with headers/@scope is less time consuming for developers; second, the new HTML5 code is much leaner, which means faster page loads and so on. Also, the use of @scope give you the potential to mark up more complex data tables.

> ■ **Note** A few years ago, the HTML5 working group took a stance that data tables didn't need headers and that @scope was enough to build data tables. Headers on data tables were going to be dropped from the specification. Thankfully, this didn't happen because this move would have been disastrous for older users of AT (and there are many). If you are interested in the details of the debate, check out the HTML5 Working Group ESW wiki:[2]

New Ways of Describing HTML5 Tables

Some new ways for describing the table are suggested in the specification, and I am including examples of them here for the sake of completeness. You can use them if you want. However, I take issue with some of them, and currently support for the new elements like <figcaption> and the <details> element is poor. In time, this will change. You need to make a call as to whether you want to provide a textual description of the table before or after it, and then create some programmatic link between them. The argument for this kind of model is that it helps people with cognitive impairments understand the table better, and there is certainly some truth in this. However, often it is unnecessary for simple tables, and more complex tables benefit more from @summary descriptions (which is unfortunately invalid in HTML5) or some equivalent.

Some ways that the specification suggests to describe a data table, which might be either simple or more complex, follow.

Method #1: In Prose, Surrounding the Table

The example in Listing 7-6 uses the <p> element above the table as a verbose text description of what follows. The idea is that the description will suffice for all users because it is presented within the browser.

Listing 7-6. Verbose Text Description of a Data Table

```
<section>
<p>In the next table the number of animals we have in care are given in the first column,
Number in Care, the animal type is in the second column, Animal Type, and the third column
shows the number that are available currently.</p>
<table>
<caption>The number of animals in care that we have and that are available for immediate re-
housing.</caption>
<thead>
<tr>
<th id="number"> Total in Care
<th> Animal Type<th> Number available
<tbody>
<tr>
<td headers="number row1"> 12
```

---

[2] www.w3.org/html/wg/wiki/IssueTableHeaders

```
<th id="row1"> Older Dog<td> 7
<tr>
<td headers="number row2"> 9
<th id="row2"> Aging Cat<td> 6
<tr>
<td headers="number row3"> 14 <th id="row3"> Young Puppy<td> 9
<tr>
<td headers="number row4"> 23
<th id="row4"> Kitten <td> 15
<tr>
<td headers="number row5"> 5
<th id="row5"> Pony<td> 4
<tr>
<td headers="number row6"> 3
<th id="row6"> Horse<td> 1
</table>
</section>
```

■ **Note** Listing 7-6 has two headers because the markup is used to reference both the header at the top of the table and one that is inline. The HTML5 spec allows multiple headers to be referenced in this way.

Although having a verbose description immediately above the table is a good idea (and users of screen readers, if they need to, will be able to discover it more easily because it is very close to the table), it is still flawed. This is because there is no programmatic association that is explicit in the code. As you know by now, screen-reader users can bounce around web content using their AT, so an explicit association is very helpful, because it will be announced as soon as the table receives focus. This happens with the <caption> in Listing 7-6.

Method #2: Using aria-describedby with a Data Table

A way around this previously was to add a @summary element that describes the table. It is hidden from sighted users but very useful for screen-reader users. How can you provide a more explicit description that is programmatically associated? You can use a @summary, but you get an error from the Validator (available at http://validator.w3.org). If you can live with that, then fine. An alternative is to use aria-describedby to point at a description on the page. The code is shown in Listing 7-7.

Listing 7-7. Using aria-describedby to Describe the Table

```
<section>
<p id="desc">In the next table the number of animals we have in care are given in the first
column, Number in Care, the animal type is in the second column, Animal Type, and the third
column shows the number that are available currently.</p>
<table aria-describedby="desc">
<caption>The number of animals in care that we have and that are available for immediate re-
housing.</caption>
<thead>
```

```
<tr>
<th id="number"> Total in Care
<th> Animal Type<th> Number available
<tbody>
<tr>
<td headers="number row1"> 12
<th id="row1"> Older Dog<td> 7
<tr>
<td headers="number row2"> 9
<th id="row2"> Aging Cat<td> 6
<tr>
[…]
```

Coding your table like this allows the screen reader to point to the on-page description. Note that it doesn't have to be directly above or below the table to work, as long as the description is anywhere on the same page as the table it will work.

Method #3: In the Table's <caption>

The HTML5 specification suggests that you can provide these descriptions in the <caption> element. This is similar to the code shown in Listing 7-8.

Listing 7-8. Describing the Table in the <caption>

```
<section>
<table>
<caption>Table outlining the number of animals we have in care are given in the first column,
Number in Care, the animal type is in the second column, Animal Type, and the third column
shows the number that are available currently.</caption>
<thead>
<tr>
<th id="number"> Total in Care
<th> Animal Type<th> Number available
<tbody>
<tr>
<td headers="number row1"> 12
<th id="row1"> Older Dog<td> 7
<tr>
```

[…]

Although the example in Listing 7-8 is valid HTML5, I feel it overloads the <caption> with too much information and also changes the purpose of any caption as a short description to a much longer one. Presenting information like this as a longer description might be better marked up using aria-describedby, or it would be perfect for a @summary.

Method #4: In the Table's Caption, in a <details> Element

The HTML5 specification also recommends that the table's <caption> be used in conjunction with the new <details> element to provide a description as shown in Listing 7-9.

Listing 7-9. Using the <details> Element to Describe the Table

```
<section>
<table>
<caption>
<strong>The number of animals in care that we have and that are available for immediate re-
housing.</strong>
<details>
<summary>Help</summary>
<p>the number of animals we have in care are given in the first column, Number in Care, the
animal type is in the second column, Animal Type, and the third column shows the number that
are available currently.</p>
</details>
</caption>
<thead>
<tr>
<th id="number"> Total in Care
<th> Animal Type<th> Number available
<tbody>
<tr>
<td headers="number row1"> 12
<th id="row1"> Older Dog<td> 7
<tr>
```

[…]

In the example in Listing 7-9, note two new elements: <summary> and <details>.

The new <details> element represents a disclosure widget from which the user can obtain additional information or controls. You can use it to create accordion-style show/hide controls, for example. Note that it is not appropriate for footnotes. This new element is currently supported by the newer versions of Firefox, IE9, and Safari 5. These descriptions, again, are visible in the browser by default, but they can be hidden using CSS if required.

The <summary> element is a child of the <details> element and is used to represent the summary or legend. It is different from the @summary of the table element from earlier versions of HTML5.

Method #5: Next to the Table, in the Same Figure

This next method, shown in Listing 7-10, wraps the entire table in a <figure> element and uses <figcaption> to provide the initial short description and the <p> element to provide the longer description.

Listing 7-10. Using <figcaption> to Describe the Table

```
<figure>
<figcaption>The number of animals in care that we have and that are available for immediate
re-housing.</figcaption>
<p>the number of animals we have in care are given in the first column, Number in Care, the
animal type is in the second column, Animal Type, and the third column shows the number that
are available currently.</p>
<table>
<thead>
```

```
<tr>
<th id="number"> Total in Care
<th> Animal Type<th> Number available
<tbody>
<tr>
<td headers="number row1"> 12
<th id="row1"> Older Dog<td> 7
<tr>
[…]
</table>
</figure>
```

The current problem with this method is that apart from the entire <table> being wrapped in a <figure> (a method that is currently not very well supported by AT), there is no other programmatic association between the descriptive text and the table element. So it won't be wise to use this method until support for the <figure> element improves. At the time of writing this, there is some support in Firefox for <figure> and <figcaption>.

Conclusion

As you can see from the preceding examples, there are lots of ways to describe data tables using HTML5 and to make them more accessible. The more tried and trusted methods are usually the best, and the old adage captured in the acronym KISS (Keep It Simple, Stupid) certainly applies. In the next chapter, we will look at HTML5 forms and some of the new elements and form controls you can use to make your forms more responsive, usable, and accessible.

CHAPTER 8

HTML5 and Accessible Forms

In this chapter, you'll learn about creating accessible forms in HTML5. The good news is that many techniques you might have used previously to create accessible forms using HTML 4 still apply when using HTML5. You'll also have a look at some new elements, as well as how the new HTML5 elements allow you to do more form validation natively within the browser, without the need for complex scripting.

If you don't know about creating accessible forms in HTML4, don't worry—I'll cover it all from scratch.

Designing an Accessible Form User Interface

Many of the principles you learned from the last chapter about creating accessible data tables also apply to the creation of accessible forms using HTML5. In general, the mantra "KISS" applies—and not just to accessible forms!

Forms really do benefit from a clear, simple, and concise layout. At all times, you should avoid adding any unnecessary complexity, and under the hood of your forms you need to create programmatic associations between the input fields, check boxes, and other elements and their corresponding labels. These practices are at the heart of creating accessible forms with HTML5.

Forms are, of course, very different from data tables. Forms are interactive, and data tables aren't. Their interactive nature does add a level of complexity when it comes to making your forms more accessible. In particular, the interactive nature of forms brings up questions about how you should approach form validation, as well as what you should do when there is an error on the part of the end user. How do you make sure the error message is accessible? There are two parts to the answer: you must first let the user know there is an error, and then inform the user of what she needs to do to correct the error. I'll say more about that later, but these are the principle concerns of accessible error recovery.

Some Forms Good Practices

You already saw some simple forms in Chapter 3, as well as some form-validation techniques using scripting. To be polite about it, doing form validation using some of the JavaScript-heavy techniques isn't a lot of fun. It's often complex and awkward. The technique of creating more accessible error messages using earlier versions of HTML isn't as bad.

First, I'll introduce some of the new input types and elements in HTML5. You'll see how these new elements are designed to be easier to author and how they reduce the need for complex validation using scripting. You'll also see accessible error messaging and learn some practices that lead you to create more accessible and usable forms—forms that are, again, both easier to author and use. So it's a win-win approach.

> ■ **Note** Much of what you'll come across in HTML5 is ported over from the Web Forms 2.0 spec of the Web Hypertext Application Technology Working Group (WHATWG). The idea was that Web Forms 2.0 was an extension to the forms features found in HTML 4. Web Forms 2.0 provided new input fields, as well as attributes for defining constraints, a repeating model for declarative repeating of form sections, new DOM interfaces, as well as DOM events for validation and dependency tracking. Web Forms 2.0 was also an attempt to document existing practices. If you fancy some nerd train spotting, point your browser to `www.whatwg.org/specs/web-forms/current-work`.

Differences in FORM Elements Between HTML 4 and HTML5

In HTML5, there are 13 new elements, and a host of new attributes. However, there are also many existing elements that might well be familiar to you from HTML 4 and are still valid. So it's worthwhile to look at them again.

In HTML 4, there were a number of elements you could use to create your various input boxes, combo boxes, and so on. These were used in conjunction with the FORM element to specify:

- The layout of the form (defined by the controls used in the form, their order, and position).

- The page or script that would handle the completed and submitted form (which takes the form of the `action` attribute).

- The method by which user data would be sent to the server (the `method` attribute, such as post).

In HTML 4, a FORM action would take the following general form:

```
<FORM action="http://yoursite.com/contact" method="post">
...form details...
</FORM>
```

This basic syntax remains the same in HTML5. Within the form itself, various controls could (and, indeed, still can) be defined to allow the user to interact with the form, to specify the nature of the interactions, and to spell out relevant requirements that each control could impose. We'll review these controls and the criteria for their use in the following sections.

The INPUT Element

The INPUT element is used for the user to enter data such as text strings (name, address, and so on) or numbers. In HTML 4, the INPUT element has various attributes that determine what type of INPUT the form control is. There are several HTML 4 INPUT element types, as listed here:

- text

- password

- checkbox

- radio

- submit

- reset

- file

- hidden

- image

- button

All of these INPUT element types create a control within the browser, and the browser has certain behaviors that are inherited with these types. If an input type is "password," the browser displays a series of asterisks (****) instead of the real text. We'll look at the new HTML5 input types a little later.

The syntax for the INPUT types takes the following form:

```
<input type = "text">
<input type = "password">
<input type = "checkbox">
```

The syntax in HTML5 for the new types follows the same structure.

SELECT, OPTGROUP, and OPTION Elements

In HTML 4, you find the SELECT, OPTGROUP, and OPTION elements.

The SELECT element creates a menu in the browser. Each of the choices in the menu is represented by an OPTION element. If any of the OPTION element items need to be grouped together, the OPTGROUP element can be used by authors to group choices logically. This is useful if there is a long list of options for the user and you want to break them up into related sections.

This takes the form shown in Listing 8-1.

Listing 8-1. SELECT, OPTGROUP, and OPTION Elements

```
<select>
  <optgroup label="Electric Guitars">
    <option value="Fender">Fender</option>
    <option value="Gibson">Gibson</option>
<option value="Rickenbacker">Rickenbacker </option>
  </optgroup>
  <optgroup label="Acoustic Guitars">
<option value="Gretsch">Gretsch</option>
    <option value="Martin">Martin</option>
    <option value="Lowden">Lowden</option>
  </optgroup>
</select>
```

The fieldset and legend Elements

The idea behind the `<fieldset>` and `<legend>` elements in HTML 4 is that they give more structure to your forms. The `<fieldset>` element is used to group form controls thematically, and the `<legend>` is like a caption for the contents of the `<legend>` element's parent `<fieldset>`. A bit of a mouthful! If you remember, we already looked at using these elements in the Chapter 3.

■ **Note** All the preceding elements are still valid in HTML5.

The <label> Element

The `<label>` is very important for the creation of accessible form controls. The `<label>` element is used to create a specific label for a control. This label allows you to create (you guessed it) a *programmatic association* between the `<label>` name and the control itself. This allows assistive technologies (AT) such as a screen reader to understand what the purpose of the INPUT element is. A suitable label for the INPUT control is important because as soon as the INPUT field has focus, if it's labeled correctly, the `<label>` name will be announced by the screen reader.

The for/id Method

Accessible, well-labeled form controls in HTML 4 use a method called the for/id method. This is where the label that you use to identify the INPUT element takes the form `<label for="somename">`, and it is programmatically associated with the INPUT control by giving the same value to the INPUTs id, `<input id="somename">`. Listing 8-2 details this method.

Listing 8-2. Using for/id Combinations to Make an INPUT Text Box Accessible

```
<h1>Create new account</h1>
<form>
<label for="username">E-mail address:</label>
<input id="username" type=email name=mail>

<label for="password1">Password:</label>
<input id="password1" type=password name=pass>

<input type="submit" value="Login">
</form>
</body>
</html>
```

The name attribute is also designed to specify the name of the INPUT element and is useful for identifying groups of controls. It's also used for form submission. It isn't announced by AT.

So the text that is contained between `<label>[…]</label>` is announced by AT as soon as the corresponding INPUT field has been given focus via the keyboard. When you want to be sure that a screen reader user will be able to access some information in your form, you can include it in the form's `<label>`.

HTML5 Labeling of Form Controls

The HTML5 specification outlines another way of labeling a form control that doesn't use the preceding for/id method. This way isn't actually new, and it's where you literally wrap the form control in a <label>. It takes the following general form:

```
<label>Text to label control<input type="text"></label>
```

■ **Note** As mentioned, this method isn't new and was in HTML 4. In HTML 4, you can also technically assign several label elements to a form control by using the for attribute of various labels to point at the control. - However, you can no longer do this in HTML5. Also, this method was poorly supported by AT.

In the HTML5, the specification suggested that you use either the for/id method or wrap the label in the control. In the following line of code, I combined the two methods and wrapped the control in a label, while also using the for/id method. This takes the form shown next:

```
<label for="a11y_label"> Text to label control <input type="text" id="a11y_label"> <label>
```

This worked fine for me when testing it in Safari 5.1 using VoiceOver on Mac 10.7 (Lion). I also tried running some more text beyond the input box, and this was also announced by the screen reader. For example:

```
<label for="a11y_label"> Text to label control <input type="text" id="a11y_label"> some extra useful info!</label>
```

The interesting thing is that Steve Faulkner, a friend and an accessibility expert with The Paciello Group (TPG), ran some extensive tests and found that neither method worked very well on Safari 5 with VoiceOver, but I find that it now does (or seems to). So it's possibly a sign of improvement in terms of support for these structures.

■ **Caution** Jared Smith published a very interesting article on WebAIM titled "Semantic Automation." Semantic automation is used by VoiceOver to repair certain broken web content. This can mean that the test results I found are a product of advanced *heuristic evaluation* and not the application of HTML5 markup. I'm referring here *not to the for/id method* (which is tried and tested and bulletproof), but to the method recommended in the HTML5 specification for wrapping a control in a label. For more detail, see the WebAIM blog at http://webaim.org/blog/semantic-automation.

Although this newer (sic) method suggested by the HTML5 specification to identify a control by wrapping it in a label doesn't use the explicit association of the for/id method, as mentioned, I found it to work OK with VoiceOver (but see the earlier Caution). However, in terms of making your forms more bulletproof and working with older legacy AT, I recommend sticking with the for/id method for now. Don't see this as a limitation. The markup is straightforward as you can see, and the for/id method is very well supported. You can use it with confidence, knowing that screen-reader users will also be able to easily use your forms.

Also, HTML5 has the same radio buttons, check boxes, and so on that you will recognize from HTML4.

New HTML5 Elements

The following is a list of the new HTML5 form elements and attributes.

The <datalist> Element and the list Attribute

HTML5, to expand on what the SELECT and OPTION elements can do, gives you the ability to present the user with suggested predefined options. You do this by using the new <datalist> element and list attribute.

You use the @list value to point to the same ID in the <datalist> element. In Listing 8-3, I added a title attribute to give the screen-reader user a heads up about how to use the control.

Listing 8-3. Using <datalist>

```
<input type="text" list="suggested_DAW_options" title="Press down arrow to see selections">
<datalist id="suggested_DAW_options">
<option value="Logic">
<option value="Ableton Live">
<option value="Digital Performer">
<option value="Cubase">
<option value="Sonar">
<option value="Cockos Reaper">
</datalist>
```

The <output> Element

This new element represents the result of a calculation. It's used in conjunction with the for attribute. You can add values from various form elements, for example. Listing 8-4 is inspired by an example on the W3Schools.com web site.

Listing 8-4. Using <output>

```
<form oninput="z.value=parseInt(x.value)+parseInt(y.value)">
Enter Value 1: <input type="number" name="x" value="0" />
Enter Value 2: <input type="number" name="y" value="0" />= <output name="z" for="x y">
</output>
</form>
```

▓ **Note** There are some interesting examples of the <output> element in use at http://html5doctor.com/the-output-element.

The <progress> and <meter> Elements

Both the <progress> and <meter> elements display similarly in the browser. Figure 8-1 shows a screen shot from Firefox 9. Figure 8-2 shows the same progress bar in Opera 11.6.

This is a progress bar

Figure 8-1. The <progress> element in Firefox 9

This is a progress bar

Figure 8-2. The <progress> element in Opera 11.6

▓ **Note** Neither of the preceding examples displays the <progress> data in a way that is accessible out of the box, and I haven't seen an accessible implementation. The closest thing to one that I have seen is a part of the excellent work that Hans Hillen (TPG) and Chris Blouch (AOL) are doing as a part of the Aegis project in developing JQuery-powered, accessible WAI-ARIA-enabled widgets and controls. For more information, point your browser to http://access.aol.com/aegis/#goto_progressbar.

New HTML5 INPUT Types

One of the really cool things about HTML5 is the new form controls—in particular, the various input types. These are going to be very useful for authors because they take away some of the complexity of validation (which isn't a lot of fun). These controls have particular behaviors and models of interaction, as you shall see. We are used to rather simple input types in earlier versions of HTML, such as Text, Password, or Search, for example.

▓ **Note** You can write the following types with or without the opening double quotes (") or closing double quotes ("). So both <input type="tel"> and <input type=tel> are valid. I wrote them here as <input type="tel"> because it's my preference. When a user agent comes across a type that it doesn't understand, it will default to displaying the control as generic text-type input.

In HTML5, the *type* state determines what kind of input the control is. All of the new types pretty much do what they say on the tin. The full list of types is described in the following short sections.

Hidden (type=hidden)

This takes the following form:

```
<input type="hidden">
```

The hidden type represents some value that isn't to be seen by the end user.

Telephone (type=tel)

This takes the following form:

```
<input type="tel">
```

Although this type is obviously for inputting a phone number, no particular phone pattern is required. This is because various valid types of phone numbers are available around the world.

URL (type="url")

This takes the following form:

```
<input type="url">
```

This control is for inputting a URL. Both this input type and the next one (for email) do expect (and enforce) the expected syntax. This is useful for client-side validation.

Email (type="email")

This takes the following form:

```
<input type="email">
```

This control is for inputting an email address. As mentioned, both this input type and the previous type (for a URL) do expect (and enforce) the expected syntax.

Password (type="password")

This takes the following form:

```
<input type="password">
```

This is used for inputting a password. The form for this is shown in Figure 8-3, and it should be familiar to you.

Password: ●●●●●●●●●

Figure 8-3. The password input type

What you might not be familiar with is how a screen reader behaves when it gives focus to the password control. Consider the following code used to generate the control:

```
<form>
<label for="pword"> Password:</label>
<input type="password" id="pword" name="pswrd">
</form>
```

A `<label>` for the control informs the screen-reader user about the purpose of the control. Then when it receives focus and the screen-reader user starts to input some characters, the output is (depending on the screen reader) a series of clicking noises that sound after each key is pressed. If a series of asterisks appear in the control, the output is "star, star, star" and so on. In other words, the actual characters that are being output are not announced so that a blind user's privacy is maintained.

Date and Time Controls

The following are new input types for adding date and time controls to HTML5 forms. They take the following form:

```
<input type="datetime">
<input type="date">
<input type="month">
<input type="week">
<input type="time">
<input type="datetime-local">
```

Let's put them together into a simple form, as detailed in Listing 8-5, and see how the different browsers render them.

Listing 8-5. Using Date and Time Controls

```
<form>
<label for="type_datetime">Datetime:</label>
<input type="datetime" id="datetime">

<label for="type_date">Date:</label>
<input type="date" id="type_date">

<label for="type_month">Month:</label>
<input type="month" id="type_month">

<label for="type_week">Week:</label>
<input type="week" id="type_week">

<label for="type_time">Time:</label>
<input type="time">

<label for="type_datetime-local">Time:</label>
<input type="datetime-local" id="type_datetime-local">
</form>
```

Listing 8-6 shows some simple Cascading Style Sheets (CSS) used to hold it together.

Listing 8-6. *CSS for the Date/Time Form*

```
label            {
width: 3em;
display: block;
margin:5px;
}

input    {
width: 5.5em;
float: left;
display: block;
margin-top:-25px;
margin-left:90px;
padding:5px;
}
```

And finally, Figures 8-4, 8-5, and 8-6 are screen shots of the form in Safari 5.1, Firefox 9, and Opera 11.6, respectively.

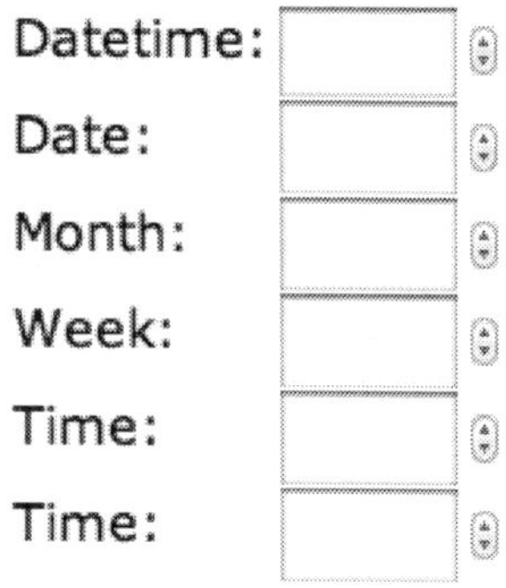

Figure 8-4. *New date and time controls in Safari*

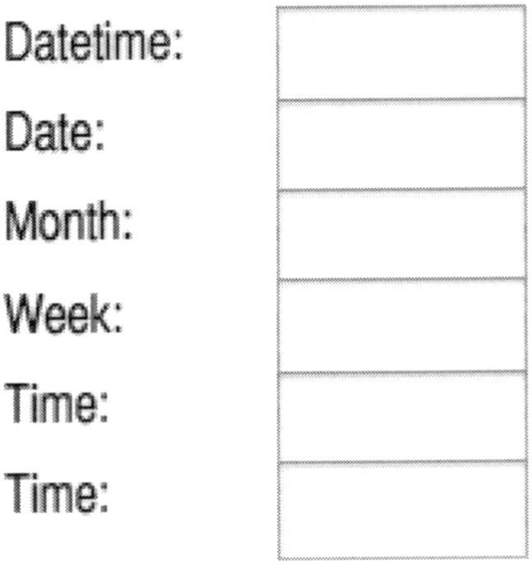

Datetime:

Date:

Month:

Week:

Time:

Time:

Figure 8-5. New date and time controls in Firefox

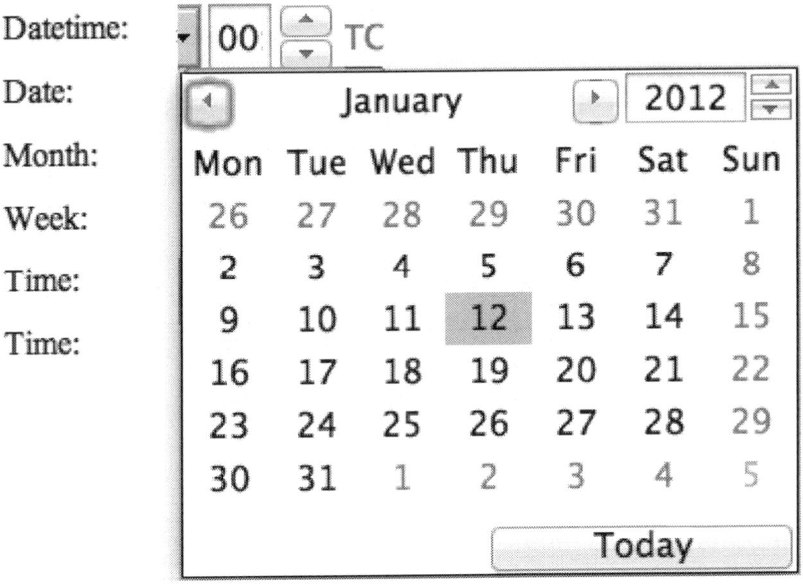

Datetime: 00 ▲▼ TC

Date:

Month:

Week:

Time:

Time:

◄ January ► 2012 ▲▼

Mon	Tue	Wed	Thu	Fri	Sat	Sun
26	27	28	29	30	31	1
2	3	4	5	6	7	8
9	10	11	12	13	14	15
16	17	18	19	20	21	22
23	24	25	26	27	28	29
30	31	1	2	3	4	5

Today

Figure 8-6. New date and time controls in Opera

Notice the difference between how the three browsers render the controls. Safari displays a spinner control to the right of each of the input controls. Firefox doesn't, and Opera gives both a spinner control for the <datetime> input as well as the time and datetime-local controls.

■ **Note** A spinner control is used to adjust values up or down by selecting the appropriate arrow. At the time of this writing, they are not natively accessible or focusable via the keyboard in Safari 5.1 (Mac). They don't display in IE9, or Firefox 8 (PC). Although the calendar date picker does display in Opera, Opera isn't a very screen reader friendly browser. By the time you read this Internet Explorer 10 will have shipped, and it promises better HTML5 support. Will it do so in practice? Time will tell.

Number (type="number")

The number input control takes the following form:

```
<input type="number">
```

It's a new type of control for representing a number. If you build it using the following code and look at it in some different browsers, you'll see the variability in the way browsers render HTML5 by default:

```
<form><label for="type_number">Enter a Number:</label>
<input type="number" id="type_number">
</form>
```

Figures 8-7, 8-8, and 8-9 show how various browsers render this code.

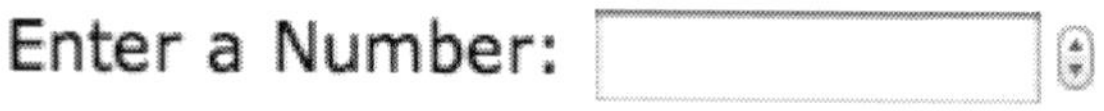

Figure 8-7. The "number" input type in Safari

Enter a Number:

Figure 8-8. The "number" input type in Opera

Enter a Number:

Figure 8-9. The "number" input type in Firefox

Range (type="range")

The range input type is an interesting new control. It allows the user to enter values into a form using a slider control. This code takes the following form:

```
<form>
<label for="type_range">Use slider to enter a value:</label>
<input type="range" title="You use the left and right arrow keys to move the values up an
down." id="type_range">
</form>
```

The range input control is displayed visually in browsers that support it, as shown in Figures 8-10 and 8-11.

Use slider to enter a value: ▬▬▬○▬▬▬

Figure 8-10. The range input in Safari

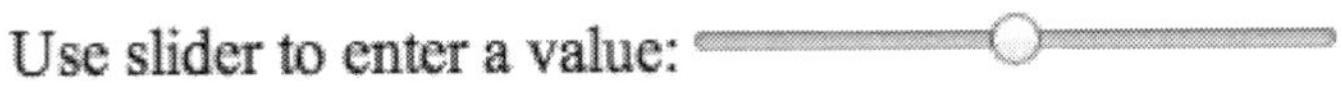

Use slider to enter a value: ▬▬▬○▬▬▬

Figure 8-11. The range input in Opera

Range isn't supported, at the time of this writing, in IE9 (PC) or Firefox 9 (MAC/PC). Chrome (PC) does support it, however. What is interesting is that, in testing, the Chrome browser not only has native keyboard access to the control, but it also feeds back the current value of the slider. As far as I can tell, no other browser currently does that. To make the slider control more accessible, you might have to provide a scripted solution in order for AT to be able to announce the current value of the slider so that the screen-reader user can know where they are at.

▪ **Note** For some really good examples of accessible and unobtrusive JavaScript-powered, HTML5, range-type controls, point your browser at www.frequency-decoder.com/demo/fd-slider. You can see how these *polyfills* often don't use the native *range*, but use a combination of CSS to style the control, WAI-ARIA to add the semantics, and JavaScript to capture interactions.

Both the number and range input types can take the following new HTML5 attributes: min and max. These attributes allow you to set both minimum and maximum values that a numerical control or, indeed, the range control can accept.

They take the following form:

```
<input type="range" min="1" max="5">
```

There is also the new step attribute, which allows you to set in a granular way the amount that input values jump up or down. If you want user input to jump, up or down, by a value of 5, you use code like the following:

```
<input type="number" step="5">
```

Color (type="color")

This control takes the following form:

```
<input type="color">
```

This is a color picker type input. To my mind, it's a strange control for forms because I struggle to think of uses for it. At time of this writing, only Opera has an interesting rendering of the control in the browser (shown in Figure 8-12).

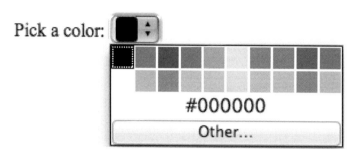

Figure 8-12. The color input in Opera

The rest of the controls should be familiar to you from HTML 4, such as check boxes, radio buttons, file upload controls, Submit buttons, Reset buttons, and Search inputs.

New HTML5 Form Attributes

The following sections list attributes taken from the "HTML5 differences from HTML4" document that are new to HTML5. You can find the document at `www.w3.org/TR/html5-diff`.

The autofocus Attribute

A new autofocus attribute (@autofocus) can be specified on the input control (except when the type attribute is hidden) and on the select, textarea, and button elements. It provides a declarative way to focus a form control during page load.

Using the @autofocus attribute takes the following general form:

```
<input type="text" name="firstname" autofocus>
```

It's very easy to author and add to your projects. The @autofocus attribute is an interesting new attribute in HTML5, and it has the potential to be useful in creating accessible error recovery. This can be achieved by using it to autofocus on the first field that has an error message after the form has been validated. If this method is used, it is important to ensure that any inline description of the error message is also included as a part of the label of the control, or that aria-described by is used to point at the error if that exists on another part of the page.

It isn't enough to just use the autofocus attribute to position the focus on a field, even if it's the correct field where the error occurs, and not clearly explain what the error is and how to fix it.

New INPUT Element Attributes

The INPUT element has several new attributes to specify constraints: autocomplete, min, max, multiple, pattern, and step. Some of these attributes were discussed in the section about the range input type. There is also a new list attribute that can be used together with the datalist element.

The dirname Attribute

The input and textarea elements have a new attribute, named dirname, that causes the directionality of the control as set by the user to be submitted as well.

New TEXTAREA Element Attributes

The TEXTAREA element also has two new attributes: maxlength and wrap. These attributes control the maximum input length and the submitted line-wrapping behavior.

The novalidate Attribute

The FORM element has a novalidate attribute that is used when you don't want to perform any validation and just submit the form, in all circumstances.

New input and button Element Attributes

The input and button elements have formaction, formenctype, formmethod, formnovalidate, and formtarget as new attributes. If present, they override the action, enctype, method, novalidate, and target attributes on the FORM element.

The placeholder Attribute

A new placeholder attribute can be specified on the input and textarea elements. It represents a hint intended to aid the user with data entry, as shown here:

```
<input type=email placeholder="mr.pussels@bigcat.com">
```

The new @placeholder has codified the use of placeholder text within form fields. I have mixed feelings about this. Traditionally, placeholder text performed a couple of tasks. First, to aid a sighted person in understanding what the input control is for by displaying a sample of the kind of content it requires. It was also used to describe the purpose of the control to AT (when it didn't in the early days of the Web), support the title attribute of the input type, or other labeling mechanisms.

However, this hasn't been the case for quite some time, and adding placeholder text like this created several problems—such as the contents of the INPUT control not being cleared if scripting was disabled, for example. Clearing the content of the input field on focus is certainly a useful technique, but in older user agents it begs the question of what happens when JavaScript is off. I'll tell you what happens. The text that's input from the user gets mixed with the placeholder content. For example, if you have an input type like the one just shown, for email, in earlier versions of HTML, and you input the string "josh@animalsanctuary.com", if you didn't use script to clear the field or if it was off, you would get a string like the example in Figure 8-13.

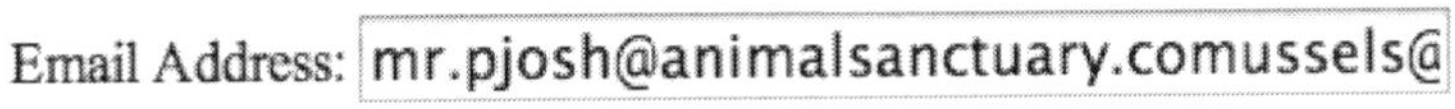

Email Address: `mr.pjosh@animalsanctuary.comussels@`

Figure 8-13. Placeholder text mixed with user input text

The good news is that when most older user agents, such as browsers, come across the placeholder attribute or any new HTML5 input types that they doesn't understand, most will just display an input box by default. For example, consider the code in Listing 8-7 and the resulting screen capture (Figure 8-14).

Listing 8-7. An HTML5 Input Type

```
<!DOCTYPE HTML>
<html>
<head>
<meta charset="UTF-8">
<title>HTML5 forms:Placeholder</title>
</head>
<body>
<h1> HTML5 Form placeholder</h1>
<form>
<label>Address: <input type="email" name="address" placeholder="mr.pussells@bigcat.com">
</label>
</form>
</body>
</html>
```

The resulting rendering in the browser is shown in Figure 8-14.

HTML5 Form placeholder

Address: [   ]

Figure 8-14. HTML5 rendered as a text field by an older browser

---

■ **Note** In newer HTML5 browsers that support the @placeholder, the contents get cleared on focus, without the need for any scripting at all. This makes authoring easier. Also, the default behavior for older user agents means that you can use it without worrying too much about older user agents having problems.

One issue to be aware of, however, is the poor color contrast of the placeholder text. This will be problematic for low-vision computer users. For example, consider the screen shots from Safari 5.1 (Figure 8-15) and then Opera 11.5 (Figure 8-16).

HTML5 Form placeholder

Email Address: [mr.pussells@bigcat.c]

Figure 8-15. Color contrast of placeholder text in Safari

HTML5 Form placeholder

Address: mr.pussells@bigcat.com

Figure 8-16. Color contrast of placeholder text in Opera

Did you notice how poor the color contrast is? Poor color contrast can make it very difficult for people with vision impairments to see content on screen. Bear in mind that lots of people with vision impairments don't use AT at all. They get by using the browser controls to resize text or by using systemwide, high-visibility options and so on. So having good, strong color contrast in your web content is a great help.

In HTML5, you can style various input types, but you must target specific browsers, as well as mention the attribute that you want to style.

To style an input box to darken the placeholder text, you can use CSS3 selectors, which take the following form:

```
::-webkit-input-placeholder {
    color: #333333;
}

:-moz-placeholder {
    color: #333333;
}
```

■ **Note** There are vendor-specific prefixes for webkit browsers such as Safari and Chrome, as well as the prefixes for Mozilla or Gecko-based browsers. At the time of this writing, many browser manufacturers are starting to drop the need for a prefix on some CSS3 declarations. So rather than having to write vendor specific declarations, soon you might be able to just declare something like "border-radius" and the browser will just handle it correctly. IE9 is impressive in this regard but will need the "ms" prefix for some selectors.

The New form Attribute

The new form attribute for input, output, select, textarea, button, label, object, and fieldset elements allows for controls to be associated with a form. The idea is that the elements can be placed anywhere on a page, not just as descendants of the form element, and still be associated with a form. The specification gives the following example:

```
<label>Email:
 <input type=email form=foo name=email>
</label>
<form id=foo></form>
```

However, this example doesn't really get across what the potential of this new pattern is. Now the form control can be separated from its parent and placed outside the <form>[...]</form> markup, if the author has a need to do this.

The example in Listing 8-8 should make this a little clearer.

Listing 8-8. Using the New form Attribute

```
<div id="form_container">
<form id="contact_1" action="post">
<label for="first_name"> First Name:</label>
<input type="text" id="first_name" name="fname">

<label for="second_name"> Last Name:</label>
<input type="text" id="second_name" name="lname">
<label for="mail">Your Email:</label>
<input type="email" id="mail" name="mail">
<input type="submit" id="submit" value="Contact Us!">
</form>
</div>

<div id="content_2">
<textarea id="extra_info" title="Enter extra Info here and tab back to submit form"
form="contact_1" placeholder="Something more to say?">
</textarea>
</div>
```

Listing 8-9 provides a little CSS to render the form and give it some basic positioning and styling.

Listing 8-9. CSS for the form

```
<style type="text/css">

#form_container {
display:block;
width:100%;
max-width:190px;
font-family: Lucida Sans Unicode, Lucida Grande', sans-serif;
color: #C90;
background-color:#333;
margin:10px;
padding:10px;
border-radius: 19px;
}

#content_2            {
display:block;
max-width:190px;
font-family: Lucida Sans Unicode, Lucida Grande', sans-serif;
color: #C90;
background-color:#333;
margin:10px;
padding:10px;
```

```
border-radius: 15px;
}

label           {
width: 3em; display: block; margin:5px;
}

input               {
width: 9.5em;
float: right;
display: block;
margin-top:-40px;}

#extra_info {
width:90%;
max-width:inherit;
display: block;
font-family: Lucida Sans Unicode, Lucida Grande', sans-serif;
color: #C90;
background-color:#333;
border-radius: 15px;
}

#submit             {
margin:10px;
}

::-webkit-input-placeholder {
color: #ffffff;
}

:-moz-placeholder {
color: #ffffff;
}
</style>
```

Figure 8-17 is a screen shot of the form taken from the Safari browser.

Figure 8-17. The form attribute at work

This kind of pattern might become more popular, and certainly the ability to refer to an element outside of the traditional <form> structure has the potential to create, well, new forms (pardon the pun) of interaction. In this case, because I can add a title attribute to the text area the screen reader will be able to provide supplementary information to the user. The contents of the title attribute on a form control are output when the control is given focus, in the absence of a label. Giving a form control a title, instead of a label, is an acceptable way of providing accessible information to the end user provided that the purpose of the control is apparent also from its visual rendering. In this case, the text "Something more to say?" acts as a visual cue. You might find that you have other controls when building forms that you might not want to label.

As mentioned, this new form attribute can be added to input, output, select, textarea, button, label, object, and fieldset elements. As always, the issue is one of support for them in both the browser and the AT. In time, as this new pattern gains ground, support undoubtedly will improve.

■ **Note** The use of the title attribute or (@title) on form controls is different from using the @title attribute on an image. Although you cannot be sure if the screen reader will pick up on the contents of the @title on an image or graphic, when used on form controls it's a lot more robust. So you can use it with confidence.

The New required Attribute

The new required attribute (or @required) applies to input, select, and textarea controls and plays an important part in form validation and, indeed, error recovery. It indicates that the user has to fill in a value in order to submit the form. For a select control, the first option element has to be a placeholder with an empty value, as shown in the following snippet:

```
<label>Color: <select name=color required>
 <option value="">Choose one
 <option>Red
 <option>Green
 <option>Blue
</select>
</label>
```

Support for the HTML5 @required is pretty good with new screen readers. The attribute won't be picked up by older screen readers at all. A way around this is to use a combination of the WAI-ARIA property aria-required="true" in conjunction with the HTML5 @required. The idea is that the older screen reader that supports WAI-ARIA but not HTML5, will pick up on the aria-required="true" property, and the net result will be that they will be informed that they have focused on a required control. The code for that (based on the preceding example from the spec) is as follows:

```
<label>Color: <select name=color required aria-required="true">
 <option value="">Choose one
 <option>Red
 <option>Green
 <option>Blue
</select>
</label>
```

There are some drawbacks from the example. First, a screen reader that understands both the HTML5 code required and the WAI-ARIA code aria-required="true" will output "Required" twice. This can be a pain, in particular when there are lots of required fields. You can argue that it's a bulletproof method, but the user experience might leave a lot to be desired. Also, with this method, what about screen readers that don't understand either the HTML5 code or the WAI-ARIA code? In this case, they won't be able to do anything useful for the end user.

Unfortunately, there is no way for you as an author to detect what kind of AT a person is using. A more robust way of being backward compatible with older technology is to include the word "Required" within the label of the control. This takes the following form:

```
<label> Choose a color [Required] </label>
```

It's rather simple and will work for both older user agents and newer ones. It's also an older method of making forms accessible that still has some traction—there are a few! However, you might not want to have the word "[Required]" in the label of your control, but that's your call. The advantage is that it will work for both sighted users and screen-reader users with both old and new screen readers.

This issue in particular is suitable to highlight how there are similarities between some WAI-ARIA code forms and HTML5. In this case, there certainly seems to be a degree of redundancy between the two. The advantage of aria-required="true" in this case (as it will be in a lot of ARIA 1.0 cases) is that support was implemented in screen readers over the last couple of years, and at time of this writing is slightly ahead of HTML5. I am pretty sure, however, that this will all change when HTML5 support grows (as it currently is). Ultimately, how you decide to author should be based on testing and what is best for your needs. In the end, go with whatever works, though you might have to compromise somewhere along the line.

263

■ **Note** The @required isn't to be used when the type attribute is hidden or when an image or some button type such as a submit button is used.

The disabled Attribute

The fieldset element now allows the disabled attribute, which disables all descendant controls when specified, and the name attribute, which can be used for script access.

HTML5 Form Validation

Form validation is an important part of the under-the-hood mechanics of both getting good data from your users, as well ensuring that when there are errors you can be accurate when you inform the user of what went wrong. So validation plays a part as a stage-one process in error recovery also.

First (as mentioned earlier), you can use the required attribute and/or aria-required="true" (or a combination if the two).

Opera has an interesting implementation of the required attribute if the form is submitted without a required field being filled in, as shown in Figure 8-18.

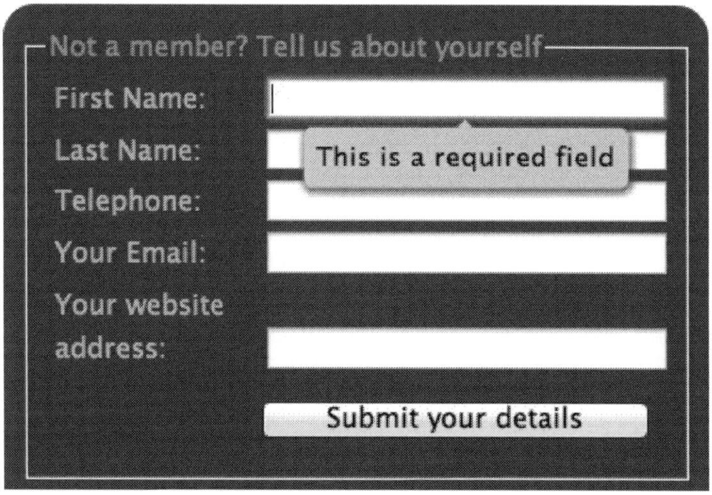

Figure 8-18. Opera 11.6 required field

Firefox also has an interesting implementation in such cases: it also highlights the required field in red by default. You can see the effect in Figure 8-19.

Figure 8-19. Firefox 9 required field

In terms of "in the browser" validation, Firefox also has a very nice feature: the message "Please fill out this field" is announced by the screen reader—at least in my testing with JAWS 12 and Firefox 9 (PC). This is excellent. Not only does the field that the error occurs on receive focus, but the label is also read out again when focus is brought to the field. This is a perfectly acceptable, and it's an accessible way of performing both validation and error recovery. Chrome also displays an error message similar to the other browsers mentioned, but it's not accessible out of the box in the same way as it is in Firefox 9.

Sadly, none of these features are supported in IE9.

The Use of Patterns in HTML5 Forms

Within HTML5 forms, you can also check that the user input matches what is expected—so that you don't get a text string in a numeric field or so that you do get a proper email address. You can use the new pattern attribute to help with validation. This attribute tells the browser to look for a pattern after user input, so this can be a range of numeric characters or a particular text string. For example, a UK postal code can take the following form:

UK Postal Code   [A-Z]{1,2}[0-9R][0-9A-Z]? [0-9][ABD-HJLNP-UW-Z]{2}

Or the date pattern can be the following:

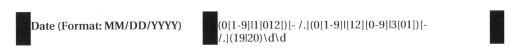
Date (Format: MM/DD/YYYY)   (0[1-9]|1[012]])[- /.](0[1-9]|[12][0-9]|3[01])[-/.](19|20)\d\d

Don't worry if this seems complex. There are lots of resources online, and I came across this one via the Thinkvitamin.com website, called "html5pattern.com," that contains loads. So point your browser over there if you want to include these kinds of patterns in your projects.

Accessible Error Recovery

Accessible error recovery is a very important technique in the creation of forms that can be used by the widest possible audience. Therefore, it's important that any new methods you use in HTML5 have some degree of backward compatibility because not everyone is using the latest browsers or, as I have indicated time and again, the latest AT. So while the new HTML5 language is very powerful, the issue of user-agent support is a recurring limitation you have to provide for.

There are couple of stages to accessible error recovery you should be aware of:

1. Let the user know there is an error.

2. Let the user access the error, and provide instructions on how to fix it.

3. Allow the user to resubmit the form.

As you saw in the section on validation, some browsers do support the new HTML5 attributes like `required` and can provide focus to each field (depending on the source order in the code) that has an error. When the input field is marked up correctly with a proper `<label>`, in supporting browsers this is often enough information for a screen-reader user to fix the error. However, in tests this worked only in Firefox 9 with JAWS (from a screen-reader user's perspective). However, this is a good sign. Where there is support for these HTML5 methods to help with validation and, to some degree, error recovery, there is the possibility of being able to do both without authoring more complex error-recovery methods.

However, lots of browsers don't support this method at all. So how can you support the important issue of accessible error messaging in a way that will work with both older and newer browsers?

The following is a method of accessible error recovery that will work with both older and newer browsers.

■ **Note** While I came across a similar method on the WebAIM web site many years ago, this implementation comes from the "Standards Schmandards" website developed by Peter Krantz. Many thanks to Peter for allowing me to reproduce it here. As an aside, Peter is also doing lots of other interesting work in data visualization and systems interoperability. For more information, point your browser at `www.peterkrantz.com`.

This is a simple method that is pretty bulletproof. Consider the form shown in Figure 8-20.

Figure 8-20. *A registration form with required fields*

Listing 8-10 shows the HTML for the form.

Listing 8-10. *Code for the Registration Form*

```
<p>Please complete the following form to create your account. </p>
<form name="registrationform" id="registrationform" method="post" action="index.php">
<fieldset>
<legend>Personal details</legend>
<div class="formrow"><div class="labelcontainer">
<label for="name">* Name:</label>
</div>
<div class="field">
<input name="name" type="text" id="name" maxlength="55" style="width:200px" title="Your name.
Required information." />
</div>
</div><div class="formrow">
<div class="labelcontainer">
<label for="age">* Age:</label>
</div>
<div class="field">
<input name="age" type="text" id="age" maxlength="3" title="Your age. Required
information."/></div>
</div>
<div class="formrow">
<div class="labelcontainer">
<label for="country">Country:</label>
</div>
<div class="field">
<select name="select" id="country" title="Your country of residence.">
<option value="1">Sweden</option>
```

```
<option value="2">United States</option>
<option value="3">Japan</option>
</select>
</div>
</div>
<div class="formrow">
<input type="submit" style="float:right;" value="Register" name="registerbtn"/>
</div>
</fieldset>
</form>
```

Now, if the form was submitted and both fields were left blank, the error message in Figure 8-21 would be displayed.

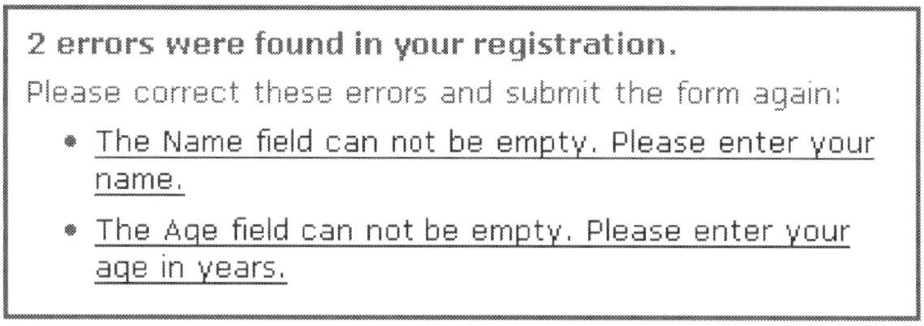

2 errors were found in your registration.

Please correct these errors and submit the form again:

- The Name field can not be empty. Please enter your name.

- The Age field can not be empty. Please enter your age in years.

Figure 8-21. Error message for required fields

The code to produce this error message is shown in Listing 8-11.

Listing 8-11. Code for the Error Message

```
<div id="validationerror">
  <h2 id="errorsummary">2 errors were found in your registration.</h2>
  <p>Please correct these errors and submit the form again:</p>
  <ul>
    <li id="er_128">
    <a href="#name" onclick="setfocus('name')">
    The Name field can not be empty.
    Please enter your name.</a></li>
    <li id="er_215">
    <a href="#age" onclick="setfocus('age')">
    The Age field can not be empty.
    Please enter your age in years.</a></li>
  </ul>
</div>
```

Some JavaScript is used to focus on the relevant field the user can use to address the problem:

```
function setfocus(objectid) { if(document.getElementById(objectid))
{ document.getElementById(objectid).focus(); }
 }
```

The preceding code can be triggered via the keyboard, so it's perfectly accessible. The error messages are also very clear and give the user an overview of both the error and what can be done to remedy it. Pretty neat!

Using JQuery for Form Validation

There is also a good JQuery form-validation plug-in you can use to validate your forms and provide accessible error messages. Point your browser at the NOMENSA blog for an excellent tutorial on how to do it: www.nomensa.com/blog/2010/accessible-forms-using-the-jquery-validation-plug-in.

Conclusion

In this chapter, we looked some old, as well as new, HTML elements and attributes you can use to build accessible forms. Not all of the new elements are supported as of yet, but this will change. Also, you saw how to do some client-side validation, as well as some accessible error messaging. In the next chapter, we'll look at usability and user-centered design.

HTML5, Usability, and User-Centered Design

While a large part of this book has focused on the technical aspects of the HTML5 language, there are others aspects you should consider to ensure that your project is usable by the widest possible audience. This chapter covers areas you'll find useful, such as iterative development methods, participatory design, using focus groups and surveys for research, expert evaluation, and use of personas.

First, if *accessibility* is mostly about people with disabilities, what is *usability*?

What Is Usability?

Usability is a subset of human/computer interaction (HCI) that looks at the quality of the user experience and attempts to understand how to improve it. Usability as a discipline attempts to determine how successfully a user can complete a task and how satisfying a device or interface might be to use. This can be determined for any diverse group that you can think of, such as vision-impaired or blind people and older people, but it also can be determined for users without disabilities.

■ **Note** The area of *UX*, or *user experience*, is expanding these days. This is largely due to the power of consumer choice, such as potential customers being able to easily access alternatives to your service if they aren't 100 percent happy with yours.

There are different definitions of *usability*, and we'll look at several because they are nuanced and have individual implications. One popular definition of usability is the following:

> *"A measure of how easy it is for a user to complete a task. In the context of Web pages this concerns how easy it is for a user to find the information they require from a given Web site."* [1]

---

[1] www.webarch.co.za/jargon.html

This definition is focused on the user being able to complete a specific task , which is obviously very important. However, is it the full picture?

Another interesting definition is this one:

"The ease with which a system can be learnt or used. A figure of merit or qualitative judgment of ease of use or learning. Some methods of assessing usability may also express usability as a quantitative index." [2]

I like this one, and I mention it here because it talks about how easily the system can be learned by the user. For me, a good rule of thumb in user-interface design is this: if you have to provide instructions on how to use it, it's already too complicated!

The user of your web sites and applications ideally should intuitively *get it*. This is, of course, not possible in many domains. The user won't just get how to fly a plane, for example. In fact, there are stories of disasters that befell pilots and surgeons, for example (or more explicitly the passengers and the patients) because of complexity in a UI. No one wants to have to hunt for and decipher a manual when the plane is going down in order to figure out what the obscure error message flashing on the dashboard means.

▥ **Tip** For a really interesting read that documents these kind of techno horror stories, as well as discussing the wider need for more "human" technologies, have a look at the book *Leonardo's Laptop: Human Needs and the New Computing Technologies* by Ben Schneiderman. It shows that *user friendly* is a far from wooly notion.

This third definition is one of the most interesting because it goes beyond dryly looking at the tasks the user needs to do and mentions the level of satisfaction the user will feel when using a web interface.

"The effectiveness, efficiency, and satisfaction with which specified users can achieve specified goals in a particular environment. Synonymous with 'ease of use'." [3]

This final definition takes the usability ideal to a higher level by looking at the quality of the user experience and not merely taking a mechanical, task-based approach. This is where user testing is very useful because it is a fantastic way of assessing the quality of the user experience.

---

[2] www.sqatester.com/glossary/index.htm
[3] www.jnd.org

■ **Note** I'll say more on user testing later. User testing is a great tool for meeting end users and getting really useful feedback from them on the quality of your user interface. Nothing says "success" like hearing one of your users happily say, "I found using that web site really easy, and I could do what I wanted. I'll be back." Also, nothing says "fail" quite as loudly as the user threatening to throw the monitor out the window in frustration. User testing is the key to this kind of feedback.

Donald Norman, one of the fathers of usability, has this to say on his web site about the best ways to get user feedback about the usability of a system:

> *"I caution that logical analysis is not a good way to predict people's behavior (nor are focus groups or surveys): observation is the key [...] For both products and services I'm a champion of beauty, pleasure and fun, coupled with behavioral and functional effectiveness."* [4]

Usability is about looking at how usable, intuitive, user friendly, and simply satisfying an interface is to use. As a discipline, it also examines the psychology of user interaction, or *cognitive ergonomics*. It is an attempt to understand how users perceive the instructions they receive from looking at or interacting with a user interface or device.

■ **Note** Although accessibility and usability are two different fields, there is a very strong relationship between the two. The following techniques are often used in the preparatory phase of a project and, if sufficient care is taken to use these techniques well, these requirements-gathering and prototyping phases can help authors avoid very serious mistakes in a UI design further on in the project.

I also highly recommend books by Donald Norman. In particular, the excellent (both fun, short, and easy to read) *The Design of Everyday Things* (with its distinctive teapot on the cover). He talks about the psychology of design and lays down some ground rules for good interaction design. For example, a couple of simple but profound ideas he puts forth are called the "Gulf of Evaluation" and the "Gulf of Execution." I'm sure you have come across both online unaware, and becoming aware of them will help you to design better HTML5 interfaces.

According to his book, the "Gulf of Evaluation" is small "when the system provides information about its state in a form that is easy to get, is easy to interpret, and matches the way the person thinks of the system." This gulf describes situations where a web site doesn't tell you, in a way that is intuitive and

---

[4] www.jnd.org

easy to understand, either what it is doing or what state it is in—or it doesn't even give you any feedback at all!

The "Gulf of Execution" outlines the difference between what your users think they need to do, to perform some task such as booking tickets or finding information, and what the system requires them to do.

I come across them both all the time! I often spend time shouting at my computer, "Why did they do it *that* way? It doesn't make sense! It's so obvious that all they needed to do was [insert better design by Josh here]," and then I try to calm down. See if you can spot either gulf online, and be aware that when you design a UI you need to translate the idea of how you think the system should work that's in your head to a mental model your users will understand. When your users *get it* easily, that's good usability and good interaction design.

▦ **Note** While we are on the subject of good books, you should also read *Don't Make Me Think* by Steve Krugs and *About Face 3: The Essentials of Interaction Design*," by Robert Reimann, Alan Cooper, and Dave Cronin.

Universal Design

One of the most exciting developments in designing for inclusion in recent times has been universal design.

Universal design can be defined as follows:

> *"The design of products and environments to be usable by all people, to the greatest extent possible, without the need for adaptation or specialized design."* [5]

The "7 Principles of Universal Design," which are illustrated in Figures 9-1 through 9-7, were developed in 1997 by a working group of architects, product designers, engineers, and environmental design researchers, led by the late Ronald Mace at North Carolina State University. [6] The purpose of the principles is to guide the design of environments, products, and communications. According to the Center for Universal Design at NCSU, the principles "might be applied to evaluate existing designs, guide the design process and educate both designers and consumers about the characteristics of more usable products and environments."

---

[5] www.ncsu.edu/dso/general/universal-design.html

[6] Copyright © 1997 NC State University, The Center for Universal Design, College of Design

░ **Note** You might see some similarities between these principles and the WCAG 2.0, and there are. See which ones you can spot! The universal design (UD) guidelines are designed to span several domains from product design to information and communcation technologies (ICT) and the built environment. They are useful food for thought, even for your HTML5 projects.

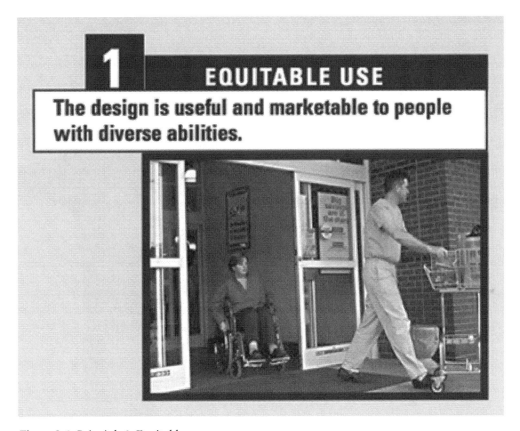

Figure 9-1. Principle 1: Equitable use

Here are the guidelines for this principle:

- 1a. Provide the same means of use for all users: make it identical whenever possible and equivalent when not.

- 1b. Avoid segregating or stigmatizing any users.

- 1c. Provisions for privacy, security, and safety should be equally available to all users.

- 1d. Make the design appealing to all users.

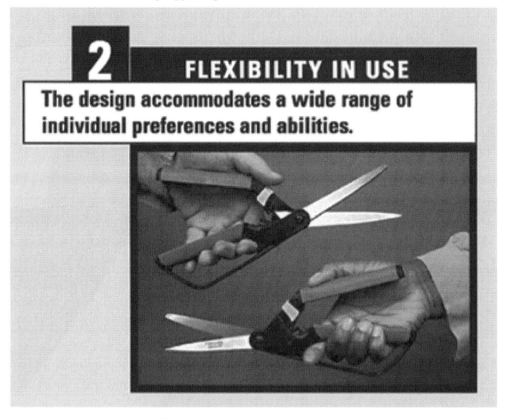

Figure 9-2. Principle 2: Flexibility in use

Here are the guidelines for this principle:

- 2a. Provide choice in methods of use.

- 2b. Accommodate right-handed and left-handed access and use.

- 2c. Facilitate the user's accuracy and precision.

- 2d. Provide adaptability to the user's pace.

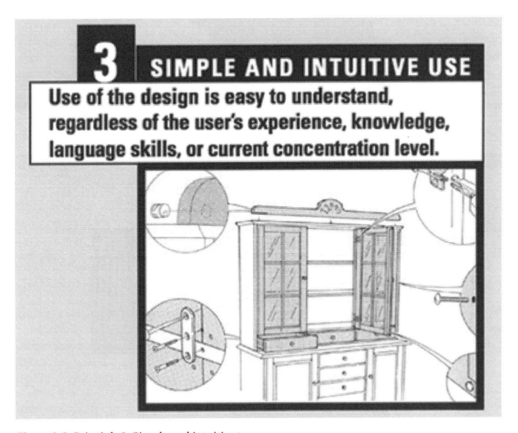

Figure 9-3. Principle 3: Simple and intuitive to use

Here are the guidelines for this principle:

- 3a. Eliminate unnecessary complexity.

- 3b. Be consistent with user expectations and intuition.

- 3c. Accommodate a wide range of literacy and language skills.

- 3d. Arrange information consistent with its importance.

- 3e. Provide effective prompting and feedback during the task and after task completion.

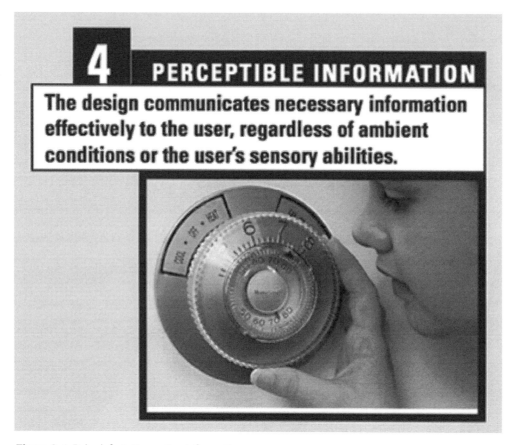

Figure 9-4. Principle 4: Perceptive information

Here are the guidelines for this principle:

- 4a. Use different modes (pictorial, verbal, tactile) for redundant presentation of essential information.

- 4b. Provide adequate contrast between essential information and its surroundings.

- 4c. Maximize legibility of essential information.

- 4d. Differentiate elements in ways that can be described (that is, make it easy to give instructions or directions).

- 4e. Provide compatibility with a variety of techniques or devices used by people with sensory limitations.

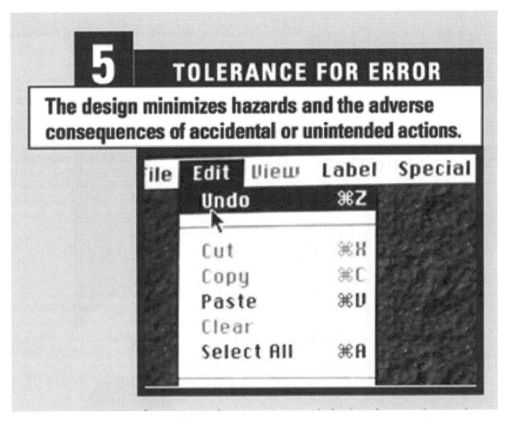

Figure 9-5. Principle 5: Tolerance for error

Here are the guidelines for this principle:

- 5a. Arrange elements to minimize hazards and errors. Possible arrangement include ordering by most used elements or the most accessible ones; eliminating, isolating, or shielding hazardous elements.

- 5b. Provide warnings of hazards and errors.

- 5c. Provide fail-safe features.

- 5d. Discourage unconscious action in tasks that require vigilance.

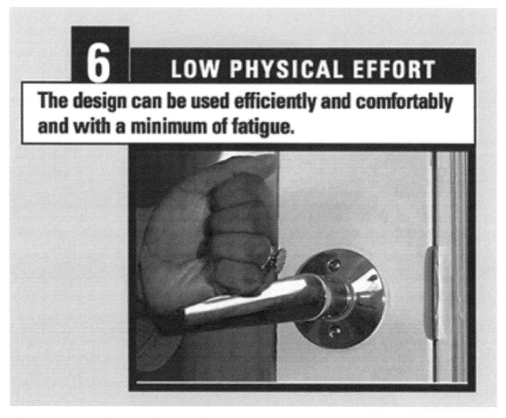

Figure 9-6. Principle 6: Low physical effort

Here are the guidelines for this principle:

- 6a. Allow user to maintain a neutral body position.
- 6b. Use reasonable operating forces.
- 6c. Minimize repetitive actions.
- 6d. Minimize sustained physical effort.

Figure 9-7. Principle 7: Size and space for approach and use

Here are the guidelines for this principle:

- 7a. Provide a clear line of sight to important elements for any seated or standing user.

- 7b. Make reach to all components comfortable for any seated or standing user.

- 7c. Accommodate variations in hand and grip size.

- 7d. Provide adequate space for the use of assistive devices or personal assistance.

■ **Tip** The HTML5 spec does make some claim to support "universal design." How would you do this in your projects? Think about it when you are building an HTML5 interface and when you have finished a prototype you are happy with. Go back to the UD principles and see if your web site adheres to them. It can be fun, as well as very instructive to do this.

Participatory Design

Jeffery Rubin (an influential usability expert) outlines participatory design as a technique where there might be one or more end users on the design team itself. The user is put at the heart of the process by having his knowledge, skill set, and emotional responses tapped by the designers.

In practice, you might not always have the resources (both financially and in terms of time) to do this, but if you are fortunate enough to work in a company with deep pockets, it could be worthwhile to explore this option. Rubin warns, however, that the user can get "consumed" by the process because teams that work closely together can end up in a sort of bubble—erroneously thinking that once everyone in the team can happily use or understand the system, it's ready for prime time!

Focus Group Research

Focus group research aims to evaluate the project's basic concepts at an early stage in the development process. It can be used to identify and confirm the characteristics of the user, and also to validate the projected effectiveness of the product. It usually involves multiple participants.

The concepts to be explored can be presented to the group in many forms, such as paper-and-pencil drawings, storyboards, PowerPoint presentations, 3D prototypes and models, and so on. The idea is to identify how acceptable the concepts are to the group participants and in what ways they can be improved.

Focus groups are certainly very useful and a worthwhile way of figuring out what the user wants from the project. It also can be an effective way of doing quick prototype testing of UI components or getting feedback on wireframe or other aspects of your HTML5 design.

Surveys

Surveys are often used to understand users' preferences about an existing product or a potential product. The survey is in some ways a more superficial way of collecting data than the focus group, but it is useful in particular to draw a picture of the views of a larger population. They can be used at any time but are often used at the beginning of a product development cycle.

Thorough survey design is very important, and a great deal of thought must go into survey design to ensure that questions are clear and unambiguous to get the best use from the returned data. It might not be practical for you to do a survey, but it is worth mentioning as a method of gaining information from end users. If you work on a university campus or in a large organization where there is an intranet, a survey is something you could do internally.

The Cognitive Walkthrough

The cognitive walkthrough is a common technique for evaluating the design of a user interface, with special attention paid to how well the interface supports *exploratory learning*—that is, successful first-time use without formal training. This evaluation can be performed by the system designer in the early stages of design—for example, before user testing is possible.

Early versions of the walkthrough method relied on a detailed series of questions to be answered on paper or electronic forms. These could take the form of "paper and pencil evaluations," which are a useful way of learning user preferences for certain attributes of a user interface, such as the organization and layout of menus or other controls.

Paper and pencil evaluations, which are literally drawings of your interface, - are useful because designers can find out critical information very quickly. They are also inexpensive and allow you to get some real feedback about how intuitive a user interface might be before any development work has taken place. This technique can be used as often as necessary and can be used in conjunction with, or instead of, prototyping software such as Serena Prototype Composer or Axure.

Expert Evaluations

Expert evaluations refers to bringing in a usability specialist who has little to do with the project to assess its usability. The expert applies usability principles to assess the quality of the system and any potential problems it might have. This type of evaluation can be performed in conjunction with an accessibility audit of the system to see how usable it would be by people with disabilities using assistive technology (AT).

Expert Accessibility Audits

An *accessibility audit* tests a web site or application for technical accessibility problems against guidelines such as WCAG 2.0. This is a really powerful way of seeing what is right or wrong with the system, from an independent party. It generally takes the form of a list of recommendations framed against a list of each of the WCAG 2.0 checkpoints.

However, the feedback from an audit must be actively incorporated in the project. This really happens only when it is done as a part of an *iterative* development process; it is not effective if the recommendations are tagged on at the end. The accessibility audit is one of the most useful tools if it's used properly. However, there is often a culture of minimum compliance—a "We'll get to it later, we have the audit" attitude that makes the exercise hollow and pointless.

The ideal path is to first create a well-designed site that incorporates best practice and, if possible, uses feedback from users—ideally incorporating that feedback in the development process at various stages, or *iterations*, of the project. When a stage of the project is in a steady state, it should then be accessibility audited by a third party (which is important for objectivity). After the results of the test have been incorporated, a user test should be done.

The user test is not just the icing on the cake, it's the acid test of success or failure.

Using Personas

In some instances, it might not be feasible to do a user test at all. This is where using personas can be useful. A *persona* is a distilled archetype of a certain user group's qualities and attributes. These attributes are models of the various qualities a user-experience professional thinks might epitomize a certain user group, such as blind people. They, therefore, build a persona around them.

Persona use aims to simulate what the experience of using a web site might be like for this group of users. If various personas are accurate, the simulation of their experience will likely be accurate also. Personas can be used to justify the modification of an application design, based on the perceived needs of the persona.

Building Personas

Personas are created from the gathered research about a target group. This can be from surveys, interviews, and so on. It is possible to build personas that represent an average user. These various groups can include older people, young people, blind users, and so on. A good persona comes from real-world feedback that has been gathered from real users.

Does Using Personas Work?

Although personas are widely used, there is little empirical evidence to support the claim that using personas actually improves the quality of the user-interface design. However, in a very interesting field study conducted by Frank Long of Frontend (an excellent Irish user experience and interface design company), the effectiveness of using personas was investigated. This took the form of an experiment conducted over a period of five weeks using students from the National College of Art and Design in Dublin. The results showed that, through using personas, designs with superior usability characteristics were produced. The results also indicated that using personas provides a significant advantage during the research and conceptualization stages of the design process (supporting previously unfounded claims).

The study also investigated the effects of using different presentation methods to present personas and concluded that photographs worked better than illustrations, and that visual storyboards were more effective in presenting task scenarios than text-only versions.

■ **Note** You can read the full paper "Real or Imaginary: The effectiveness of using personas in product design" by Frank Long at `www.frontend.com/products-digital-devices/real-or-imaginary-the-effectiveness-of-using-personas-in-product-design.html`.

Measuring the Effectiveness of Using Personas

Long's study produced objective evidence to support the key claims made by Cooper et al. (who invented them) for using personas in the product-design process. Using personas seemed to strengthen the focus by designers on the end user and the user's tasks, goals, and motivation. Personas make the needs of the end user more explicit and thereby can direct decision-making within design teams more toward those needs. The study also suggests that using personas can improve communication between teams and facilitate more constructive and user-focused design discussion.

The use of personas doesn't always get the thumbs-up, however. Research by Chapman and Milham aiming to critically evaluate the use of persona expressed concern about the claim that the use of personas was effective. They suggested that personas actually could be harmful and lead to skewed and incorrect conclusions, and they were therefore unreliable. They asked, "How many users are represented by this persona?", "Is this persona relevant for a group?", "Are personas a valid method at all (and how can this be verified)?" [7]

These are valid questions. Long also found that using illustrations instead of photographs of the persona seem to reduce effectiveness and reduce empathy toward the illustrated persona. Also, the use of a storyboard task scenario was more effective than the text version and facilitated more detailed design solutions.

Long concluded that using personas offers several benefits for user-centered design in product development, such as enhancing the possibility of incorporating user-centered features at the product-specification stage. And he provided some objective evidence that using personas does work.

Field Studies

Field studies is a term that refers to testing a product or interface in its natural setting, which is the ideal. This setting can be an office, home, or any other environment that realistically reflects how the product will be used. A field study might or might not be possible to do, and when undertaken late in the product cycle it should be viewed not as an indicator of significant issues with the product or interface but as a way of refining it.

Traditional Usability Testing

Traditional usability testing involves testing with a random sample of the public or a sample of representative users, who will in practice be using a web application or web site. This type of testing is an attempt to assess the quality of the user experience. The outcomes of the test—such as whether a user can successfully complete a certain task or set of tasks, the ease of use with which could the user completed the tasks, and other user feedback and observations made during the test—are all noted by the test facilitator. This recorded information is valuable because it allows an experienced usability analyst to gain a detailed picture of what is or is not working for the end user in a particular user-interface design.

Although traditional usability testing is very useful, it usually captures only a small sample of issues. It is not exhaustive, but any difficulties become immediately apparent during the test. An experienced usability professional understands exactly how the design or implementation contributes to these problems and what can be done to fix them.

User Testing with People with Disabilities

Although user testing with people who do not have disabilities often yields many positive results that can certainly improve the user experience, these users generally have more standard requirements and might not need or use AT.

Therefore, involving people with disabilities in user testing is often the best way to get a detailed picture of how usable an interface, application, or web site is for people who use AT. There are also many people with mild to moderate disabilities who don't use AT and rely on the accessibility settings of their

---

[7] Chapman, C.N, and Milham, R. P (2006) The persona's new clothes: methodological and practical arguments against a popular method Proceedings of the Human Factors and Ergonomics Society 50th Annual Meeting, pp. 634 –636. Available online at:
http://cnchapman.files.wordpress.com/2007/03/chapman-milham-personas-hfes2006-0139-0330.pdf

operating system, their browser, and good keyboard accessibility. By closely studying the experience of a user with a disability, it is possible to gain deep insight into how your design choices and decisions impact the user experience.

If you do user testing *iteratively*—that is, by involving people with disabilities in the full development and design cycle of a project—you can form a much more rounded picture of the user experience and make effective design decisions early on.

Formal vs. Informal User Testing

Formal usability analysis and user testing conjures images of the stern scientist with a white coat taking notes behind a one-way, glass observation screen—while the test participant is relayed commands and tasks via a talkback system or feedback relay. These instructions, of course, must be given in a voice drained of any hint of emotion or semblance of humanity to avoid the sin of bias within the test. These images, while obviously caricatures, are what many people think of when they hear the words "observation," "testing," and "analysis." However, it's a rather outdated view that's at odds with the current trends and habits in the field of user testing.

Formal user testing is very much associated with the *scientific method.* Although this approach is certainly valid in certain domains, it is not what we are concerned with here. The formal method is associated with statistical analysis and control experiments. In terms of road testing your HTML5 projects, what we are concerned with here is the more real-world approach of *informal user testing.* This is where testing often has to be done quickly, as a part of an iterative development cycle (in the best of cases) and as an add-on at the end of a project as some attempt at validation, at worst.

More informal user testing is where there is a *test script* and a series of tasks that have been outlined beforehand. The test facilitator might also have a relationship that has been built up over the years where the test facilitator and participant have done many, many tests together.

Measuring User-Testing Outputs

User tests have certain outputs. These are varied and can be the accumulated notes of the test facilitator, the video footage collected during the test for later analysis, the collective impression of uninvolved observers of the test, and so on. Some outputs are more tangible, such as video that can be archived and viewed later. Some are less tangible but are still very valuable, such as the lasting impressions a user test can leave on the observers when they have watched someone use their web site.

These less tangible impressions and subjective experiences, however, can result in very real outputs. A product can be dropped, a software iteration cycle abandoned, and so on if a project manager sees a live, real-time negative user response to one of a product's interfaces. Conversely, a designer can be vindicated because the results of her design efforts and attention to detail come to fruition when a user says, "Yes, that web site is great. I can find the information I need really easily. I like the way the page is designed." This experience can be more profound when the person being observed has a disability.

It is not by observing the average, user-experience testing where a usability expert gets the interesting information. It is the extreme cases—both positive and negative—where the really interesting aspects of user-testing analysis take place. This is where both positive and negative experiences are amplified and made quite explicit, so there is often no ambiguity. The language is often less than neutral, so there can be little doubt of the user's impression and feelings about a particular user interface or application.

How Does User Testing Work?

Figure 9-8 is an example of a user-testing facility (the one where I work at the NCBI Centre for Inclusive Technology). The figure shows the layout of the rooms and equipment.

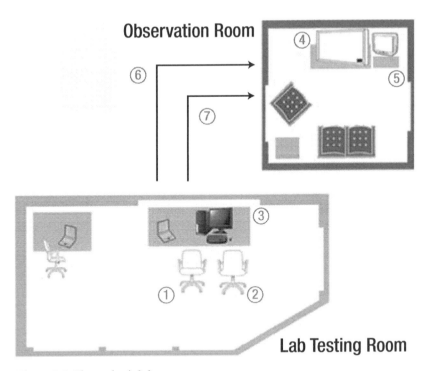

Figure 9-8. The author's lab

The User Environment

The user test participant (1) sits in a typical office environment within the testing room, which is controlled for sound. The test facilitator (2) sits with the user, explaining the tasks, taking notes, and critically observing the user's interactions. The test is conducted using a standard PC (3) with assistive hardware and software. Dedicated user test recording software such as Morae, together with discreet cameras and microphones, capture and record every aspect of the user-testing session for later analysis.

The Observation Environment

Observers can watch the test in real time from the comfort of observation room couches. The video from the user's monitor (6) is displayed on a flat screen TV (4), while a second signal from the camera and microphone (7) shows the user's gestures, facial expressions, body language, and vocalizations on a television monitor (5).

Through these links, observers can see everything the user does and says, as well as the interaction between the user and the facilitator.

Test Details

A typical user test consists of eight separate user sessions of one to one and a half hours each. The types of use that are tested cover a broad range of disabilities and assistive technologies. It also allows us to include younger and older users with people with different levels of experience. This results in a more representative sample of attitudes and approaches. Figure 9-9 shows one participant at the center.

Figure 9-9. *A user test participant in the NCBI Centre for Inclusive Technology usability lab*

Each user carries out a set of realistic tasks that have been agreed on beforehand with the client. These usually include the most common tasks for which the product is used, as well as the most critical tasks and any tasks that the test facilitator might anticipate causing problems for users. Tests are carefully designed and run to yield the most realistic user behavior possible. Figure 9-10 shows a facilitator and user together in the testing lab.

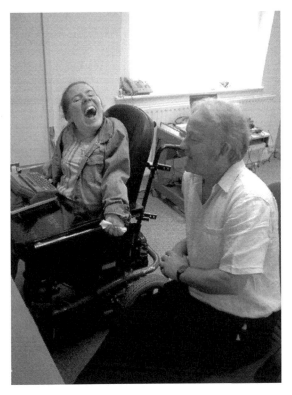

Figure 9-10. User test facilitator and participant in the NCBI Centre for Inclusive Technology lab

Basic Elements of User Testing

Rubin outlines a basic methodology and standard elements for more informal testing [8]:

- Develop problem statements or test objectives rather than hypotheses.
- Use a representative sample of end users, which might or might not be randomly chosen.
- Use a representation of the work environment.
- Observe end users (with a representative product).

---

[8] Handbook of Usability Testing: How to Plan, Design, and Conduct Effective Tests (Wiley Technical Communications Library)

- Use controlled interrogation and probing of the participants by a test monitor (facilitator).

- Collect both quantitative and qualitative performance and preference measures.

- Recommend improvements to the design of the product.

The preceding points form an outline of the core aspects of user testing. When I undertake a test, I talk to the client first and ask him or her what the core areas of the site are that he or she wants me to look at. Remember that your client will be far more familiar with the system than you are (unless you built it, of course!). Then I draw up a test script based on some of this feedback and my own testing of the site, which I do beforehand to identify any possible problem areas. I then recruit users with different types of disabilities such as low-vision, blindness, limited mobility, or cognitive/sensory disabilities. I try to mix up the age range of the test participants also, because this gives better results.

■ **Note** Although it is great to have as diverse a group as possible, don't try to do too much, either. It is good to have a smaller group that gives good feedback and do several iterations of tests. Practical things like availability are often a big issue, and the logistics can be awkward because people promise to take part and then drop out and so on. You've just got to roll with it!

When performing tests, initially I was very conscious of not leading the user and tried to be very scientific about the whole thing. I soon realized, however, that this wasn't always necessary or wise. I had to face the fact that the whole test is artificial and contrived—trying to make it not so, or to ignore the reality of the situation in the name of some science, seemed to me to be rather shallow and pointless. When you acknowledge that the test is artificial, you put both yourself and the test participant at ease and you might find that you enjoy the process. In my opinion, this is healthy and can result in better data.

"Why?" you might ask. For a start, test participants might be more inclined to be more honest when they are relaxed. Also, they'll be more inclined to take chances and try new things that they might not try if they are uptight. The reason for this is interesting, and it took me a long time to realize it: the user test participants often want to please the test facilitator and don't want to be seen as not being able to do something. This is even more true when testing with people with disabilities—they might be very self-conscious, so you need to be aware of this and clearly explain that *they* are not being tested. If a person can't perform some task, they might feel there is something wrong with them, and the issue could well be an accessibility and usability issue that even Steve Hawking couldn't understand! So try to relax and even have fun. It's worth it. And if you do more testing with the same people, you'll build a rapport with them and understand their interaction patterns. If you are at ease, that will be a great help to them.

Observing a User Test

Observing user tests, as shown in Figure 9-11, is one of the best ways to gain a firsthand understanding of what accessibility and usability really mean. Designers and developers in particular can get huge benefits from the insights they gain from observing users.

Some facilities have a dedicated observation room, like ours. Using a wide screen TV and a small video monitor, clients can watch and listen to the user tests via a remote link without disturbing the users in their tasks.

Figure 9-11. Observing a user test in the NCBI Centre for Inclusive Technology observation room

Digital video recordings of user sessions are then often used to review the sessions after the test and to illustrate key issues. The emphasis is on building an understanding of how the design of the site contributes to users' difficulties and what practical steps can be taken to alleviate these problems.

Goals and Benefits of User Testing

There are several areas where a user test will help your HTML5 projects. One of the main goals is that it will help you identify problems your site users might have and give you the opportunity to fix them before you go live.

Some questions to bear in mind are the following:

- Is your site both easy to learn and to use?

- Is it satisfying to use?

- Will the site be valued by the user by providing the functionality that the user needs?

Here are some of the benefits of user testing:

- User testing your projects and documenting the results will give you a point of reference for later versions of your site.

- The amount of time spent on supporting/maintaining your site will be reduced if it is a quality project from the start. So the effort you put into gaining feedback from your users will pay for itself in the long run.

- A better site will result in more sales or greater use of your site, as well as fewer complaints.

- A better site gives you an advantage over your competitors.

■ **Note** It is interesting that there has been a large increase in demand for the services of usability professionals over the last few years, as the Internet has become more pervasive and the consumer has gained far more choices. Usability comes into its own when the quality of the user experience is a determinant of what your site users will buy and the services that they will use.

Limitations of Testing

Although user testing is undoubtedly useful and an important part of the user-centered design development cycle, there are some drawbacks to testing that you should be aware of:

- **User tests are contrived environments:** No matter how you slice it, user testing and observing people using a product or service is artificial. What you see is only a facsimile of real usage, and users often will not behave the way they would in their own environment. The act of observing something changes it.

- **User test results might not actually prove that your HTML5 web site really works:** To do *statistically significant* testing, you have to do a lot of it. Most of the resources at our disposal don't allow us to do this. Also, end users might often miss very obvious errors in your site that are apparent to you (if you built it or are an experienced test facilitator), even in larger test samples.

- **Your user-test participants don't often truly represent your target audience:** Even when you are being very careful to choose the right people, the test results might be skewed from the start because you might have too many more advanced users or too many users with only a basic level of digital literacy. Finding the right balance is often very hard. Again, to do tests that are more representative of the wider audience, you need to recruit a lot more than is practical for most developers to do.

- **Is user testing always the best technique to use?** This is an important question. For example, an expert evaluation in the form of a usability evaluation might be the best approach for your project. There might be expertise needed to use the system in the first place, so testing with novice users isn't ideal in this situation.

Digital Literacy

One recurring issue is that of the level of fluency a person has with both the AT he uses, as well as with the Web and technology in general. In the early days of your testing process, if you are inexperienced you might see a user having problems and think it is the fault of the user interface or the site design. But is it? You need to be sure. This is where using an experienced test facilitator can pay off—in particular, using someone who understands deeply how AT works. There aren't many around, but if you can find them, they are worth work with. This is because the knowledge such an expert brings to your project will be invaluable when it comes to understanding and analyzing your test results. You have to remember that you will need to make design decisions based on these outcomes.

So What's the Best Method for Me to Assess My HTML5 Project?

As you can see from what we have covered, there are a wide range of user evaluation methods available. It can be very difficult, even for usability professionals, to get a true picture of the user evaluation method—user testing, focus groups, prototyping, or other method—that is best suited to any given project. Here are some of the main issues:

- **The evaluator effect.** This is where different test facilitators or evaluators come up with varying results for the same data set.

- **Lack of scientific rigor when applying usability evaluation techniques.** This has the net effect of greatly diluting the reliability of much user data that is collected during a user test or other usability evaluation method.

- **A general lack of appropriate standards or metrics that can be used to compare evaluation methods.**

In short, there is no "one size fits all" method, so you have to approach your projects in the context of what you need from testing and the resources you have. It does get easier in time, and you'll learn what to ignore and what to pay attention to as you gain experience.

Iterative Design Processes

There is also much made in usability circles of the importance of a *responsive*, or iterative, design process. (You might have noticed the references to that in this chapter.) In practice, however, there is often little agreement on exactly how to achieve this.

■ **Note** The essence of the iterative design process is to include user involvement as early as possible in each stage of the build. If you break the project into three stages—such as the Initial Stage, the Prototype Stage, and the Final Stage, ideally the outcome of usability testing from each stage is fed into each consecutive stage. This results in a site that has a core of real-world feedback from users at its heart.

Is Usability the New Economics?

There is an old joke, that if you ask four economists the same question, you get five answers. To some degree, it is similar in the area of usability. Even the most seasoned professionals looking at the same data often come up with very different analyses of what a critical issue is. There are often cases where they come up with very few similar issues.

However, this isn't to say that the user-centered design processes discussed in this chapter aren't useful. They are, but it isn't an exact science. If you want to take the plunge and start using some of these methods, I strongly encourage you to go for it. You will make mistakes, but trust your instincts and learn from the mistakes. It is very worthwhile and satisfying to build humane technologies that help people do what they want to or, indeed, need to online.

▦ **Note** Much of the advice I give in this chapter is based on a combination of years of experience doing user testing myself, and being influenced by the work of people like Donald Norman and, in particular, Jeffery Rubin. I highly recommend Rubin's book *Handbook of Usability Testing: How to Plan, Design, and Conduct Effective Tests* for further reading.

Conclusion

This chapter was an introduction to many user-centered design processes and methodologies. You should feel free to pick and choose whatever works for your particular needs and circumstances. There is no "one size fits all" method. However, I strongly recommend that you start to try incorporating them into your HTML5 projects as best you can.

One of the most ironic things for me, as someone who has for years been doing user testing of web sites and applications involving people with disabilities, is that often the simple act of letting a developer meet with and observe people with disabilities using their system is very powerful. There is often an epiphany for the developer. A realization dawns that all the talk of accessibility, usability, and the application of various guidelines are not empty or esoteric exercises. The good and (indeed) bad coding and design decisions you and I make do have an impact on people's lives, in ways that we might not initially have the capacity to perceive.

CHAPTER 10

Tools, Tips, and Tricks: Assessing Your Accessible HTML5 Project

In this chapter, you'll look at some tools and techniques available to help you make your accessible HTML5 site be the best it can be. By spending a little time with the some of the tools I'll outline here, you can avoid some common pitfalls, as well as test your work (or indeed the work of others) to get some idea of its level of accessibility and assess some aspects of its usability.

■ **Note** The good news is there are lots of plugins for your favorite browser; the bad news is that there are lots of plugins for your favorite browser! In this chapter, I'll outline some that I am most familiar with or that I use in my day-to-day assessment of web sites for my clients.

We'll discuss topics such as *validation* and *automated accessibility checking*, and you'll see how to use a screen reader in testing (both how to do it and how not to do it). You'll also look at how to do quick "Guerilla User Testing" (which should be fresh in your mind after the last chapter). And, in the event that you don't have the facility to do user testing with real people, the chapter shows some simple simulation techniques that might help you understand how people with disabilities might experience your web site.

Useful Tools for Developers

Coming up now we will look at some indispensable tools that you can use to improve the accessibility of your HTML5 projects.

The Chris Pederick Web Developer Toolbar

I'm sad to say that the first tool you'll look at no longer is being maintained by the developer. However, it was one of best. It's the Chris Pederick Web Developer Toolbar for Firefox, shown in Figure 10-1.

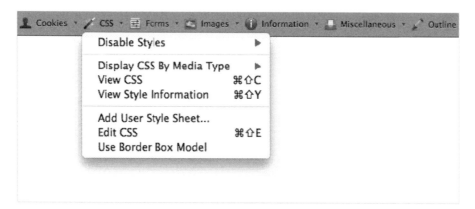

Figure 10-1. The Web Developer Toolbar in Firefox

This was an elegant tool you could use to test pages for the presence of HTML headings, unlabeled form controls, images with missing @alt, and many other very useful accessibility-related things. The last official release of it was for Firefox 4, and there was a Chrome release also. Having said that, the plugin still works in one of my instances of Firefox 9 (that I use), but it might be buggy. I hope that in the future an updated plugin will be released that will work with newer browsers. It is worth mentioning purely because it was so good. For more details, keep an eye on http://chrispederick.com/work/web-developer.

WAT-C Web Accessibility Toolbar (Internet Explorer and Opera)

The Web Accessibility Tools Consortium (WAT-C) developed the tool that Jim Thatcher (who developed one of the first screen readers) described as, "The best thing that has happened for accessibility in recent years." Developed by Steve Faulkner (of TPG) and Jun (of WAT-C), the WAT-C Web Accessibility Toolbar is shown in Figure 10-2.

Figure 10-2. The Web Accessibility Toolbar in Internet Explorer

This is a great tool for both identifying the various components of a webpage and giving you access to alternate views of page content. You can use it to get an overview of the structure (or lack of structure), how well tables are marked up (for example, if they have table headers, suitable captioning, or summary data), and so on. The Web Accessibility Toolbar is available in languages such as English, French, Italian, German, and Chinese. WAT-C is always working on new versions of its tools—a full range of which can be found on the WAT-C web site at www.wat-c.org/tools.

Colour Contrast Analyser

Another excellent tool that I use often is the Colour Contrast Analyser, shown in Figure 10-3.

■ **Note** I first came across this tool as a browser plugin for Firefox that was originally developed by Gez Lemon (of TPG, Juicy Studio).

I'm on a Mac (most of the time), so I like to use tools native to that platform (although I do a lot of testing on a PC also). I was really glad when Cédric Trévisan (of TPG) developed the Colour Contrast Analyser for Mac, a really nice tool I use to check the foreground and background color of a user interface. It can tell me if these colors might be problematic for vision-impaired people.

The tool checks foreground and background color combinations to determine if they provide good color visibility. It also contains functionality to create simulations of certain visual conditions, such as color blindness.

The idea of *color visibility* is based on the Contrast Ratio algorithm suggested by the Worldwide Web Consortium (W3C).

■ **Note** The contrast ratio is a W3C recommendation to help determine whether or not the contrast between two colors can be read by people with color blindness or other visual impairments.

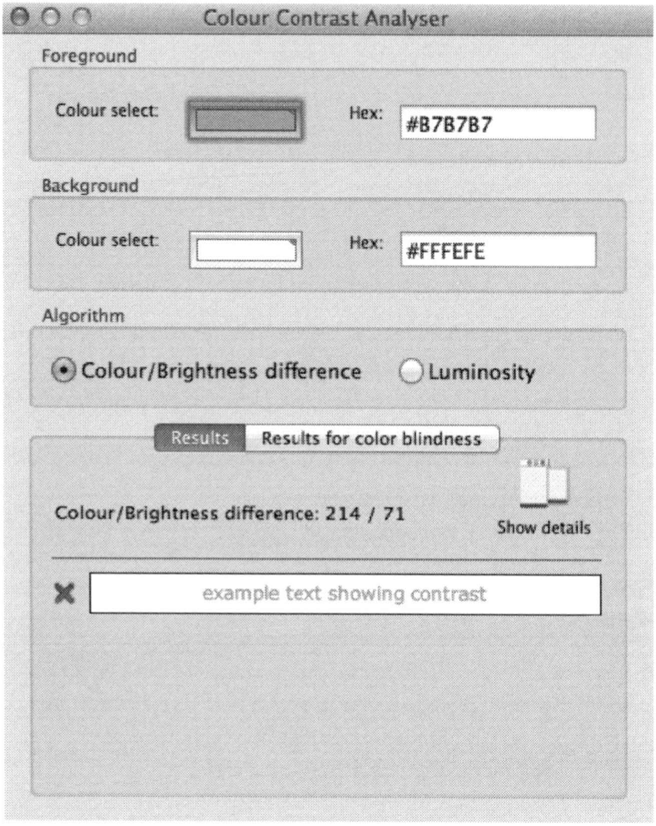

Figure 10-3. The Colour Contrast Analyser (Mac version)

You can use the tool to help determine, in particular, the legibility of text on a webpage and the legibility of image-based representations of text. It is particularly useful when you want to see if your content is compliant with Web Content Accessibility Guidelines (WCAG). For example, the WCAG2.0 Guideline 1.4, which addresses making content distinguishable, states that you should do the following:

> *"Make it easier for users to see and hear content including separating foreground from background."* [1]

Guideline 1.4.3 Contrast (Minimum) states the following:

---

[1] www.w3.org/TR/UNDERSTANDING-WCAG20/visual-audio-contrast.html

The visual presentation of text and images of text has a contrast ratio of at least 4.5:1, except for the following (Level AA):

- **Large Text:** *Large-scale text and images of large-scale text have a contrast ratio of at least 3:1.*
- **Incidental:** *Text or images of text that are part of an inactive user interface component, that are pure decoration, that are not visible to anyone, or that are part of a picture that contains significant other visual content, have no contrast requirement.*
- **Logotypes:** *Text that is part of a logo or brand name has no minimum contrast requirement.*

Guideline 1.4.6: Contrast (Enhanced) states this:

The visual presentation of text and images of text has a contrast ratio of at least 7:1, except for the following: (Level AAA):

- **Large Text:** *Large-scale text and images of large-scale text have a contrast ratio of at least 4.5:1.*

- **Incidental:** *Text or images of text that are part of an inactive user interface component, that are pure decoration, that are not visible to Logotypes: Text that is part of a logo or brand name has no minimum contrast requirement.*

The Colour Contrast Analyser is really useful to help you test if your color contrast is sufficient to satisfy these two points. It proves a clever way of providing you with instant feedback, as you can see in Figure 10-4.

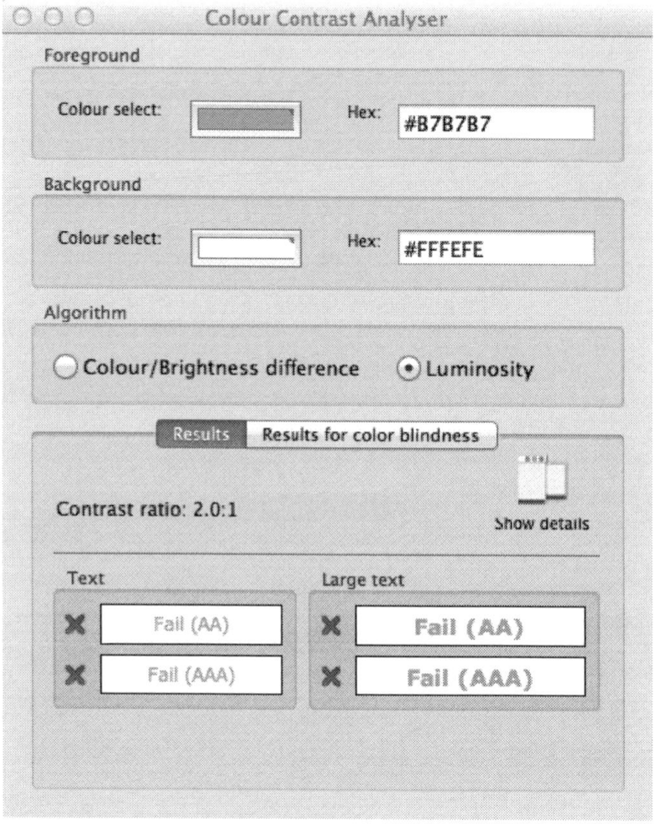

Figure 10-4. *Colour Contrast Analyser feedback (Mac version)*

WAVE

WAVE is my current favorite tool for checking webpage accessibility and quickly spotting potential problems. It is one that I turn to again and again these days. It is a free accessibility evaluation tool developed by the WebAIM crew (whose work you can explore at the excellent www.WebAIM.org web site). The WebAIM site itself is a fantastic resource for all things related to accessibility, and it has become a hub for the accessibility community worldwide, including practitioners, experts, and newbies alike. I highly recommend you point your browser in that direction.

So what does WAVE do? The idea is that WAVE is used to aid humans in the web-accessibility evaluation process. Rather than providing a complex technical report, WAVE shows the original webpage with embedded icons and indicators that reveal the accessibility of that page.

There are a few different ways to *WAVE* a page. You can use the web site and enter a URL, upload a file, or input HTML code directly. Figure 10-5 is a screen shot of the WAVE web site.

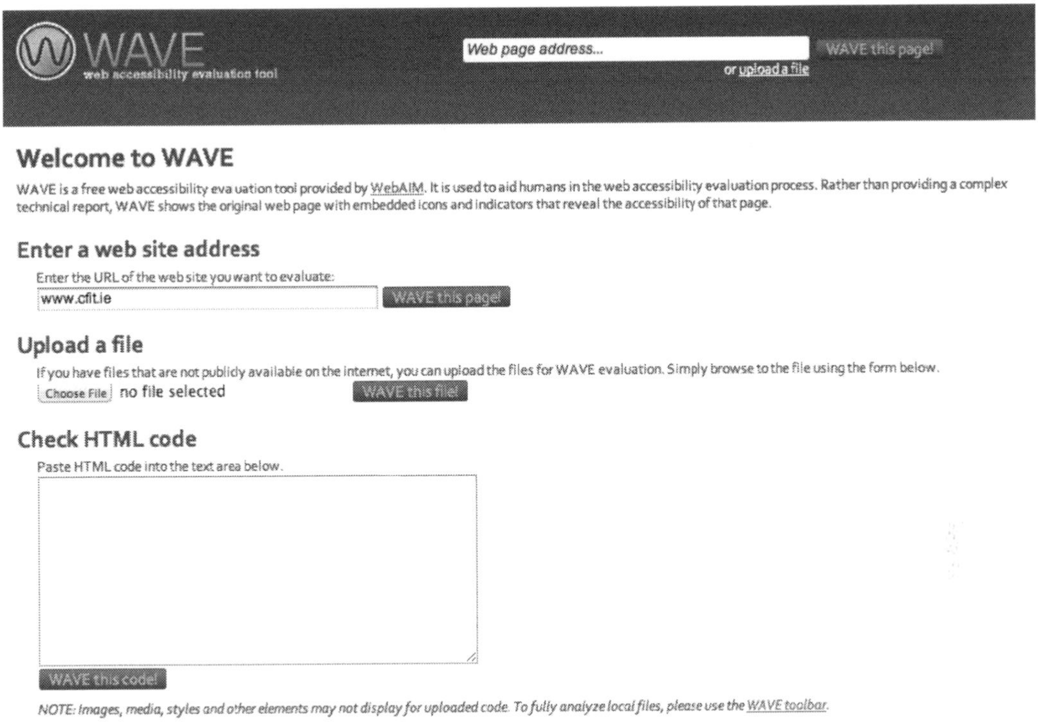

WAVE
web accessibility evaluation tool
Web page address...
WAVE this page!
or upload a file
Welcome to WAVE
WAVE is a free web accessibility evaluation tool provided by WebAIM. It is used to aid humans in the web accessibility evaluation process. Rather than providing a complex technical report, WAVE shows the original web page with embedded icons and indicators that reveal the accessibility of that page.
Enter a web site address
Enter the URL of the web site you want to evaluate:
www.cfit.ie
WAVE this page!
Upload a file
If you have files that are not publicly available on the internet, you can upload the files for WAVE evaluation. Simply browse to the file using the form below.
Choose File
no file selected
WAVE this file!
Check HTML code
Paste HTML code into the text area below.
WAVE this code!
NOTE: Images, media, styles and other elements may not display for uploaded code. To fully analyze local files, please use the WAVE toolbar.

Figure 10-5. *The WAVE home page at http://wave.webaim.org*

If you have some local files that you want to evaluate for accessibility, you can download and install the WAVE plugin for Firefox, and there is also a Dream Weaver extension. There are other options too, such as adding WAVE into your webpages via links or WAVE buttons. You can create quick links and bookmarks for automatically processing pages in WAVE, or you can implement WAVE in other tools, such as the Google toolbar.

My preference is to use the WAVE tool as a plugin for Firefox. This approach is shown in Figure 10-6.

NCBI Centre for Inclusive Technology
NCBI Centre for Inclusive Techn...
cfit.ie
Google
WAVE
Errors, Features, and Alerts
Structure/Order
Text-only
Outline
Reset Page
Disable Styles
Icons Key
Tools

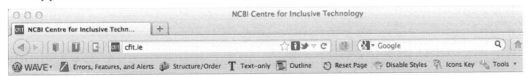

Figure 10-6. *WAVE plugin for Firefox*

The great thing about WAVE for me is that I find that it functions in a very elegant way. If you take a web site, such as my own for the NCBI Centre for Inclusive Technology (CFIT), you can see before and after pictures of a WAVE evaluation. Figure 10-7 is the page before WAVE is applied.

Figure 10-7. *The CFIT web site pre-WAVE*

Later, by adding the URL to the WAVE tool, you see the result shown in Figure 10-8. This shows how WAVE evaluates the page giving you excellent visual feedback highlighting both errors and aspects of the site that are accessible.

Figure 10-8. The CFIT web site post-WAVE

So my work home page gets a pretty good bill of health. You can see that the tool has added useful icons to indicate where there are headings present on the page, as well as some null @alt text, which I added. The WAVE tool also gives you the option to look at structural outlines of a page in more detail. When the Outline option is activated, the WAVE tool displays the page shown in Figure 10-9.

h1 Home

h2 Creating an inclusive Future Internet: Web 2.0 applications for all

h2 CFIT at Include 2011

h2 Notes from #CSUN11

h2 Inclusive Teaching of Inclusive Design

h3 What We Do

h3 Consultancy

h3 About Us

h3 News and commentary

h3 What we're doing now

h3 CFIT is also involved in...

Figure 10-9. The WAVE page outline feature

■ **Note** The tool has other options you might find useful, such as being able to explore the Structure/Order option, or see text only. The most common option is to activate errors, features and alerts. This option gives you exactly that, doing just what it says on the tin.

How about testing the Errors, Features And Alerts options on a page that might have some accessibility errors? By running the Irishtimes.com web site through the WAVE tool, you get the results shown in Figure 10-10. It's fair to say that the site is actually not too bad from an accessibility perspective, but there is always room for improvement.

Figure 10-10. Using WAVE on the Irishtimes.com home page

You can see that the WAVE tool has detected 15 possible accessibility errors. These are brought to your attention by the really useful little icons that are embedded in the page by the evaluation tool.

■ **Note** WAVE also shows you good things about your site! It's the red icons that are possibly problematic.

You can see that the search box area on the Irish Times web site needs some attention and might be problematic, so let's explore that a little further. Figure 10-11 shows the error detail that appears when you mouse over an icon.

Figure 10-11. Mouse over an error to see more details

By moving your mouse over the icon, you'll get more info about the potential problem. You can see from Figure 10-11 that the search <input> text box is missing a suitable label. The absence of a label makes it harder for screen-reader users to know what the <input> is for. So this is important. This easy way of being able to quickly spot problem areas makes the WAVE tool very usable and effective.

You can find explanations of the icons that WAVE uses by clicking the Icons Key button in the toolbar. Doing so will give you the icon legend shown in Figure 10-12, which outlines the icons used for Errors and Alerts (such as HTML, scripting-related, and media alerts). By clicking this button, you also can see the structural and semantic elements of a site as well as some accessibility features.

Index of WAVE Icons

Hover over the icons with your mouse for a brief description or click on an icon for a detailed description.

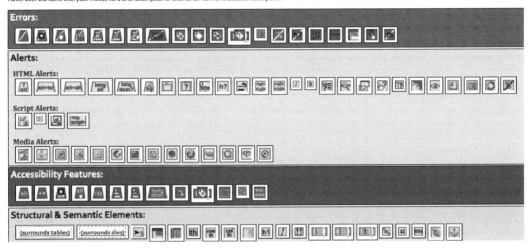

Figure 10-12. The index of WAVE icons

■ **Tip** Something that I really like about WAVE is that it quickly implemented support for some WAI-ARIA roles, states, and other items. It's great to be able to also detect these easily using WAVE.

Firebug

Another current jewel in the crown of "really useful tools that you just gotta use" is Firebug. You can see the home page of the company's web site in Figure 10-13.

Figure 10-13. Go to www.getfirebug.com. Now!

This tool really is a game-changer, and I was delighted when I first came across it. It has many useful things to recommend it.

Firebug is a browser plugin that allows you to edit and debug CSS, HTML, and JavaScript live in your webpages. You can view and edit your code within Firebug. You can examine your own code (as well as other people's code) to help you improve what you are building as well as reverse engineer how others do things. Firebug has other nifty features you can use to accelerate your JavaScript runtimes as well as debug JavaScript. You can use it to check HTTP header data and do *XMLHttpRequest* monitoring. I could just go on saying how great it is, but I won't. Just point your browser at getfirebug.com/ and check it out of yourself.

Tools in the Browser

Note that browsers such as Safari (Figure 10-14) and Opera (Figure 10-15) have built-in DOM and CSS inspection tools. What you use ultimately comes down to your preferences and whatever fits the way you like to work.

Figure 10-14. Safari Web Inspection Tool

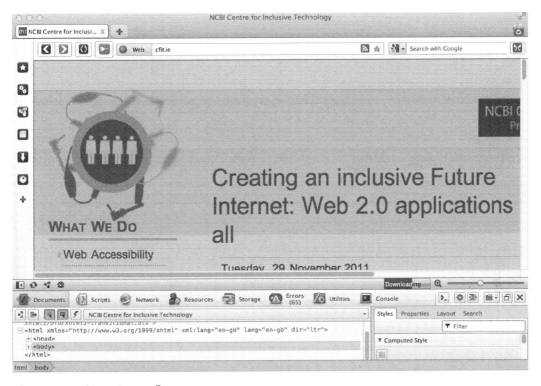

Figure 10-15. *Opera Dragonfly*

Automated Accessibility Evaluation Tools

There are actually many automated accessibility tools. One of the first tools I used after reading Jeffery Zeldmans' book *Designing with Web Standards* (New Riders Press, 2009) and Joe Clark's book *Building Accessible Websites* (New Riders Press, 2002)—which, by the way, are both great reads—were A-Prompt and A-Checker. Both were developed by the Adaptive Technology Resource Center (ATRC) at the University of Toronto.

A fairly comprehensive list of automated accessibility tools, "Complete List of Web Accessibility Evaluation Tools," is available at `www.w3.org/WAI/RC/tools/complete`. In reality, these tools are a varied bag, and what you use in your projects really comes down to personal preference.

You might find the output from some of these tools difficult to parse. When I first started to become interested in Web accessibility, the greatest challenge for me was knowing what was a serious error and what was not. Ultimately, I caution you against being overly reliant on or zealous about the output from these tools. An expert evaluation of the site or, ideally, a user test with someone who has a disability might lead you to discover that the issue isn't critical. Having said that, tools like WAVE are winners for me, because they are very intuitive and simple and fit in nicely with my own workflow. You might find that if you are working on very large sites that the enterprise-level solution fits your needs. When you use any of these tools (big or small), I recommend you do so only as part of your total evaluation suite and not take their output as gospel. Ideally, you should use a combination of methods when checking for accessibility and usability, because a skilled accessibility expert will be able to spot false positives and read the nuances of an issue in the way that software just cannot do.

■ **Note** Some automated accessibility checkers have *lite* versions that are free to use and give you the choice of upgrading your subscription for more enterprise-level solutions if you need to.

Want to Examine Accessibility APIs? Try AccProbe or Inspect32

If you want to get more under-the-hood detail about how a control is exposed to an accessibility API, a couple of useful tools (for Windows) are AccProbe and Inspect32. These tools perform simple but useful tasks, such as exposing an HTML element's properties (such as its name, role, and state).

Inspect32 has been around for some time and focuses on the accessibility-related properties of an HTML component.

Other tools similar to Inspect32 are the newer AccEvent (or "Accessible Event watcher"). AccEvent allows developers to validate that an application's UI elements raise proper Microsoft UI Automation and Microsoft Active Accessibility events when UI changes occur. There are many changes that can happen on a focus change, for example, or when a webpage component has some property or state change.

■ **Note** The preceding tools come as part of the Microsoft Windows SDK.

AccProbe is a standalone, Eclipse Rich-Client Product (RCP) application that provides a view of the Microsoft Active Accessibility (MSAA) or IAccessible2 hierarchy, exposing the properties of the accessible objects of that application or document. It can also serve as an event monitor for tracking the events fired by these accessible objects.

Developers are meant to combine the functionality of tools like Microsoft Inspect32, AccExplore, and AccEvent into one easy-to-use application for accessibility testing and debugging. See `http://accessibility.linuxfoundation.org/a11yweb/util/accprobe/` for more information.

For UIAutomation API testing, you can use UISpy (`http://msdn.microsoft.com/en-us/library/ms727247.aspx`). UISpy enables developers to explore, view, and interrogate the structure, property values, and so on of their page content. It is useful for checking things like UI Automation event information, whether an element is navigable, and whether it can receive keyboard focus.

■ **Note** Michael Squillace of IBM wrote an interesting article from the perspective of blind users' experience of using these tools. His article, "Writing accessible accessibility tools" is available at `www-03.ibm.com/able/resources/accessible_tools.html`.

Disability Simulation Tools: aDesigner

There are some disability simulation tools you can look into, in particular aDesigner. With these tools, you can get an idea of the accessibility and usability of a webpage for a person who is blind or who has low vision.

■ **Note** Get aDesigner at `www.eclipse.org/actf/downloads`.

I have mixed feelings about these simulation tools because you cannot beat getting feedback directly from real people when you do user testing. However, this just isn't always possible. My view is that simulation tools are the poor second cousin to user testing; however, if these tools have the net effect of helping you to be more aware of the needs of people with disabilities, as well as helping you to identify possible problem areas with your designs, then they have done their job and are worthwhile.

Guerilla User Testing

This is the "Using what ya' got DIY punk rock approach" to user testing we covered in Chapter 9. It's where you literally use the people around you (the more diverse the better in terms of age, level of computer literacy, colleagues with disabilities if they are agreeable, and so on), as well as using any equipment you can beg for or borrow or open source software, to do some quick-and-dirty user testing of your web sites or prototypes. If you can video tape the session with a hand-held camera, that's even better.

Enjoy these informal sessions, and over time you'll find that they can be useful. If you are relaxed while running these tests, your users will pick up on that and also relax and give you good feedback. You'll also find that your ability to quickly come up with a "test script" (that outlines some tasks) and spot possible usability fails will improve. Have fun and don't be shy! People like to get involved and feel they are helping. Don't worry about being scientific or too formal. In my experience, even the best user-testing environment is totally contrived. By acknowledging this, you'll get better results.

Validation

Code validation via the W3C validator (available at `http://validator.w3.org` and shown in Figure 10-16) is a way of checking that your document conforms to a particular style of grammar. This could be a version of HTML, CSS, XHTML, MathML, and more.

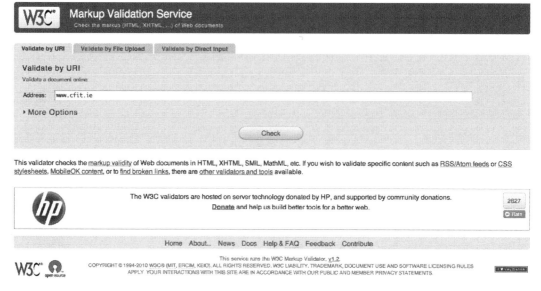

Figure 10-12. *The W3C validator*

In my early days in the field of accessibility, I loved the validator. This seemed to be a tool that gave you feedback (totally incomprehensible, but feedback nonetheless) you could use to help to make sites more accessible. Also, if you were assessing webpages for accessibility, it was a go-to resource you could use to show your clients errors it threw up that just had to be fixed. Lots of people who knew little about accessibility or, indeed, web development started to turn to it to test how accessible their web sites were. There were complaints if you saw the little red x's (as shown in Figure 10-17) that just had to be fixed ASAP!

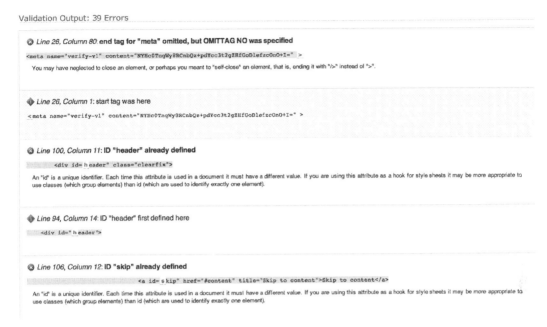

Figure 10-13. *Sample validation errors spotted by the W3C validator*

But did they really need to be fixed ASAP? Were these errors critical? How could you tell what was a serious problem and what wasn't? The maxim, "A little knowledge is a dangerous thing," springs to mind. A real lack of awareness about what the validator is (and isn't) caused confusion for everyone. I think it came to be relied on in a way that was almost counterproductive, because the tool made it easy for a person to become a validation zealot. You could hide behind the validator and mask deficiency in your own knowledge of real accessibility issues. The truth is that there just isn't a one-to-one mapping between the validator and accessibility. So while you might like to think validation is equivalent to a11y - it isn't the case. In reality, just because your page passes the validator doesn't mean it is accessible. Not passing the validator also doesn't mean that your page is inaccessible.

The validator checks that your page content conforms to the grammar you defined in the DOCTYPE (DTD). It runs algorithms that check if you have stuck to best practice for that language as defined in its specification. This is certainly very useful, and the validator can help with *well-formedness* and indicate if a page is more likely to be accessible. However, this likelihood is only a probability and not a certainty. So try to treat the validator as it is intended: as a way of assessing document conformance and not as an accessibility checker.

Cascading Style Sheets

You might have noticed that there isn't a lot of CSS3 covered in this book. This is really by design. There are many excellent books available on the topic and tutorials online that will give you up-to-date tips and techniques on CSS3. This book focused on the semantics that assistive technologies (AT), such as a screen reader, that are provided by HTML5 and WAI-ARIA. CSS doesn't provide any of these and operates in a different layer.

However, using CSS to help make your page content suitable for people with vision impairments by ensuring sufficient color contrast is a great help, as well as using CSS to ensure your text can be resized from the keyboard by using relative font sizes (em or %).

A welcome big leap forward with CSS3 is its more sophisticated typography. Using media queries to resize page content is also neat. However, there are effects I just don't like, such as nausea-inducing CSS transforms where webpages can now fly in and out of your browser, or up and down, for no good reason other than "You can do this now!" Also, CSS offers accordion menus that are so jumpy, dynamic (in a bad way), or clever-clever as to be practically unusable. These all get the thumbs-down from me. Use all this stuff with caution. A little restraint never hurt anybody.

Simulation Exercises

As mentioned in Chapter 1, a good way to experience your web content the way a disabled person might is to turn off all the bells and whistles in your browser. This section provides some simple exercises you can use to get a feel for what accessing a webpage would be like if you couldn't use some of the features as you would normally. They are an attempt to get you to put yourself in another person's shoes by turning off many of the features within the browser that you might just take for granted or use without a second thought.

Simulation Exercise 1:No-Frills Browsing

To kick off the no-frills experience, I suggest that in your browser of choice you turn off the following items:

- Style sheets
- Images
- Sound
- JavaScript
- Java
- Support for Flash/Silverlight
- Pop-up windows

You don't have to do this all at once, but doing so can certainly help you get a feel for the core of your page content and experience what a limited browsing experience can be like for someone with a disability.

Blocking JavaScript/Java and Flash Content with NoScript

A useful plugin for Firefox is NoScript, shown in Figure 10-18. While its main usage or purpose is for increased security, it can be good to use as a part of the no-frills browsing experience. It is easy to install and use. This can be useful as a simulation exercise because you can experience how JavaScript-powered menus or widgets behave if they have been coded in a way that they don't degrade gracefully.

Figure 10-18. *NoScript in action*

Disabling Pop-ups

Pop-up windows can be rather disorienting for people with cognitive impairments. They can be both confusing and distracting, and therefore make it hard to understand what is going on. They can also be problematic for nonsighted users because a blind user might have to toggle between the pop-up and the main browser window when inputting data. Or there might be a disconnect between where data is entered and the page *state*. For more advanced computer users, this might not be a significant problem apart from a usability hit, but for a novice user it can be disorienting. A person with low vision might not be aware that the pop-up even exists. They might not see the pop-up. A rule of thumb is that if there are <input> controls and similar that your user needs to log in and perform other such tasks, just include them in the main browser window. It is good practice to try to avoid pop-ups completely, and certainly do avoid spawning many instances or browser windows. This also means you really shouldn't link to external sites in new browser windows/instances if you can at all avoid it. If you must do it, however, you should inform the user that this is going to happen by including the notification "[Opens in new Browser Window]" or similar in your link text.

Working Without Your Mouse

Now I want you to throw away your mouse.

Then browse the Web doing what you usually do, and see how you get on with booking your concert tickets! It can be a good idea to browse a mix of sites you are familiar with (for a new perspective on them) and then follow that with some sites you haven't been to before.

Try it for 30 minutes or so at a time, and you should get a good sense of what the Web can be like for many people with different disabilities who rely on the keyboard, or who can't get at Flash content, or who have JavaScript off (for whatever reason), and so on.

This brief experiment should provide enough food for thought. You'll also find that no-frills browsing is a good way of finding possible problems.

Simulation Exercise 2: Turning Off Your Display and Using a Screen Reader

To really try to simulate and understand what the Web is like for blind screen-reader users, you can try some browsing using a screen reader. If you have no experience using a screen reader, it isn't an easy task and does require a certain determination (on your part) to stick with it. The screen reader is a complex application. Before you even start the software, I recommend that you read up on it (most have quick start guides) and stick with some basic browsing. If you have a Mac. you already have the excellent VoiceOver installed, and I recommend that you spend time using it. It can be equally fun and frustrating, as well as enlightening. If you are using a PC, there are demos of JAWS that can be downloaded from the Freedom Scientific web site, or free options like NVDA that you can try. They all perform variations of a similar theme.

▨ **Note** The demo option of JAWS runs for 40 minutes, which is a good time for a learning session while you test drive a screen reader.[2]

You should practice as often as possible using your screen reader of choice. If you do need some help, I urge you to contact your local service provider for people with vision impairments. They will be really glad to help. This could also be a great way to get to know people who are blind and understand their browsing strategies.

For your early screen-reader road tests, I recommend some short task-based sessions. For example, focus on an aspect of a site and try to do something like buy concert tickets, as mentioned previously. This will focus your attention on one aspect of the site (such as how accessible the forms are) and give the session some structure. It might also help you feel a little less all over the place as you find your way around the Web using a screen reader.

---

[2] www.freedomscientific.com/downloads/jaws/jaws-downloads.asp

▓ **Note** As previously mentioned, screen-reader users have different browsing strategies as well as levels of digital literacy. This is really important to remember. Although testing on your own can be both frustrating and fun, it is no substitute for user testing by people who really are blind and really need to use the screen reader. The psychology is also different if you are sighted—you can just choose to turn on the display or pick up the mouse the moment you become frustrated. Your tests are just a shadow of the real experience, no matter how proficient you become in your testing.

Conclusion

This chapter marks the end of the book. I really hope you learned a thing or two. Accessibility is really a continuum—an evolving line and not a mountain top to be conquered. Just do your best, and people will appreciate that. Finally, don't be shy about getting involved with the accessibility community to learn more and share what you do know. There is a vibrant Web community worldwide of good-hearted people who gladly share expertise and knowledge to try to make the Web a better and more inclusive place for everyone.

WCAG 2.0 Client-Side Scripting Techniques[1]

- SCR1: Allowing the user to extend the default time limit
- SCR2: Using redundant keyboard and mouse event handlers
- SCR14: Using scripts to make nonessential alerts optional
- SCR16: Providing a script that warns the user a time limit is about to expire
- SCR18: Providing client-side validation and alert
- SCR19: Using an onchange event on a select element without causing a change of context
- SCR20: Using both keyboard and other device-specific functions
- SCR21: Using functions of the Document Object Model (DOM) to add content to a page
- SCR22: Using scripts to control blinking and stop it in five seconds or less
- SCR24: Using progressive enhancement to open new windows on user request
- SCR26: Inserting dynamic content into the Document Object Model immediately following its trigger element
- SCR27: Reordering page sections using the Document Object Model
- SCR28: Using an expandable and collapsible menu to bypass block of content
- SCR29: Adding keyboard-accessible actions to static HTML elements
- SCR30: Using scripts to change the link text
- SCR31: Using scripts to change the background color or border of the element with focus

---

- SCR32: Providing client-side validation and adding error text via the DOM

- SCR33: Using script to scroll content, and providing a mechanism to pause it

- SCR34: Calculating size and position in a way that scales with text size

- SCR35: Making actions keyboard accessible by using the onclick event of anchors and buttons

- SCR36: Providing a mechanism to allow users to display moving, scrolling, or auto-updating text in a static window or area

- SCR37: Creating custom dialogs in a device-independent way

SCR1: Allowing the user to extend the default time limit

Description

The objective of this technique is to allow the user to extend the default time limit by providing a mechanism to extend the time when scripts provide functionality that has default time limits. To allow the user to request a longer time limit, the script can provide a form (for example) that allows the user to enter a larger time limit or indicate that more time is needed. If the user is being warned that a time limit is about to expire (see "SCR16: Providing a script that warns the user a time limit is about to expire"), this form can be made available from the warning dialog. The user can extend the time limit to at least 10 times the default time limit, either by entering a value into the form to indicate how much additional time is needed or by repeatedly extending the time limit.

Examples

A webpage contains current stock market statistics and is set to refresh periodically. When the user is warned prior to the first refresh, the user is provided with an option to extend the time period between refreshes.

In an online chess game, each player is given a time limit for completing each move. When the player is warned that time is almost up for this move, the user is provided with an option to increase the time limit.

SCR2: Using redundant keyboard and mouse event handlers

Description

The objective of this technique is to demonstrate using device-independent events to change a decorative image in response to a mouse or focus event. Use the onmouseover and onmouseout events to change a decorative image when the mouse moves on top of or away from an element on the page. Also, use the onfocus and onblur events to change the image when the element receives and loses focus.

The example in Listing A-1 has a decorative image in front of an anchor element. When the user mouses over the anchor tag, the decorative image in front of the anchor is changed. When the mouse moves off the anchor, the image is changed back to its original version. The same image-change effect occurs when the user gives keyboard focus to the anchor element. When focus is received, the image changes; when focus is lost, the image is changed back. This is accomplished by attaching onmouseover, onmouseout, onfocus, and onblur event handlers to the anchor element. The event handler is a JavaScript function called updateImage(), which changes the src attribute of the image. The updateImage() is called in response to the onmouseover, onmouseout, onfocus, and onblur events.

Each image is given a unique Id. This unique ID is passed to updateImage() along with a boolean value indicating which image is to be used: updateImage(imgId, isOver);. The boolean value of true is passed when the mouse is over the anchor element or it has focus. A false value is passed when the mouse moves off the anchor element or it loses focus. The updateImage() function uses the image id to load the image and then changes the src attribute based on the boolean value. Note that since the image is for decorative purposes, it has a null alt attribute.

■ **Note** It is best to use images that are similar in size and to specify the height and width attributes on the image element. This will prevent any changes to the layout of the page when the image is updated. This example uses images that are identical in size.

Listing A-1. Swapping Images

```
<!DOCTYPE HTML PUBLIC "-//W3C//DTD HTML 4.01 Transitional//EN"
"http://www.w3.org/TR/html4/loose.dtd">
<html lang="en">
<head>
<meta http-equiv="Content-Type" content="text/html; charset=ISO-8859-1">
<title>Changing Image Source in a Device Independent Manner</title>
<script type="text/javascript">
/* This function will change the image src of an image element.
 * param imgId - the id of the image object to change
 * param isOver - true when mouse is over or object has focus,
 *                false when mouse move out or focus is lost
*/
function updateImage(imgId, isOver) {
  var theImage = document.getElementById(imgId);
  if (theImage != null) { //could use a try/catch block for user agents supporting at least
JavaScript 1.4
                          // These browsers support try/catch - NetScape 6, IE 5, Mozilla,
Firefox
      if (isOver) {
        theImage.setAttribute("src","yellowplus.gif");
      }
      else {
        theImage.setAttribute("src","greyplus.gif");
      }
  }
}
</script>
</head>
<body>
<p>Mouse over or tab to the links below and see the image change.</p>
```

```
<a href="http://www.w3.org/wai" onmouseover="updateImage('wai', true);"↵
onfocus="updateImage('wai', true);"
  onmouseout="updateImage('wai',false);" onblur="updateImage('wai',false);">
<img src="greyplus.gif" border="0" alt="" id="wai">
  W3C Web Accessibility Initiative</a> &
<a href="http://www.w3.org/International/" onmouseover="updateImage('i18n', true);"
  onfocus="updateImage('i18n',true);" onmouseout="updateImage('i18n',false);"
  onblur="updateImage('i18n',false);">
  <img src="greyplus.gif" border="0" alt="" id="i18n">
  W3C Internationalization</a>
</body>
</html>
```

Tests

Procedure

1. Load the webpage, and test the events using a mouse and via the keyboard.

2. Check that the standard image is displayed as expected when the webpage is loaded.

Using the Mouse

1. Move the mouse over the element containing the event handlers (in this example, it is an anchor element). Check that the image changes to the expected image.

2. Move the mouse off the element. Check that the image changes back to the standard image.

Using the Keyboard

1. Use the keyboard to set focus to the element containing the event handlers. Check that the image changes to the expected image.

2. Use the keyboard to remove focus from the element (generally by moving focus to another element). Check that the image changes to the standard image.

3. Verify that the layout of other elements on the page is not affected when the image is changed.

Expected Results

All of the steps for the previous checks are true.

If this is a sufficient technique for a success criterion, failing this test procedure does not necessarily mean that the success criterion has not been satisfied in some other way, only that this technique has not been successfully implemented and cannot be used to claim conformance.

SCR16: Providing a script that warns the user a time limit is about to expire

Example

A page of stock market quotes uses a script to refresh the page every five minutes in order to ensure the latest statistics remain available. Twenty seconds before the five minute period expires, a confirmation dialog appears asking if the user needs more time before the page refreshes. This allows the user to be aware of the impending refresh and to avoid it if desired. Listing A-2 creates the described behavior.

Listing A-2. Using a Script to Refresh the Page

```
<!DOCTYPE html PUBLIC "-//W3C//DTD HTML 4.01 Transitional//EN"
    "http://www.w3.org/TR/html4/loose.dtd">
<html lang="en">
<head>
<title>Stock Market Quotes</title>
<script type="text/javascript">
<!--
function timeControl() {
        // set timer for 4 min 40 sec, then ask user to confirm.
        setTimeout('userCheck()', 280000);
}
function userCheck() {
        // set page refresh for 20 sec
        var id=setTimeout('pageReload()', 20000);
        // If user selects "OK" the timer is reset
        // else the page will refresh from the server.
        if (confirm("This page is set to refresh in 20 seconds.
        Would you like more time?"))
        {
        clearTimeout(id);
        timeControl();
        }
}
function pageReload() {
        window.location.reload(true);
}
timeControl();
-->
</script>
</head>
<body>
<h1>Stock Market Quotes</h1>
...etc...
```

323

```
</body>
</html>
```

SCR21: Using functions of the Document Object Model (DOM) to add content to a page

Description

The objective of this technique is to demonstrate how to use functions of the Document Object Model (DOM) to add content to a page instead of using document.write or object.innerHTML. The document.write() method does not work with XHTML when served with the correct MIME type (application/xhtml+xml), and the innerHTML property is not part of the DOM specification and thus should be avoided.

If the DOM functions are used to add the content, user agents can access the DOM to retrieve the content. The createElement() function can be used to create elements within the DOM. The createTextNode() is used to create text associated with elements. The appendChild(), removeChild(), insertBefore(), and replaceChild() functions are used to add and remove elements and nodes. Other DOM functions are used to assign attributes to the created elements.

▦ **Note** When adding elements that will receive focus into the document, do not add tabindex attributes to explicitly set the tab order as this can cause problems when adding focusable elements into the middle of a document. Let the default tab order be assigned to the new element by not explicitly setting a tabindex attribute.

Example

This example demonstrates use of client-side scripting to validate a form. If errors are found, appropriate error messages are displayed. The example uses the DOM functions to add error notifications consisting of a title, a short paragraph explaining that an error has occurred, and a list of errors in an ordered list. The content of the title is written as a link so that it can be used to draw the user's attention to the error using the focus method. Each item in the list is also written as a link that places the focus onto the form field in error when the link is followed.

For simplicity, the example just validates two text fields, but it can easily be extended to become a generic form handler. Client-side validation should not be the sole means of validation, and should be backed up with server-side validation. The benefit of client-side validation is that you can provide immediate feedback to the user to save them waiting for the errors to come back from the server, and it helps reduce unnecessary traffic to the server.

Here is the script that adds the event handlers to the form. If scripting is enabled, the validateNumbers() function will be called to perform client-side validation before the form is submitted to the server. If scripting is not enabled, the form will be immediately submitted to the server, so validation should also be implemented on the server.

Listing A-3. Adding Event Handlers to the Form

```
window.onload = initialise;
function initialise()
{
  // Ensure we're working with a relatively standards compliant user agent
  if (!document.getElementById || !document.createElement || !document.createTextNode)
    return;

  // Add an event handler for the number form
  var objForm = document.getElementById('numberform');
  objForm.onsubmit= function(){return validateNumbers(this);};
}
```

Here is the validation function. Note the use of the createElement(), createTextNode(), and appendChild() DOM functions to create the error message elements.

Listing A-4. Form Validation

```
function validateNumbers(objForm)
{
  // Test whether fields are valid
  var bFirst = isNumber(document.getElementById('num1').value);
  var bSecond = isNumber(document.getElementById('num2').value);
  // If not valid, display errors
  if (!bFirst || !bSecond)
  {
    var objExisting = document.getElementById('validationerrors');
    var objNew = document.createElement('div');
    var objTitle = document.createElement('h2');
    var objParagraph = document.createElement('p');
    var objList = document.createElement('ol');
    var objAnchor = document.createElement('a');
    var strID = 'firsterror';
    var strError;
    // The heading element will contain a link so that screen readers
    // can use it to place focus - the destination for the link is
    // the first error contained in a list
    objAnchor.appendChild(document.createTextNode('Errors in Submission'));
    objAnchor.setAttribute('href', '#firsterror');
    objTitle.appendChild(objAnchor);
    objParagraph.appendChild(document.createTextNode('Please review the following'));
    objNew.setAttribute('id', 'validationerrors');
    objNew.appendChild(objTitle);
    objNew.appendChild(objParagraph);
    // Add each error found to the list of errors
    if (!bFirst)
    {
      strError = 'Please provide a numeric value for the first number';
      objList.appendChild(addError(strError, '#num1', objForm, strID));
      strID = '';
```

```
      }
      if (!bSecond)
      {
        strError = 'Please provide a numeric value for the second number';
        objList.appendChild(addError(strError, '#num2', objForm, strID));
        strID = '';
      }
      // Add the list to the error information
      objNew.appendChild(objList);
      // If there were existing errors, replace them with the new lot,
      // otherwise add the new errors to the start of the form
      if (objExisting)
        objExisting.parentNode.replaceChild(objNew, objExisting);
      else
      {
        var objPosition = objForm.firstChild;
        objForm.insertBefore(objNew, objPosition);
      }
      // Place focus on the anchor in the heading to alert
      // screen readers that the submission is in error
      objAnchor.focus();
      // Do not submit the form
      objForm.submitAllowed = false;
      return false;
    }
    return true;
  }

  // Function to validate a number
  function isNumber(strValue)
  {
    return (!isNaN(strValue) && strValue.replace(/^\s+|\s+$/, '') !== '');
  }
```

Listing A-5 details the helper functions used to create the error message and to set focus to the associated form field.

Listing A-5. *Helper Functions*

```
// Function to create a list item containing a link describing the error
// that points to the appropriate form field
function addError(strError, strFragment, objForm, strID)
{
  var objAnchor = document.createElement('a');
  var objListItem = document.createElement('li');
  objAnchor.appendChild(document.createTextNode(strError));
  objAnchor.setAttribute('href', strFragment);
  objAnchor.onclick = function(event){return focusFormField(this, event, objForm);};
  objAnchor.onkeypress = function(event){return focusFormField(this, event, objForm);};
  // If strID has a value, this is the first error in the list
  if (strID.length > 0)
    objAnchor.setAttribute('id', strID);
```

```
  objListItem.appendChild(objAnchor);
  return objListItem;
}

// Function to place focus to the form field in error
function focusFormField(objAnchor, objEvent, objForm)
{
  // Allow keyboard navigation over links
  if (objEvent && objEvent.type == 'keypress')
    if (objEvent.keyCode != 13 && objEvent.keyCode != 32)
      return true;
  // set focus to the form control
  var strFormField = objAnchor.href.match(/[^#]\w*$/);
  objForm[strFormField].focus();
  return false;
}
```

Listing A-6 shows the HTML for the example form.

Listing A-6. Example Form

```
<!DOCTYPE HTML PUBLIC "-//W3C//DTD HTML 4.01//EN" "http://www.w3.org/TR/html4/strict.dtd">
<html>
<head>
        <title>ECMAScript Form Validation</title>
        <meta http-equiv="Content-Type" content="text/html; charset=utf-8">
        <script type="text/javascript" src="validate.js"></script>
</head>
<body>
<h1>Form Validation</h1>
<form id="numberform" method="post" action="form.php">
<fieldset>
<legend>Numeric Fields</legend>
<p>
<label for="num1">Enter first number</label>
<input type="text" size="20" name="num1" id="num1">
</p>
<p>
<label for="num2">Enter second number</label>
<input type="text" size="20" name="num2" id="num2">
</p>
</fieldset>
<p>
<input type="submit" name="submit" value="Submit Form">
</p>
</form>
</body>
</html>
```

This example is limited to client-side scripting and should be backed up with server-side validation. The example is limited to the creation of error messages when client-side scripting is available.

A working version of the form can be found at www.w3.org/TR/WCAG20-TECHS/working-examples/SCR21/ex1.html.

SCR24: Using progressive enhancement to open new windows on user request

Description

The objective of this technique is to avoid confusion that might be caused by the appearance of new windows that were not requested by the user. Suddenly opening new windows can disorient users or be missed completely by some users. If the document type does not allow the target attribute (it does not exist in HTML 4.01 Strict or XHTML 1.0 Strict) or if the developer prefers not to use it, new windows can be opened with ECMAScript. The following example demonstrates how to open new windows with script: it adds an event handler to a link (a element) and warns the user that the content will open in a new window.

Example

Markup

The script is included in the head of the document, and the link has an ID that can be used as a hook by the script, as shown in Listing A-7.

Listing A-7. Opening a New Window

```
<script type="text/javascript" src="popup.js"></script>
...
<a href="help.html" id="newwin">Show Help</a

// Use traditional event model whilst support for event registration
// amongst browsers is poor.
window.onload = addHandlers;

function addHandlers()
{
  var objAnchor = document.getElementById('newwin');

  if (objAnchor)
  {
    objAnchor.firstChild.data = objAnchor.firstChild.data + ' (opens in a new window)';
    objAnchor.onclick = function(event){return launchWindow(this, event);}
    // UAAG requires that user agents handle events in a device-independent manner
    // but only some browsers do this, so add keyboard event to be sure
    objAnchor.onkeypress = function(event){return launchWindow(this, event);}
  }
}
```

```
function launchWindow(objAnchor, objEvent)
{
  var iKeyCode, bSuccess=false;

  // If the event is from a keyboard, we only want to open the
  // new window if the user requested the link (return or space)
  if (objEvent && objEvent.type == 'keypress')
  {
    if (objEvent.keyCode)
      iKeyCode = objEvent.keyCode;
    else if (objEvent.which)
      iKeyCode = objEvent.which;

    // If not carriage return or space, return true so that the user agent
    // continues to process the action
    if (iKeyCode != 13 && iKeyCode != 32)
      return true;
  }

  bSuccess = window.open(objAnchor.href);

  // If the window did not open, allow the browser to continue the default
  // action of opening in the same window
  if (!bSuccess)
    return true;

  // The window was opened, so stop the browser processing further
  return false;
}
```

SCR26: Inserting dynamic content into the Document Object Model immediately following its trigger element

Description

The objective of this technique is to place inserted user-interface elements into the Document Object Model in such a way that the tab order and screen-reader reading order are set correctly by the default behavior of the user agent. This technique can be used for any user-interface element that is hidden and shown, such as menus and dialogs.

The reading order in a screen reader is based on the order of the HTML or XHTML elements in the DOM, as is the default tab order. This technique inserts new content into the DOM immediately following the element that was activated to trigger the script. The triggering element must be a link or a button, and the script must be called from its onclick event. These elements are natively focusable, and their onclick event is device independent. Focus remains on the activated element and the new content, inserted after it, becomes the next thing in both the tab order and screen-reader reading order.

Note that this technique works for synchronous updates. For asynchronous updates (sometimes called AJAX), an additional technique is needed to inform the assistive technology that the asynchronous content has been inserted.

Example

This example creates a menu when a link is clicked and inserts it after the link. The onclick event of the link is used to call the ShowHide script, passing in an ID for the new menu as a parameter, as shown in the following snippet:

```
<a href="#" onclick="ShowHide('foo',this)">Toggle</a>
```

The ShowHide script creates a div containing the new menu and inserts a link into it. The last line is the core of the script. It finds the parent of the element that triggered the script and appends the div it created as a new child to it. This causes the new div to be in the DOM after the link. When the user presses the Tab key, the focus will go to the first focusable item in the menu, which is the link we created. (See Listing A-8.)

Listing A-8. *Using ShowHide*

```
function ShowHide(id,src)
{
        var el = document.getElementById(id);
        if (!el)
        {
                el = document.createElement("div");
                el.id = id;
                var link = document.createElement("a");
                link.href = "javascript:void(0)";
                link.appendChild(document.createTextNode("Content"));
                el.appendChild(link);
                src.parentElement.appendChild(el);
        }
        else
        {
                el.style.display = ('none' == el.style.display ? 'block' : 'none');
        }
}
```

Cascading Style Sheets are used to make the div and link look like a menu.

Tests: Procedure

1. Find all areas of the page that trigger dialogs that are not pop-up windows.

2. Check that the dialogs are triggered from the click event of a button or a link.

3. Using a tool that allows you to inspect the DOM generated by script, check that the dialog is next in the DOM.

Expected Results

#2 and #3 are true.

If this is a sufficient technique for a success criterion, failing this test procedure does not necessarily mean that the success criterion has been satisfied in some other way, only that this technique has not been successfully implemented and cannot be used to claim conformance.

SCR28: Using an expandable and collapsible menu to bypass block of content

Description

This technique allows users to skip repeated material by placing that material in a menu that can be expanded or collapsed under user control. The user can skip the repeated material by collapsing the menu. The user invokes a user interface control to hide or remove the elements of the menu.

▩ **Note** Similar approaches can be implemented by using server-side scripting and reloading a modified version of the webpage.

Example 1

The navigation links at top of a webpage are all entries in a menu implemented using HTML, CSS, and JavaScript. When the navigation bar is expanded, the navigation links are available to the user. When the navigation bar is collapsed, the links are not available. The code in Listing A-9 details this functionality.

Listing A-9. Expandable Menu

```
<script type="text/javascript">
function toggle(id){
  var n = document.getElementById(id);
  n.style.display = (n.style.display != 'none' ? 'none' : '' );
}
</script>

...

<a href="#" onclick="toggle('navbar')">Toggle Navigation Bar</a>

<ul id="navbar">
<li><a href="http://target1.html">Link 1</a></li>
<li><a href="http://target2.html">Link 2</a></li>
<li><a href="http://target3.html">Link 3</a></li>
<li><a href="http://target4.html">Link 4</a></li>
</ul>
```

A working example of this code is available at www.w3.org/TR/WCAG20-TECHS/working-examples/SCR28/toggle-navbar.html.

Example 2

The table of contents for a set of webpages is repeated near the beginning of each webpage. A button at the beginning of the table of contents lets the user remove or restore it on the page.

Listing A-10. *A Table of Contents*

```
<script type="text/javascript">
function toggle(id){
  var n = document.getElementById(id);
  n.style.display =  (n.style.display != 'none' ? 'none' : '' );
}
</script>

...

<button onclick="return toggle('toc');">Toggle Table of Contents</button>
<div id="toc">
  ...
</div>
```

A working example of this code can be found here: www.w3.org/TR/WCAG20-TECHS/working-examples/SCR28/toggle-toc.html.

SCR32: Providing client-side validation and adding error text via the DOM

Description

The objective of this technique is to demonstrate the display of an error message when client-side validation of a form field has failed. Anchor elements are used to display the error messages in a list and are inserted above the fields to be validated. Anchor elements are used in the error messages so that focus can be placed on the error message(s), drawing the user's attention to it. The href of the anchor elements contain an in-page link that references the fields where error(s) have been found.

In a deployed application, if JavaScript is turned off, client-side validation will not occur. Therefore, this technique is sufficient only in situations where scripting is relied upon for conformance or when server-side validation techniques are also used to catch any errors and return the page with information about the fields with errors.

Example

This example validates required fields as well as fields where a specific format is required. When an error is identified, the script inserts a list of error messages into the DOM and moves focus to them, as shown in Figure A-1.

Validating Form

2 Errors in Submission

Please review the following

1. Please enter your age
2. Please enter your email address

Personal Details

Please enter your forename [Joe]

Please enter your age [ ]

Please enter your email address [joesmith]

[Sign up]

Figure A-1. Accessible Validation Sample Form

HTML and JavaScript Code

The HTML for the example form appears in Listing A-11.

Listing A-11. *HTML for Client-Side Validation*

```
<!DOCTYPE HTML PUBLIC "-//W3C//DTD HTML 4.01//EN" "http://www.w3.org/TR/html4/strict.dtd">
<html>
    <head>
        <title>Form Validation</title>
        <meta http-equiv="Content-Type" content="text/html; charset=utf-8"/>
        <link href="css/validate.css" rel="stylesheet" type="text/css"/>
        <script type="text/javascript" src="scripts/validate.js"/>
    </head>
    <body>

        <h1>Form Validation</h1>

        <p>The following form is validated before being submitted if scripting is available,
            otherwise the form is validated on the server. All fields are required, except↩
            those marked optional. If errors are found in the submission, the form is
            cancelled and a list of errors is displayed at the top of the form.</p>

        <p> Please enter your details below. </p>

        <h2>Validating Form</h2>

        <form id="personalform" method="post" action="index.php">
            <div class="validationerrors"/>
            <fieldset>
                <legend>Personal Details</legend>
                <p>
                    <label for="forename">Please enter your forename</label>
                    <input type="text" size="20" name="forename" id="forename" class="string"
                        value=""/>
                </p>
                <p>
                    <label for="age">Please enter your age</label>
                    <input type="text" size="20" name="age" id="age" class="number" value=""/>
                </p>
                <p>
                    <label for="email">Please enter your email address</label>
                    <input type="text" size="20" name="email" id="email" class="email"↩
value=""/>
                </p>
            </fieldset>
            <p>
                <input type="submit" name="signup" value="Sign up"/>
            </p>
        </form>
        <h2>Second Form</h2>
        <form id="secondform" method="post" action="index.php#focuspoint">
            <div class="validationerrors"/>
            <fieldset>
                <legend>Second Form Details</legend>
```

```
        <p>
            <label for="suggestion">Enter a suggestion</label>
            <input type="text" size="20" name="suggestion" id="suggestion"
              class="string" value=""/>
        </p>
        <p>
            <label for="optemail">Please enter your email address (optional)</label>
            <input type="text" size="20" name="optemail" id="optemail"
                class="optional email" value=""/>
        </p>
        <p>
            <label for="rating">Please rate this suggestion</label>
            <input type="text" size="20" name="rating" id="rating"
              class="number" value=""/>
        </p>
        <p>
            <label for="jibberish">Enter some jibberish (optional)</label>
            <input type="text" size="20" name="jibberish" id="jibberish" value=""/>
        </p>

    </fieldset>
    <p>
        <input type="submit" name="submit" value="Add Suggestion"/>
    </p>
    </form>
</body>
</html>
```

The JavaScript that performs the validation and inserts the error messages is detailed in Listing A-12.

Listing A-12. Validation JavaScript

```
window.onload = initialise;

function initialise()
{
    var objForms = document.getElementsByTagName('form');
    var iCounter;

    // Attach an event handler for each form
    for (iCounter=0; iCounter<objForms.length; iCounter++)
    {
        objForms[iCounter].onsubmit = function(){return validateForm(this);};
    }
}


// Event handler for the form
function validateForm(objForm)
{
    var arClass = [];
    var iErrors = 0;
```

335

```
var objField = objForm.getElementsByTagName('input');
var objLabel = objForm.getElementsByTagName('label');
var objList = document.createElement('ol');
var objError, objExisting, objNew, objTitle, objParagraph, objAnchor, objPosition;
var strLinkID, iFieldCounter, iClassCounter, iCounter;

// Get the id or name of the form, to make a unique
// fragment identifier
if (objForm.id)
{
   strLinkID = objForm.id + 'ErrorID';
}
else
{
   strLinkID = objForm.name + 'ErrorID';
}

// Iterate through input form controls, looking for validation classes
for (iFieldCounter=0; iFieldCounter<objField.length; iFieldCounter++)
{
   // Get the class for the field, and look for the appropriate class
   arClass = objField[iFieldCounter].className.split(' ');
   for (iClassCounter=0; iClassCounter<arClass.length; iClassCounter++)
   {
      switch (arClass[iClassCounter])
      {
         case 'string':
            if (!isString(objField[iFieldCounter].value, arClass))
            {
               if (iErrors === 0)
               {
                  logError(objField[iFieldCounter], objLabel, objList, strLinkID);
               }
               else
               {
                  logError(objField[iFieldCounter], objLabel, objList, '');
               }
               iErrors++;
            }
            break;
         case 'number':
            if (!isNumber(objField[iFieldCounter].value, arClass))
            {
               if (iErrors === 0)
               {
                  logError(objField[iFieldCounter], objLabel, objList, strLinkID);
               }
               else
               {
                  logError(objField[iFieldCounter], objLabel, objList, '');
               }
               iErrors++;
```

```
            }
            break;

        case 'email' :
            if (!isEmail(objField[iFieldCounter].value, arClass))
            {
                if (iErrors === 0)
                {
                    logError(objField[iFieldCounter], objLabel, objList, strLinkID);
                }
                else
                {
                    logError(objField[iFieldCounter], objLabel, objList, '');
                }
                iErrors++;
            }
            break;
        }
    }
}

if (iErrors > 0)
{
    // If not valid, display error messages
    objError = objForm.getElementsByTagName('div');

    // Look for existing errors
    for (iCounter=0; iCounter<objError.length; iCounter++)
    {
        if (objError[iCounter].className == 'validationerrors')
        {
            objExisting = objError[iCounter];
        }
    }

    objNew = document.createElement('div');
    objTitle = document.createElement('h2');
    objParagraph = document.createElement('p');
    objAnchor = document.createElement('a');

    if (iErrors == 1)
    {
        objAnchor.appendChild(document.createTextNode('1 Error in Submission'));
    }
    else
    {
        objAnchor.appendChild(document.createTextNode(iErrors + ' Errors in Submission'));
    }
    objAnchor.href = '#' + strLinkID;
    objAnchor.className = 'submissionerror';

    objTitle.appendChild(objAnchor);
```

```
        objParagraph.appendChild(document.createTextNode('Please review the following'));
        objNew.className = 'validationerrors';

        objNew.appendChild(objTitle);
        objNew.appendChild(objParagraph);
        objNew.appendChild(objList);

        // If there were existing errors, replace them with the new lot,
        // otherwise add the new errors to the start of the form
        if (objExisting)
        {
            objExisting.parentNode.replaceChild(objNew, objExisting);
        }
        else
        {
            objPosition = objForm.firstChild;
            objForm.insertBefore(objNew, objPosition);
        }

        // Allow for latency
        setTimeout(function() { objAnchor.focus(); }, 50);

        // Don't submit the form
        objForm.submitAllowed = false;
        return false;
    }

    // Submit the form
    return true;
}

// Function to add a link in a list item that points to problematic field control
function addError(objList, strError, strID, strErrorID)
{
    var objListItem = document.createElement('li');
    var objAnchor = document.createElement('a');

    // Fragment identifier to the form control
    objAnchor.href='#' + strID;

    // Make this the target for the error heading
    if (strErrorID.length > 0)
    {
        objAnchor.id = strErrorID;
    }

    // Use the label prompt for the error message
    objAnchor.appendChild(document.createTextNode(strError));
    // Add keyboard and mouse events to set focus to the form control
    objAnchor.onclick = function(event){return focusFormField(this, event);};
    objAnchor.onkeypress = function(event){return focusFormField(this, event);};
    objListItem.appendChild(objAnchor);
```

```
    objList.appendChild(objListItem);
}

function focusFormField(objAnchor, objEvent)
{
    var strFormField, objForm;

    // Allow keyboard navigation over links
    if (objEvent && objEvent.type == 'keypress')
    {
        if (objEvent.keyCode != 13 && objEvent.keyCode != 32)
        {
            return true;
        }
    }

    // set focus to the form control
    strFormField = objAnchor.href.match(/[^#]\w*$/);
    objForm = getForm(strFormField);
    objForm[strFormField].focus();
    return false;
}

// Function to return the form element from a given form field name
function getForm(strField)
{
    var objElement = document.getElementById(strField);

    // Find the appropriate form
    do
    {
        objElement = objElement.parentNode;
    } while (!objElement.tagName.match(/form/i) && objElement.parentNode);

    return objElement;
}

// Function to log the error in a list
function logError(objField, objLabel, objList, strErrorID)
{
    var iCounter, strError;

    // Search the label for the error prompt
    for (iCounter=0; iCounter<objLabel.length; iCounter++)
    {
        if (objLabel[iCounter].htmlFor == objField.id)
        {
            strError = objLabel[iCounter].firstChild.nodeValue;
        }
    }

    addError(objList, strError, objField.id, strErrorID);
```

339

```
}

// Validation routines - add as required

function isString(strValue, arClass)
{
   var bValid = (typeof strValue == 'string' && strValue.replace(/^\s*|\s*$/g, '')
     !== '' && isNaN(strValue));

   return checkOptional(bValid, strValue, arClass);
}

function isEmail(strValue, arClass)
{
   var objRE = /^[\w-\.\']{1,}\@([\da-zA-Z\-]{1,}\.){1,}[\da-zA-Z\-]{2,}$/;
   var bValid = objRE.test(strValue);

   return checkOptional(bValid, strValue, arClass);
}

function isNumber(strValue, arClass)
{
   var bValid = (!isNaN(strValue) && strValue.replace(/^\s*|\s*$/g, '') !== '');

   return checkOptional(bValid, strValue, arClass);
}

function checkOptional(bValid, strValue, arClass)
{
   var bOptional = false;
   var iCounter;

   // Check if optional
   for (iCounter=0; iCounter<arClass.length; iCounter++)
   {
      if (arClass[iCounter] == 'optional')
      {
         bOptional = true;
      }
   }

   if (bOptional && strValue.replace(/^\s*|\s*$/g, '') === '')
   {
      return true;
   }

   return bValid;
}
```

A working example of this technique implemented using PHP, JavaScript, CSS, and XHTML can be found here: www.w3.org/TR/WCAG20-TECHS/working-examples/SCR32/index.php.

SCR35: Making actions keyboard accessible by using the onclick event of anchors and buttons

Description

The objective of this technique is to demonstrate how to invoke a scripting function in a way that is keyboard accessible by attaching it to a keyboard-accessible control. To ensure that scripted actions can be invoked from the keyboard, they are associated with *natively actionable* HTML elements (links and buttons). The onclick event of these elements is device independent. Although "onclick" sounds like it is tied to the mouse, the onclick event is actually mapped to the default action of a link or button. The default action occurs when the user clicks the element with a mouse, but it also occurs when the user focuses the element and presses Enter or the spacebar, and when the element is triggered via the accessibility API.

This technique relies on client-side scripting. However, it is beneficial to provide a backup implementation or explanation for environments in which scripting is not available. When using anchor elements to invoke a JavaScript action, a backup implementation or explanation is provided via the href attribute. When using buttons, it is provided via a form post.

Example 1

The code in Listing A-13 creates a link that runs script, but it navigates to another page when script is not available. This approach can be used to create sites that don't rely on script, if and only if the navigation target provides the same functionality as the script. This example is identical to the example shown in the previous section, except that its href is now set to a real page, dostuff.htm. The dostuff.htm page must provide the same functionality as the script. The "return false;" at the end of the doStuff() event handling function tells the browser not to navigate to the URI. Without it, the browser would navigate to dostuff.htm after the script ran.

Listing A-13. Creating a Link to Run a Script

```
<script>
function doStuff()
 {
  //do stuff
  return false;
 }
</script>
<a href="dostuff.htm" onclick="return doStuff();">do stuff</a>
```

A working example of this code is available at www.w3.org/TR/WCAG20-TECHS/working-examples/SCR35/jslink.html.

Example 2

Listing A-14 creates a button that runs a script and falls back to a form post for users without script. This approach can be used by sites that do not rely on script, if and only if the form post provides the same functionality as the script. The onsubmit="return false;" prevents the form from submitting.

Listing A-14. Creating a Button to Run a Script, with Form Post as Fallback

```
<script>
  function doStuff()
  {
      //do stuff
  }
</script>
<form action="doStuff.aspx" onsubmit="return false;">
 <input type="submit" value="Do Stuff" onclick="doStuff();" />
</form>
```

A working example of this code is available here: www.w3.org/TR/WCAG20-TECHS/working-examples/SCR35/jsbutton.html.

SCR37: Creating custom aialogs in a device-independent way

Description

Site designers often want to create dialogs that do not use the pop-up windows supplied by the browser. This is typically accomplished by enclosing the dialog contents in a div and placing the div above the page content using z-order and absolute positioning in CSS.

To be accessible, these dialogs must follow a few simple rules.

- Trigger the script that launches the dialog from the onclick event of a link or button.

- Place the dialog div into the Document Object Model (DOM) immediately after the element that triggered it. The triggering element will maintain focus, and inserting the dialog content after that element will make the content inside the dialog next in the screen-reader reading order and next in the tab order. The dialog can still be absolutely positioned to be elsewhere on the page visually. This can be done either by creating the dialog in the HTML and hiding it with CSS, as in the following example, or by inserting it immediately after the triggering element with script.

- Ensure that the HTML inside the dialog div meets the same accessibility standard as other content.

- It is also nice, but not always necessary, to make the launching link toggle the dialog open and closed, and to close the dialog when the keyboard focus leaves it.

Example

The HTML for this example includes a triggering element—in this case a button—and a div that acts as the frame for the dialog.

The triggering element is a button, and the script is triggered from the onclick event. This sends the appropriate events to the operating system so that assistive technology is aware of the change in the DOM.

In this example, the Submit and Reset buttons inside the dialog simply hide the div.

Listing A-15. An Options Button That Opens a Dialog

```
...
<button onclick="TogglePopup(event,true)"
        name="pop0001">Options</button>

<div class="popover" id="pop0001">
  <h3>Edit Sort Information</h3>
  <form action="default.htm" onsubmit="this.parentNode.style.display='none'; return false;"↵
 onreset="this.parentNode.style.display='none'; return false;">
    <fieldset>
      <legend>Sort Order</legend>
      <input type="radio" name="order" id="order_alpha" /><label↵
 for="order_alpha">Alphabetical</label>
      <input type="radio" name="order" id="order_default" checked="true" /><label↵
 for="order_default">Default</label>
    </fieldset>
<div class="buttons">
  <input type="submit" value="OK" />
  <input type="reset" value="Cancel" />
</div>
</form>

</div>
...
```

The div, heading, and form elements are styled with CSS to look like a dialog, as shown in Listing A-16.

Listing A-16. Styling Form Elements

```
...
a { color:blue; }
a.clickPopup img { border:none; width:0; }

div.popover { position:absolute; display:none; border:1px outset; background-color:beige;↵
 font-size:80%; background-color:#eeeeee; color:black; }
div.popover h3 { margin:0; padding:0.1em 0.5em; background-color:navy; color:white; }
#pop0001 { width:20em; }
#pop0001 form { margin:0; padding:0.5em; }
#pop0001 fieldset { margin-bottom:0.3em; padding-bottom:0.5em; }
#pop0001 input, #pop0001 label { vertical-align:middle; }
#pop0001 div.buttons { text-align:right; }
#pop0001 div.buttons input { width:6em; }
...
```

The script toggles the display of the popup div, showing it and hiding it. See Listing A-17.

Listing A-17. Displaying the Popup

```
...
function TogglePopup(evt,show)
```

343

```
{
        HarmonizeEvent(evt);
        var src = evt.target;
        if ("click" == evt.type)
        {
                evt.returnValue = false;
        }
        var popID = src.getAttribute("name");
        if (popID)
        {
                var popup = document.getElementById(popID);
                if (popup)
                {
                        if (true == show)
                        {
                                popup.style.display = "block";
                        }
                        else if (false == show)
                        {
                                popup.style.display = "none";
                        }
                        else
                        {
                                popup.style.display = "block" == popup.style.display ?↵
 "none" : "block";
                        }
                        if ("block" == popup.style.display)
                        {
                                //window.alert(document.documentElement.scrollHeight);
                                popup.style.top = ((document.documentElement.offsetHeight -↵
 popup.offsetHeight) / 2 ) + 'px';
                                popup.style.left = ((document.documentElement.offsetWidth -↵
 popup.offsetWidth) / 2) + 'px';
                        }
                }
        }
}

function SubmitForm(elem)
{
        elem.parentNode.style.display='none';
        return false;
}

function ResetForm(elem)
{
        elem.parentNode.style.display='none';
        return false;
}
...
```

A working example, which is an options button that opens a dialog, is available here: www.w3.org/TR/WCAG20-TECHS/working-examples/SCR37/default.htm.

As mentioned earlier the full list of techniques are available here: www.w3.org/TR/WCAG20-TECHS/client-side-script.html.

APPENDIX B

Definition of WAI-ARIA Roles

The definitions in this appendix[1] are taken from Accessible Rich Internet Applications (WAI-ARIA) 1.0 at www.w3.org/TR/wai-aria/roles#role_definitions.

The following is an alphabetical list of WAI-ARIA roles to be used by rich internet application authors.

alert

A message with important, and usually time-sensitive, information. See related *alertdialog* and *status*.

alertdialog

A type of dialog that contains an alert message, where initial focus goes to an element within the dialog. See related *alert* and *dialog*.

application

A region declared as a web application, as opposed to a web document.

article

A section of a page that consists of a composition that forms an independent part of a document, page, or site.

banner

A region that contains mostly site-oriented content, rather than page-specific content.

---

[1] Copyright © 2008-2011 W3C® (MIT, ERCIM, Keio), All Rights Reserved. W3C liability, trademark and document use rules apply.

button

An input that allows for user-triggered actions when clicked or pressed. See related *link*.

checkbox

A checkable input that has three possible values: true, false, or mixed.

columnheader

A cell containing header information for a column.

combobox

A presentation of a select control; usually similar to a textbox where users can type ahead to select an option, or type to enter arbitrary text as a new item in the list. See related *listbox*.

command (abstract role)

A form of widget that performs an action but does not receive input data.

complementary

A supporting section of the document, designed to be complementary to the main content at a similar level in the DOM hierarchy, but which remains meaningful when separated from the main content.

composite (abstract role)

A widget that can contain navigable descendants or owned children.

contentinfo

A large perceivable region that contains information about the parent document.

definition

A definition of a term or concept.

dialog

An application window designed to interrupt the current processing of an application in order to prompt the user to enter information or require a response. See related *alertdialog*.

directory

A list of references to members of a group, such as a static table of contents.

document

A region containing related information that is declared as document content, as opposed to a web application.

form

A landmark region that contains a collection of items and objects that, as a whole, combine to create a form. See related *search*.

grid

A grid is an interactive control that contains cells of tabular data arranged in rows and columns, like a table.

gridcell

A cell in a grid or treegrid.

group

A set of user interface objects that are not intended to be included in a page summary or table of contents by assistive technologies.

heading

A heading for a section of the page.

img

A container for a collection of elements that form an image.

input (abstract role)

A generic type of widget that allows user input.

landmark (abstract role)

A region of the page intended as a navigational landmark.

link

An interactive reference to an internal or external resource that, when activated, causes the user agent to navigate to that resource. See related *button*.

list

A group of noninteractive list items. See related *listbox*.

listbox

A widget that allows the user to select one or more items from a list of choices. See related *combobox* and *list*.

listitem

A single item in a list or directory.

log

A type of live region where new information is added in meaningful order and old information might disappear. See related *marquee*.

main

The main content of a document.

marquee

A type of live region where nonessential information changes frequently. See related *log*.

math

Content that represents a mathematical expression.

menu

A type of widget that offers a list of choices to the user.

menubar

A presentation of a menu that usually remains visible and is usually presented horizontally.

menuitem

An option in a group of choices contained by a menu or menubar.

menuitemcheckbox

A checkable menuitem that has three possible values: true, false, or mixed.

menuitemradio

A checkable menuitem in a group of menuitemradio roles, only one of which can be selected at a time.

navigation

A collection of navigational elements (usually links) for navigating the document or related documents.

note

A section whose content is parenthetical or ancillary to the main content of the resource.

option

A selectable item in a select list.

presentation

An element whose implicit native role semantics will not be mapped to the accessibility API.

progressbar

An element that displays the progress status for tasks that take a long time.

radio

A checkable input in a group of radio roles, only one of which can be selected at a time.

radiogroup

A group of radio buttons.

range (abstract role)

An input representing a range of values that can be set by the user.

region

A large perceivable section of a web page or document that the author feels is important enough to be included in a page summary or table of contents—for example, an area of the page containing live sporting event statistics.

roletype (abstract role)

The base role from which all other roles in this taxonomy inherit.

row

A row of cells in a grid.

rowgroup

A group containing one or more row elements in a grid.

rowheader

A cell containing header information for a row in a grid.

scrollbar

A graphical object that controls the scrolling of content within a viewing area, regardless of whether the content is fully displayed within the viewing area.

search

A landmark region that contains a collection of items and objects that, as a whole, combine to create a search facility. See related *form*.

section (abstract role)

A renderable structural containment unit in a document or application.

sectionhead (abstract role)

A structure that labels or summarizes the topic of its related section.

select (abstract role)

A form widget that allows the user to make selections from a set of choices.

separator

A divider that separates and distinguishes sections of content or groups of menuitems.

slider

A user input where the user selects a value from within a given range.

spinbutton

A form of range control that expects the user to select from among discrete choices.

status

A container whose content is advisory information for the user but is not important enough to justify an alert, often but not necessarily presented as a status bar. See related *alert*.

structure (abstract role)

A document structural element.

tab

A grouping label providing a mechanism for selecting the tab content that is to be rendered to the user.

tablist

A list of tab elements, which are references to tabpanel elements.

tabpanel

A container for the resources associated with a tab, where each tab is contained in a tablist.

textbox

Input control that allows free-form text as its value.

timer

A type of live region containing a numerical counter that indicates an amount of elapsed time from a start point, or the time remaining until an end point.

toolbar

A collection of commonly used function buttons represented in compact visual form.

tooltip

A contextual popup that displays a description for an element.

tree

A type of list that can contain sublevel nested groups that can be collapsed and expanded.

treegrid

A grid whose rows can be expanded and collapsed in the same manner as for a tree.

treeitem

An option item of a tree. This is an element within a tree that can be expanded or collapsed if it contains a sublevel group of treeitems.

widget (abstract role)

An interactive component of a graphical user interface (GUI).

window (abstract role)

A browser or application window.

WAI-ARIA States and Properties

Following is an alphabetical list of WAI-ARIA states and properties to be used by rich internet application authors. Go to `www.w3.org/TR/wai-aria/states_and_properties#state_prop_def` for more on these terms and definitions.

aria-activedescendant

Identifies the currently active descendant of a composite widget.

aria-atomic

Indicates whether assistive technologies will present all, or only parts of, the changed region based on the change notifications defined by the `aria-relevant` attribute. See related `aria-relevant`.

aria-autocomplete

Indicates whether user-input completion suggestions are provided.

aria-busy (state)

Indicates whether an element and its subtree are currently being updated.

aria-checked (state)

Indicates the current "checked" state of checkboxes, radio buttons, and other widgets. See related `aria-pressed` and `aria-selected`.

aria-controls

Identifies the element (or elements) whose contents or presence are controlled by the current element. See related `aria-owns`.

aria-describedby

Identifies the element (or elements) that describes the object. See related `aria-labelledby`.

aria-disabled (state)

Indicates that the element is perceivable but disabled, so it is not editable or otherwise operable. See related `aria-hidden` and `aria-readonly`.

aria-dropeffect

Indicates what functions can be performed when the dragged object is released on the drop target. This allows assistive technologies to convey the possible drag options available to users, including whether a pop-up menu of choices is provided by the application. Typically, drop-effect functions can be provided only after an object has been grabbed for a drag operation because the drop-effect functions available are dependent on the object being dragged.

aria-expanded (state)

Indicates whether the element, or another grouping element it controls, is currently expanded or collapsed.

aria-flowto

Identifies the next element (or elements) in an alternate reading order of content that, at the user's discretion, allows assistive technology to override the general default of reading in document source order.

aria-grabbed (state)

Indicates an element's "grabbed" state in a drag-and-drop operation.

aria-haspopup

Indicates that the element has a popup context menu or sublevel menu.

aria-hidden (state)

Indicates that the element and all of its descendants are not visible or perceivable to any user as implemented by the author. See related `aria-disabled`.

aria-invalid (state)

Indicates the entered value does not conform to the format expected by the application.

aria-label

Defines a string value that labels the current element. See related `aria-labelledby`.

aria-labelledby

Identifies the element (or elements) that labels the current element. See related `aria-label` and `aria-describedby`.

aria-level

Defines the hierarchical level of an element within a structure.

aria-live

Indicates that an element will be updated, and describes the types of updates the user agents, assistive technologies, and user can expect from the live region.

aria-multiline

Indicates whether a text box accepts multiple lines of input or only a single line.

aria-multiselectable

Indicates that the user can select more than one item from the current selectable descendants.

aria-orientation

Indicates whether the element and orientation are horizontal or vertical.

aria-owns

Identifies an element (or elements) in order to define a visual, functional, or contextual parent/child relationship between DOM elements where the DOM hierarchy cannot be used to represent the relationship. See related `aria-controls`.

aria-posinset

Defines an element's number or position in the current set of listitems or treeitems. It's not required if all elements in the set are present in the DOM. See related `aria-setsize`.

aria-pressed (state)

Indicates the current "pressed" state of toggle buttons. See related `aria-checked` and `aria-selected`.

aria-readonly

Indicates that the element is not editable, but is otherwise operable. See related `aria-disabled`.

aria-relevant

Indicates what user-agent change notifications (additions, removals, and so on) assistive technologies will receive within a live region. See related `aria-atomic`.

aria-required

Indicates that user input is required on the element before a form can be submitted.

aria-selected (state)

Indicates the current "selected" state of various widgets. See related `aria-checked` and `aria-pressed`.

aria-setsize

Defines the number of items in the current set of listitems or treeitems. It's not required if all elements in the set are present in the DOM. See related `aria-posinset`.

aria-sort

Indicates if items in a table or grid are sorted in ascending or descending order.

aria-valuemax

Defines the maximum allowed value for a range widget.

aria-valuemin

Defines the minimum allowed value for a range widget.

aria-valuenow

Defines the current value for a range widget. See related `aria-valuetext`.

aria-valuetext

Defines the human-readable text alternative of `aria-valuenow` for a range widget.

Index

IDEA, 15
PAS78, 16
Rehabilitation Act (*see* Rehabilitation Act,
    HTML5)
SENDA, 16

O

Off-screen model
    DOS-based systems, 113
    GUI-based systems, 114
    screen scraping, 114

P, Q

Participatory design, 282

R

Rehabilitation Act, HTML5
    Section 504, 13
    Section 508, 14
        enforcement, 14
        influence of, 14
        VPAT, 15

S

Screen readers, 34
    browsing point, 115
    Fangs, 57
    Forms Mode, 116
    JAWS (*see* Job Access With Speech (JAWS))
    mobile device accessibility
        Android, 59
        RIM and Blackberry accessibility, 58–59
        Talks and Symbian, 58
        VoiceOver and IPhone, 58
    NVDA, 56–57
    speech synthesis
        concatenative synthesis, 60
        formant synthesis, 60
        phonemes, 59
    virtual cursor, 115
    Window-Eyes, 56
Screen-magnification, 60
    mouse emulation, 64
    switches
        scanning software, 62

switch access, 61
working principle, 62–64
Web access, 65
Special Educational Needs and Disability Act
    2001 (SENDA), 16
Survey design, 282

T

Tools, Tips, and Tricks
    AccProbe tool, 310
    aDesigner tool, 311
    automated accessibility tools, 309
    browser
        no-frills browsing, 314
        NoScript, 314
        pop-ups, 315
        screen reader, 316
        working without mouse, 315
    Chris Pederick Web Developer Toolbar, 295–
        296
    code validation, 311
        CSS, 313
        via W3C validator, 312
    Colour Contrast Analyser, 296–300
    disability simulation tools, 311
    Firebug tool, 307–8
    Guerilla user testing, 311
    Inspect32 tool, 310
    Opera Dragonfly, 309
    Safari Web Inspection Tool, 308
    WAT–C Web Accessibility Toolbar, 296
    WAVE tool, 300
        accessibility errors, 304
        CFIT web site post-WAVE, 303
        CFIT web site pre-WAVE, 302
        error detail, mouse over, 306
        Firefox, 301
        icons, 307
        outline feature, 304
Traditional usability testing, 285

U

Universal design
    definition, 274
    principles
        equitable use, 275
        flexibility in use, 276
        low physical effort, 280

363

35462102R00219

Made in the USA
Lexington, KY
11 September 2014